The Sikhs in Canada

The Sikhs in Canada

Migration, Race, Class, and Gender

Gurcharn S. Basran
B. Singh Bolaria

OXFORD

UNIVERSITY PRESS

OXFORD
UNIVERSITY PRESS

YMCA Library Building, Jai Singh Road, New Delhi 110 001

Oxford University Press is a department of the University of Oxford. It furthers the
University's objective of excellence in research, scholarship, and education
by publishing worldwide in

Oxford   New York

Auckland   Bangkok   Buenos Aires   Cape Town   Chennai
Dar es Salaam   Delhi   Hong Kong   Istanbul   Karachi   Kolkata
Kuala Lumpur   Madrid   Melbourne   Mexico City   Mumbai   Nairobi
São Paulo   Shanghai   Taipei   Tokyo   Toronto

Oxford is a registered trade mark of Oxford University Press
in the UK and in certain other countries

Published in India
By Oxford University Press, New Delhi

ISBN   019 564886 2

Typeset by Jojy Philip in Adobe Garamond (10.5/12.9)
Printed by Roopak Printers, Delhi 110032
Published by Manzar Khan, Oxford University Press
YMCA Library Building, Jai Singh Road, New Delhi 110 001

Preface

❀

International migrations of populations have become truly a global phenomenon on an unprecedented scale. Millions of people live outside their country of birth and millions more are on the move continually to other countries primarily in quest for greater opportunities. Internationalization of production in the context of globalization of world economies and the concomitant growing demand for labour have further increased the potential for more migrations. These migrations originating from diverse places and regions, with destinations to virtually all parts of the globe, are reshaping and transforming societies around the world. Virtually all societies are being affected by movements of population with diverse racial, ethnic, and cultural backgrounds. Countries and societies which were virtually racially, culturally, and linguistically homogeneous are becoming increasingly heterogeneous in these respects. These developments are not only reshaping these societies but also their social policies and political strategies to 'control' the entry and 'manage' the presence of diverse populations within their midst. Recently global political and military strategies are being developed by powerful countries to restrict the movements and migrations of nationals of some countries, specifically the individuals with certain religious affiliations and political commitments.

In view of the sheer volume, intensity, diversity, and significance of international migration, a number of issues and questions surround this important phenomenon. The questions that have received most attention are: Why do people migrate and migratory movements persist? What are the consequences of migrations for migrants and the countries? Theories about international migrations, broadly speaking, fall into micro-level and macro-level perspectives. At its core, the focus of micro-level theorizing is on individualistic reasons or motives for migration. The primary drive behind migrants' decision is said to be self-interest and economic rationality to maximize their opportunities. Macro-level theorizing, on the other hand, focuses on structural determinants in patterned migration movements. In this approach, international migrations are seen as the product of capitalist development and the interface between the needs of capital and the characteristics of labour. Capitalism as a world system is characterized by gross disparities and unequal accummulation of capital between the core and peripheral countries. Expansion of capitalist economies into the periphery produce disruptions and dislocations which create conditions for further migrations. After the initiation, the persistence of migrations are motivated by many factors including the social networks between the immigrants and potential migrants and proliferation of institutions, agencies, and agents that facilitate migratory movements. A whole new 'immigration industry' has evolved, both in receiving and some sending countries.

The settlement patterns, socio–economic status, and mobility patterns of migrants have received considerable attention. The assimilationist school sees social and economic inequality as a product of cultural value orientation and motivational differences among various groups and their degree of assimilation into the value system of the country of immigration. The structuralists, on the other hand, see inequality as a product of differential opportunity structures, labour market segmentation, and the persistence of race, class, and gender inequalities that structure the mobility patterns of migrants.

Our analysis in this book is informed by theoretical perspectives that see international migrations as a product of gross international disparities and inequalities, and social inequality as a product of structural and institutional constraints that limit the life chances of certain social groups. The passage of Sikhs from India to Canada and their location in the Canadian mosaic are presented within broad political, economic and social contexts.

Chapter 1, by way of introduction, provides an overview of the shift in immigration policy and its impact on place of origin and characteristics of immigrants. Other sections briefly cover the role of the state and perspectives in international migrations. We expand on these general themes later in this book. Chapter 2 is intended to inform the reader about basic tenets of the Sikh religion. More specifically, the chapter discusses the social context of the emergence of the Sikh religion, religious beliefs, codes and practices, the contributions of the Gurus and the birth of the Khalsa.

The self-perception of the Sikhs, as an oppressed minority community and their desire to create political and economic conditions and a geographical entity to safeguard their religious, cultural, and linguistic rights can only be fully appreciated in the context of pre- and post-independence politics and events. It is important to discuss their political, social and religious history primarily because of the important link between conditions in Punjab, India, from where most of the Sikhs have migrated, and the formation and politics of the Sikh community in Canada. In Chapter 3, entitled 'State, Religion, Language and Politics', we focus on the historical and contemporary situation and explore the important links between religion, language, and politics. This chapter covers the pre-colonial history of the Sikh Raj, the Gurdwara reform movement, and the Sikhs in the context of the anti-colonial struggle. Much of the chapter is devoted to the post-Independent Punjab, in particular the Anandpur Sahib Resolution, political maneuvering between the central government, Punjab, and others and violence in Punjab. A section of the chapter deals with state measures which to curb violence also involved violation of basic rights and criminalization of legitimate political activities.

As the Sikh community is composed of immigrants and their Canadian-born descendents it is essential to discuss Canadian immigration policy in general and the policies specific to immigration from India. However, in order to fully understand the migratory patterns and characteristics of immigrants to Canada we expand on theoretical and conceptual debates on migration studies and on racism and racial inequality. Chapter 4, entitled 'Migration, Labour, and Racism', covers topics such as migrations, labour procurement and institutional racism and exploitation of labour.

Discussion in Chapter 4 provides a broader context for presentation in Chapter 5, entitled 'From India to Canada: Immigration Policy and Migration Patterns'. In addition to a detailed discussion of immigration, a section of the chapter is devoted to political activism and anti-colonial and anti-racist activities of 'pioneer' immigrants. They actively opposed racism and social inequality in Canada and supported anti-colonial struggle in India.

The next two chapters discuss the socio-economic status and labour force profile of Sikhs. Chapter 6, entitled 'Colonialism and Indian Labour: Work and Life in the Colonies', is primarily based upon our field research in British Columbia. The procurement of Sikh workers is discussed in the broader context of procurement of Indian labour to the various parts of the colonial empire. Racism, racial discrimination, and racist labour policies at the workplace meant super-exploitation of early Sikh workers. They also faced discrimination and inequality in their daily lives.

Chapter 7, 'Post-war Immigrants: Opportunities and Constraints', covers the contemporary socio-economic status and labour force participation of Sikh immigrants. These data are presented in the broader context of recent racial minority and other immigrants. A section of the chapter deals with the media and minorities, in particular, the media's coverage of Gurdwara politics and its impact on the public image of the Sikhs.

The nature and formation of social and cultural institutions of immigrants are profoundly affected by the structural constraints under which immigrants enter Canada. Chapter 8, 'State Policies, Family Formation and Inequality', discusses Canadian immigration policy which has had a profound impact on the formation and development of Sikh families and conjugal life in Canada. Sections of this chapter also cover the economic status of visible minority families, and race, class, and gender issues as they relate to the status of women of colour. The final chapter is primarily a summation of the content and issues raised throughout this book and some concluding observations on race, class, and gender inequality in Canada.

We would like to conclude with a personal note. We are both Punjabis and Sikhs by birth. Both of us were born in Punjab, spent our early years there, and received our undergraduate university degrees from Punjab. We both, coincidentally, came to the United States in the early 1960s as graduate students and received our MA and PhD degrees from different universities here. After brief periods of faculty appointments in the US we have been on the faculty at the University of Saskatchewan for over 30 years. That is to say, in addition to an academic interest in the subject of immigration, our interest and experiences go beyond academia. Before migration to North America we were both witness to the division of Punjab province between India and Pakistan, communal riots at the time of India's independence, and Punjab politics during the fifties. Issues of racism, racial inequality, racial discrimination, and the Civil Rights movement in the US form an intrinsic part of our experience. We are both part of the professional–skilled workforce that arrived in Canada during the mid-sixties and early seventies. Our background and experiences, as well as our academic training have had important influences on our world-view. These experiences also to some extent shaped the theoretical orientation that has guided our analysis in this volume and in most of our other academic work. This theoretical model falls under the general rubric of critical sociology or political–economy perspective which is characterized by its focus on class relations and class contradictions under capitalism. In its various forms, critical sociology has proved its utility in the analysis of a wide range of social phenomena and has made significant contributions to a number of substantive areas in sociology, more recently in the areas of gender studies and racial and cultural studies. It is hoped that the analysis presented in this volume will make a contribution to the literature on immigration studies and enhance our understanding of the various dimensions of this significant global phenomenon.

Acknowledgements

❦

A number of people and institutions have contributed to the completion of this book. First, we would like to express our sincere appreciation to the individuals who participated in our study on the work and life of pioneer Sikhs. We are grateful for their time, courtesy and hospitality, for valuable, informative and rich data which forms a major section of this book. Their names are withheld to follow the accepted research protocol and ethics.

We wish to thank Malwant Basran for translation and transcription of interviews in Punjabi. We also greatly appreciate the assistance of our colleague, Peter Li, who made available statistical data on Sikhs, regarding their socio-economic status and labour force profile.

We also acknowledge the financial assistance of the multicultural directorate, Ottawa, for field research, and 'aid to publication' from the University of Saskatchewan to assist in manuscript preparation costs.

We would of course also wish to thank the people involved at Oxford University Press, India, whose careful work greatly improved the final product. Thanks are also due to the external reviewers for their very helpful comments and suggestions.

Finally, we wish to acknowledge Kiran Bolaria for her research on 'Media and the Sikhs'. Rosemary Bolaria helped in a number of ways, including extensive research and editorial assistance, and her computer expertise was invaluable in the preparation of this manuscript for publication. We are grateful for all her contributions.

Gurcharn S. Basran
B. Singh Bolaria

Contents

Introduction
Increasing Diversity in the Canadian Mosaic

❀

Contemporary Canadian society is characterized by increasing diversity comprising various racial, ethnic, cultural, and religious communities. This is a relatively recent phenomenon and is primarily the product of changes in immigrant policy over time and the consequent shift in immigration sources. This increasing heterogeneity and the presence of a more diverse and visible population have brought into sharp focus the issue of immigration policy, volume and composition of immigrant populations; the political, economic, and social location of various groups in the Canadian mosaic and the state management of this diversity in terms of the aspirations of the component groups.

This chapter provides an overview of the shift in immigration policy in the sixties and its consequences in terms of immigrant sources and characteristics of immigrants. The influx of recent immigrants from Asia and Africa has profoundly changed the racial and ethnic composition of the Canadian population as well as the labour force characteristics. First, by way of introduction, we discuss the increasing diversity in Canada, followed by a discussion of immigrant characteristics and perspectives on migrations and the role of the state.

DERACIALIZATION AND RECENT IMMIGRANTS

It is well documented that until 1962 the Canadian immigration policy was explicitly racist (Bolaria and Li, 1988; Basran, 1983; Trumper and Wong, 1997; Satzewich, 2000). This policy was guided by a conception of Canada as a 'white' country and manifested itself in a racialized hierarchy of acceptability of immigrants where 'white' northern Europeans and Americans were preferred and actively recruited, eastern and southern Europeans were less preferable, and 'non-whites' definitely excluded from entry to Canada. Historically, various mechanisms were used in this regard, such as, nationality quotas from non-white countries; head-tax on Chinese; continuous journey legislation regarding immigration from India; and the differences in entry status and the legal–political rights of white and non-white immigrants.

By the 1960s it became difficult for the Canadian state to maintain racially discriminatory policies based upon either racial or cultural differences among immigrants. This change was necessitated by the international political (the emergence of newly independent 'non-white' states), economic considerations (foreign markets), and labour shortages in Canada, specifically professional–skilled workforce (Bolaria, 1992; Li, 1992; Trumper and Wong, 1997). To facilitate the recruitment of professional–killed labour in particular from 'non-white' countries, the immigration regulations were changed, eliminating the quota system and explicit racial discrimination practices and replacing them by 'universal standards' emphasizing educational-technical qualifications and occupational demands in Canada. These changes resulted in an increase in the number of immigrants from 'non-traditional' sources and an increasingly diverse immigrant population. Recent immigrants are increasingly from Asian and African countries (Badets and Chui, 1994; Li, 1996; Satzewich, 2000). For instance, in 1950–5, 88 per cent of immigrants were from Europe, and only 3.2 per cent from Asia and Africa. In the period 1962–7, immigrants from Asia and Africa increased to 9.4 per cent and those from Europe declined to 73.5 per cent. The major shift became more evident starting with the 1968–73 period. During the period 1968–73, the European contribution declined to less than 50 per cent and that from Asia and Africa increased to 20 per cent. By the 1980s Asian and African arrivals outstripped European immigrants. A little over 46 per cent of immigrants came from Asia and Africa in 1980–5, and just above 30 per cent from Europe during the same time period. By the 1980–91 period the European contribution further declined to about 24 per cent and the Asian and African increased to just over 54 per cent (Satzewich, 2000:60).

To put it differently, nearly 42 per cent of the immigrants who lived in Canada in 1991 were from the UK, Italy, the US, Poland, Germany, and the Netherlands (Table 1.1). The same Table shows that of arrivals to Canada between 1981 and 1991, slightly over 33 per cent came from Hong

Kong, the People's Republic of China, India, Vietnam, the Philippines, and Lebanon.

TABLE 1.1

TOP TEN COUNTRIES OF BIRTH FOR ALL IMMIGRANTS
AND RECENT IMMIGRANTS, CANADA, 1991

All Immigrants			Recent Immigrants		
Country of birth	Number	%	Country of birth	Number	%
1. UK	717,745	16.5	1. Hong Kong	96,540	7.8
2. Italy	351,620	8.1	2. Poland	77,455	6.3
3. US	249,080	5.7	3. People's Republic of China	75,840	6.1
4. Poland	184,695	4.3	4. India	73,105	5.9
5. Germany	180,525	4.2	5. UK	71,365	5.8
6. India	173,670	4.0	6. Vietnam	69,520	5.6
7. Portugal	161,180	3.7	7. Philippines	64,290	5.2
8. People's Republic of China	157,405	3.6	8. US	55,415	4.5
9. Hong Kong	152,455	3.5	9. Portugal	35,440	2.9
10. Netherlands	129,615	3.0	10. Lebanon	35,065	2.8
Total Immigrants	4,342,890	100.0	Total Immigrants	1,238,455	100.0

Source: Jane Badets and Tina W.L. Chui, *Canada's Changing Immigrant Population* (Ottawa: Minister of science, Industry and Technology, 1994), p. 14. Prentice-Hall, Statistics Canada, Cat. No. 96–311E.

This change in the Canadian population has also contributed to the diversity of the labour force. Foreign-born workers are an important component of the workforce in various sectors and occupations. In particular, since the late 1960s Asian countries have been an important source of professional, scientific, and skilled workers (Li, 1996).

The ethnic and racial diversity of the population varies considerably across the country. This is largely due to the settlement patterns of immigrants over time. Ontario and British Columbia are the primary destinations of recent immigrants. This is reflected in the growing proportion of the Asian population in these provinces (Badets and Chui, 1994). In 1991, one in nine British Columbians was of Asian origin, and in Ontario seven per cent of the population reported single Asian origins (Badets and Chui, 1994). Population diversity is also reflected in linguistic diversity. In 1991, 13 per cent of the population reported other than the two official languages as their mother tongue as compared to 11 per cent in 1986 (Badets and Chui, 1994).

In summary, the change in immigration regulation in the late 1960s is reflected in the increasing ethnic, racial, and linguistic diversity of the Canadian population. While in 1991 the British and French were the largest ethnic groups (28 per cent and 23 per cent respectively), 31 per cent of the population reported ethnic origins other than these two groups. This diversity varies across the country. British Columbia and Ontario are the most heterogeneous and diverse provinces, specifically with regard to the visible minority populations.

Diversity of the immigrant population is also reflected in increasing religious diversity in Canada. While Catholics and Protestants continued to be the largest religious groups (45 and 36 per cent respectively in 1991), in Canada, the largest increase was experienced by the Eastern non-Christian religious groups (Statistics Canada, 1993). Between 1981 and 1991, these groups as a whole increased by 144 per cent. As Table 1.2 indicates, the largest increase was of Buddhists by 215 per cent during this time period.

TABLE 1.2

EASTERN NON-CHRISTIAN RELIGIONS, CANADA, 1981 AND 1991

Religions	1981	1991	Perentage increase
Islam	98,165	253,260	158
Buddhist	51,955	163,415	215
Hindu	69,505	157,010	126
Sikh	67,715	147,440	118
Bahai	7,960	14,730	85
Other	10,890	11,600	7
Total	305,890	747,455	144

Source: Compiled from Statistics Canada, Religions in Canada, 1993, Cat. 93–319.

Other Eastern non-Christian groups also increased substantially during this time—Islam (158 per cent), Hindu (126 per cent) and Sikh (118 per cent).

The Canadian mosaic is composed not only of multi-ethnic, multiracial, and multi-cultural, but also multi-religious groups.

IMMIGRANT CHARACTERISTICS: GIVE US YOUR EDUCATED

The elimination of formal racial immigration controls and alteration of the selection criteria meant a profound change in the characteristics of immigrants after the 1960s. Because of the importance given to personal characteristics and professional qualifications, recent immigrants tend to be better educated than those who arrived before 1961. Overall, immigrants also tend to have higher educational attainments than their Canadian-born counterparts.

The data in Table 1.3 demonstrate the changes in the educational attainment of immigrants by periods of immigration. Among those who arrived in the decade 1981–91, a little over 20 per cent of men and 14.6 per cent of women had university degrees, compared to 11.5 per cent of men and 6.1 per cent of women who arrived before 1961. The data also show a decline in the proportion of immigrants with less than grade nine education over the years. Overall, a little over 17 per cent of men and nearly 12 per cent of women (last column) had university degrees. An additional 38 per cent of men and 33 per cent of women had some post-secondary education. Immigrant men tend to have more formal education than women immigrants.

Primarily because of the higher educational attainment of recent arrivals, overall, immigrants tend to be better educated than their Canadian-born counterparts (Badets and Chui, 1994; Ghalam, 1995). With regard to university graduates, 19 per cent of immigrant men and nearly 14 per cent of immigrant women aged 15–64 years had university degrees. The corresponding figures for Canadian-born men and women were 12.2 per cent and 10.5 per cent respectively (Table 1.4). In the older age group (65 and over), a slightly higher proportion of immigrant men had university degrees, compared to Canadian-born men. However, there was no difference between immigrant and Canadian-born women in this age group.

On the other hand, data in Table 1.4 also show that the immigrants are more likely than the Canadian-born to have less than grade nine education. Almost twice the proportion of immigrant women compared to Canadian-

TABLE 3
EDUCATIONAL ATTAINMENT OF IMMIGRANTS BY PERIOD OF IMMIGRATION, CANADA, 1991

(percentage)

| Educational attainment | Period of immigration | | | | | | | | | | | | |
| | Before 1961 | | 1961–70 | | 1971–80 | | 1981–90 | | Total | |
	Women	Men	Women	Men	Women	Men	Women	Men	Women	Men
Less than grade 9	30.2	26.1	21.1	16.1	15.4	10.1	16.2	11.1	21.2	16.4
Grade 9–13	36.9	25.2	30.3	23.4	33.1	30.2	34.9	33.7	34.2	28.2
Some post-secondary	26.8	37.1	35.0	40.6	37.4	40.4	34.3	34.9	32.9	38.1
University degree	6.1	11.5	13.6	20.0	14.1	19.3	14.6	20.2	11.7	17.3
Total	100.0	100.0	100.0	100.0	100.0	100.0	100.0	100.0	100.0	100.0

Source: Nancy Ghalam, 'Immigrant Women', pp. 117–32 in Statistics Canada, *Women in Canada* (Ottawa: Minister of Industry, 1995). Table 9.8, p. 128 (Statistics Canada Cat. No. 89–503E).

TABLE 1.4
EDUCATIONAL ATTAINMENT OF IMMIGRANTS AND
THE CANADIAN-BORN, BY AGE, 1991

	Persons aged							
	15–64				65 and Over			
	Immigrants		Canadian-Born		Immigrants		Canadian-Born	
Educational attainment	Women	Men	Women	Men	Women	Men	Women	Men
Less than grade 9	15.7	12.3	8.3	9.4	42.8	36.9	38.1	41.0
Grade 9–13	33.7	28.4	43.0	40.5	36.1	27.3	38.8	31.6
Some post-secondary	36.8	40.4	38.3	37.8	18.0	26.9	20.1	20.2
University degree	13.9	19.0	10.5	12.2	3.2	9.0	3.0	7.2
Total	100.0	100.0	100.0	100.0	100.0	100.0	100.0	100.0

Source: Nancy Ghalam, 'Immigrant Women', pp. 117–32 in Statistics Canada, Women in Canada, (Ottawa: Minister of Industry, 1995), Table 9.7, p. 128 (Statistics Canada Cat. No. 89–503E).

born women fell in this category. The corresponding figures for immigrant and Canadian-born men were 12.3 per cent and 9.4 per cent respectively. A significantly higher proportion of immigrants and non-immigrants in the older age group than those in the 15–64 year age category had lower educational attainment, that is, less than grade nine education.

That a higher proportion of immigrants than the Canadian-born had university educations should not be surprising given the post-1960s' focus on educational and professional training of potential immigrants to correspond with Canada's labour force needs. It should also be noted that immigrants from Asia, Africa, and the US tend to have the highest educational levels and those from southern Europe and Central America the lowest (Badets and Chui, 1994:45). Given the increasing proportion of arrivals from Asia and Africa among the recent immigrants, it would be expected that visible minority men and women are more likely to have higher educational levels than non-visible minority Canadians. The data on educational attainment for 1991 show that a little over 21 per cent of visible minority men and 15 per cent of visible minority women had university degrees, compared to 12 per cent of other men and a little over 9 per cent of other women (Chard, 1995:142).

Thus, immigrants in general and visible minorities in particular, tend to have higher educational attainment than other Canadians. The recent immigrants from India, including Sikhs, tend to follow the same patterns, that is, they are better educated and often from middle and upper class and urban backgrounds. In spite of the recent increase in immigration flows, Sikhs still constitute a small but highly visible minority. The data show that Sikhs are predominantly a young population, nearly 41 per cent in 1981 and approximately 36 per cent in 1991, under 40 years of age. The average age was 25 years in 1981 and nearly 29 years in 1991, (Statistics Canada, 1993). The data also show that Sikhs are still predominantly a foreign-born (immigrant) population. In 1991 nearly two-thirds were immigrants. The geographical settlement patterns of the Sikhs correspond to the settlement patterns of other recent immigrants to Canada. In 1991 nearly 85 per cent of the Sikhs lived in two provinces: Ontario and British Columbia. Vancouver and Toronto were the primary places of residence. For instance, 66 per cent of the Sikh population in British Columbia and 82 per cent of those in Ontario lived in the Greater Vancouver and Greater Toronto areas, respectively (Statistics Canada, 1993).

Successive waves of immigrants have been an important source of labour to respond to specific sectorial labour force demands in this country. A number of factors including educational attainment, gender, country of origin, and racial background of workers have significantly influenced labour market opportunities. Differential opportunity structures have a profound impact on employment earnings and incomes of individuals and social groups. Data presented later in this book show that returns on human capital for racial minorities remain comparatively low.

INTERNATIONAL MIGRATIONS

The volume and the direction of movement of people across national boundaries have received considerable attention from sociologists and other social scientists. Theorizing about international migrations and the social, economic, and political status of migrants in the receiving countries and their settlement patterns have been the focus of many studies. Those interested in this area approach and examine these topics and issues from various theoretical perspectives and paradigms and use varying levels of analysis. In this section, by way of introduction, we outline some of the salient aspects of debate in migration studies and the consequences of migrations across national boundaries. We expand on this in the later sections of this book.

Why do people migrate from one region to another? Until very recently, the explanation of migrations have been dominated by demographic studies and push–pull factors. The primary focus of these studies is to compile the demographic characteristics of migrants and to search for individualistic reasons or motives for migration. This type of inquiry formed the basis for the push and pull model of migration (Gardezi, 1995). Push variables include such factors as unemployment, low wages and poverty, and the pull factors include such circumstances as opportunities for employment, higher wages, and other favourable conditions (Gardezi, 1995:20). The assumption here is that because of self-interest and economic rationality individuals would decide to migrate to maximize their opportunities. This perspective has been criticized for its focus on individual interests and motivation and assumptions of a uniform international labour market and freedom of mobility across national boundaries without adequate recognition of the social, economic, and political contexts of decision-making (Gardezi, 1995). Demographic studies, with their focus on migrations as movements of people, not only distract attention from the economic role migrants play in the receiving countries but also do not explain the structural determinants involved in patterned migration movements. In essence, these studies ob-scure and devalue the essential role of migrants as labour resource and reservoirs. Recent studies have begun to analyse the processes of migrations and circulations of labour across national boundaries in this context. In-formed by Marxian tradition, these studies analyse the existence of immi-grants and migrants in many countries in the context of the dynamics of capitalist development and the interface between the needs of capital and the characteristics of labour (Portes, 1978; Bolaria and Bolaria, 1997). This type of analysis points to the historical role of migrants vis-a-vis labour force needs and the drive for capital accumulation and; '... reject[s] the various essentially bourgeois positions on immigration, which go from the moralist acceptance of immigrants on grounds of human solidarity to their reaction-ary rejection because they would "steal" jobs from indigenous workers' (Carchedi, 1979:54).

With regard to successful migrants, attention is diverted to the consequences of migrations and their incorporation into political, economic, and social spheres. Until recently, most studies dealing with settlement patterns have been dominated by the assimilationist perspective (Li and Bolaria, 1979). Within this perspective, the ability to assimilate and speed of absorption are dependent upon the personal, social, and cultural background of the newcomers. This led to the characterization of some groups as more assimilable than others and provided rationalization for controlling and restricting entry of populations on the basis of their alleged non-assimilability. In almost all instances this meant exclusionary policies against non-white immigrants in Western countries. This perspective has also been used to explain ethnic and racial inequality. In the mobility literature it is expressed in various motivational hypotheses which express value orientation differences among various groups. Social and economic inequalities, therefore, were attributed to different degrees of assimilation or inadequate socialization into the value system of the host society. This focus on migrants and their ability/capacity to assimilate tended to highlight the 'problems' of newcomers and ignored the structural inequalities in the countries of immigration. These explanations of social stratification and racial inequality have been challenged both on theoretical and empirical grounds and its assumptions that there is equality of conditions and of opportunities for migrants.

Critics further argue that the assimilationist perspective distracts attention from the economic role newcomers play, obscures and devalues their essential role as labour resource and reservoirs, ignores the labour market characteristics of the receiving countries, entry states and class background of migrants, and the contexts of their reception (Portes and Borocz, 1989). Therefore, the key elements in understanding inequality and stratification are how the differential opportunity structures, legal and political structural constraints, labour market segmentation, and the persistence of racial, class, and gender differentiation structure the mobility patterns of the migrants.

Our analysis is informed by the studies within the Marxian tradition which analyse international migrations in the context of capitalist development and capitalism as a world-system characterized by gross disparities and unequal accumulation of capital between core and peripheral countries. Also, our analysis of stratification and inequality focuses on structural and institutional constraints, inequalities in the labour market, and the persistence of race, class, and gender differentiations in Canadian society.

Role of the State

In any analysis of immigration policy and immigrant flows it is important to recognize the role of the state. The quantity and composition of immigrants as well as their legal–political status and labour force participation is regulated by the state through various immigration laws, citizenship requirements, and other entry regulations.

There has been a tendency among many social scientists to view immigration policies from a pluralist conception in which the state is seen to respond to the pressures and demands of multiple interest groups organized around the specific issues of immigration laws and policies. This view of the state as an arbitrator of the interests of different groups is contrary to the view of the state as a representative of the interests of the dominant class. Proponents of this view argue that migratory flows are regulated by the state in the interest of capital as a whole. For instance, the nation state through its control of national boundaries, its authority to determine admissibility criteria and the entry status of foreign-born nationals and workers, provides capital with the cheapest and most controllable work force (Trumper and Wong, 1997). The nation state determines whether foreign-born nationals and workers enter the country with the prospect of eventually becoming citizens (immigrant permanent settlers) or to fill particular jobs for a specified time period under state administered contractual arrangements (non-immigrant/migrant transients). Various state administered labour contracts also determine whether the foreign-born nationals are free to sell their labour power (free labour) or are confined to particular jobs and are not free (unfree labour) to circulate in the labour market (Bolaria, 1992; Trumper and Wong, 1997).

The role of the state is also important in 'managing' the racial and ethnic diversity and labour market inequalities through various policies and programmes that promote equality of opportunities for all its citizens.

Summary

The deracialization of immigration controls in the 1960s and emphasis on the personal characteristics and professional qualifications of potential immigrants have had a profound impact on the immigration sources and characteristics of recent immigrants. The proportions of immigrant arrivals from Asia, Africa, and other non-European sources have increased in recent years. Recent immigrants tend to be better educated than the earlier immigrants and the Canadian-born population. The racial minority immigrants have even higher educational attainment as measured in university education than their Canadian-born counterparts. The characteristics of recent Sikh immigrants correspond to the characteristics of other recent immigrants in regard to their educational background and settlement patterns. While the pre-immigration factors, such as educational attainment and professional training, have opened up more opportunities for racial minority immigrants, their labour market profiles still differ from those of other Canadians.

We expand in subsequent chapters on the general themes introduced above. Major sections of the book deal with divergent perspectives on international migrations, the history of immigration policy and its social and economic consequences for immigrants. The state policies also had consequences for the formation of immigrant social institutions, such as the family. The sections on Sikh religion and language and politics are intended to inform the reader about some basic tenets of the Sikh religion and contextualize the discussion on links between the Sikh community in Canada and their place of origin in Punjab. Within these broad social, economic, and political contexts our primary focus, however, remains on the procurement and use of immigrant labour, particularly Sikh workers, both in historical and contemporary contexts.

REFERENCES

Badets, Jane, and Tina W.L. Chui (1994): *Canada's Changing Immigrant Population*, Statistics Canada and Prentice Hall Canada.

Basran, Gurcharn S. (1983): 'Canadian Immigration Policy and Theories of Racism', pp. 3–14 in Bolaria B. Singh and Peter S. Li (eds), *Racial Minorities in Multicultural Canada* (Toronto: Garamond Press).

Bolaria, B. Singh (1992): 'From Immigrant Settlers to Migrant Transients: Foreign Professionals in Canada', pp. 211–28, *in* Vic Satzewich (ed.), *Deconstructing A Nation: Immigration, Multiculturalism and Racism in 90s Canada* (Halifax: Fernwood Publishing and Saskatoon: Social Research Unit, Department of Sociology).

Bolaria, B. Singh and Rosemary von Elling Bolaria (1997): 'Capital, Labour, Migrations', pp. 1–17, *in* B. Singh Bolaria and Rosemary von Elling Bolaria (eds.), *International Labour Migrations* (New Delhi: Oxford University Press).

Bolaria, B. Singh and Peter S. Li (1988): *Racial Oppression in Canada* (Toronto: Garamond Press (2nd edn)).

Carchedi, Guglielmo (1979): 'Authority and Foreign Labour: Some Notes on a Late Capitalist Form of Capital Accumulation and State Intervention', *Studies in Political Economy* 2:37–74.

Chard, Jennifer. 1995. 'Women in a Visible Minority,' pp. 133–146 in Statistics Canada, *Women in Canada,*. Ottawa: Minister of Industry.

Gardezi, Hassan N. (1995): *The Political Economy of International Labour Migrations* (Montreal: Black Rose Books).

Ghalam, Nancy (1995): 'Immigrant Women,' pp. 117–32 in Statistics Canada, *Women in Canada* (Ottawa: Minister of Industry).

Li, Peter S. (1996): *The Making of Post-War Canada* (Toronto: Oxford University Press).

Li, Peter (1992): 'The Economics of Brain Drain: Recruitment of Skilled Labour to Canada, 1954–1986', in Vic Satzewich (ed.), *Deconstructing A Nation: Immigration, Multiculturalism and Racism in 90s Canada* (Halifax: Fernwood Publishing and Saskatoon, Social Research Unit, Department of Sociology).

Li, Peter S. and B. Singh Bolaria (1979): 'Canadian Immigration Policy and Assimilation Theories', pp, 411–22, *in* John A. Fry (ed.), *Economy, Class and Social Reality* (Toronto: Butterworth's).

Portes, Alejandro (1978): 'Migrations and Underdevelopment', *Politics and Society* 8:1048.

Portes, Alejandro and Jozesf Borocz (1989): 'Contemporary Immigration: Theoretical Perspectives on Its Determinants and Modes of Incorporation', *International Labour Migration Review* 23(3):606–30.

Satzewich, Vic (2000): 'Capital Accumulation and State Formation: The Contradictions of International Migration', pp. 51–72 in B. Singh Bolaria (ed.), *Social Issues and Contradictions in Canadian Society*. Toronto: Harcourt Brace, Canada.

Statistics Canada (1993): *Religions in Canada*, The Nation. Cat. 93–319.

Trumper, Ricardo and Lloyd Wong (1997): 'Racialization and Genderization: The Canadian State, Immigration and Temporary Workers', pp. 153–91, *in* B. Singh Bolaria and Rosemary von Elling Bolaria (eds), *International Labour Migrations* (New Delhi: Oxford University Press).

Sikhs and Sikhism
The Khalsa Panth

❦

INTRODUCTION

Despite the optimistic prognosis by social thinkers that with industrialization, modernization, and secularization, the influence of religion and
religious institutions would progressively decline, empirical reality indicates
otherwise. Religious beliefs and practices form an integral part of social
structure and religion continues to be an important aspect of people's
personal lives, their ethnic identity, their social relationships, and political
behaviour.

Historical and contemporary evidence indicates that religion may often
serve contradictory functions in society: integrative (social solidarity) and
disintegrative (conflict); conservative force which supports the status quo as
well as agent of social change. For instance, religion has been a legitimizing
and conservative force in support of the status quo by providing supernatural sanctions for the existing power, wealth, and status differentials. This
social and ideological support for the existing social order serves as an
important mechanism for social control in the society. History however also
reveals that religion has also been an important emancipatory and revolutionary force (Dawson, 1993).

Religion and religious institutions do not exist in a vacuum and cannot
be indifferent to the surrounding social, political, and economic institutions. Religious movements originate within a particular societal context
and initially may be threatening to the existing social and power arrangements. However, religion also has to contend with the societal forces
that may often create contradictions and conflicts between the ideal religious tenets and everyday life experiences and individual and institutional
practices.

This brief introduction provides the context within which the origin, history, religious beliefs, practices, and institutions of the Sikh religion are discussed. More specifically, this chapter discusses the social context within which the Sikh religion emerged, life and contributions of Sikh gurus, religious beliefs, codes and practices, and the birth of the Khalsa.

SIKH GURUS AND SIKH RELIGION

A Sikh is any person whose faith consists of belief in one God, the Ten Gurus, the Guru Granth Sahib, and other scriptures of Sikh religion. Additionally, he or she must believe in the necessity and importance of Amrit––the Sikh baptism ceremony. [SGPC, 1945.]

At the birth of Guru Nanak, the founder of the Sikh religion, in the fifteenth century, India was in a period of major economic, political, and social unrest and instability. Feudalism, oppression, foreign invasions, idol worship, caste prejudice, and religious intolerance were paramount (Singh, 1983:3; de Souza, 1986:8). Under the Muslim Mughal rulers there was widespread plunder and destruction of Hindu property, conversion of Hindus to Islam by force, and extensive victimization (murder, rapes) of the population. The Hindu religion was steeped in superstitions and ritualism, and the Hindus themselves were fragmented into caste divisions and the upper-caste Brahmins exercised oppressive authority and control over the others, particularly the lowest 'untouchable' caste (de Souza, 1986). While Hindus also regarded the Muslims as untouchables, the Muslims believed that all Hindus were infidels, to be converted to Islam, by the sword if necessary (Sikh Society, 1984:3). Sikhism took birth within these circum-stances (Singh, 1963).

These briefly were the conditions when Guru Nanak was born on 15 April 1469 in the village of Talwandi near Lahore (now in Pakistan). He travelled widely and preached against ritualism, superstitions, caste system, religious intolerance, and religious oppression by the Mughal rulers. His message was one of love, equality, fraternity, and tolerance. As Harbans Singh (1983) states, the primary message of Guru Nanak included the unity of God, human brotherhood (and sisterhood), rejection of caste, and the futility of idol worship.

This message and his teachings basically questioned the then prevailing structural arrangements and were a threat to those who had power and benefitted from a system of inequality. In essence, his message was one of emancipation, equality, liberation, and change. This, of course, did not find favour with both the rulers and the dominant caste (de Souza, 1986).

After the death of the founder there was a succession of nine more Gurus (Box 2.1). The succession of each Guru was by appointment which was the prerogative of the Guru immediately preceding the successor. Guru Angad, who succeeded Guru Nanak, continued his work and was instrumental in making knowledge more accessible to the common people through his writings and teachings in the Punjabi language. This basically threatened and undermined the authority of the priests who wrote in Sanskrit, the language of the privileged classes (de Souza, 1986).

Guru Amar Das, the third Guru, continued the process of democratization by institutionalizing the practice of *langar* or free kitchen where everyone ate together regardless of religious, caste, and class background. The fourth Guru, Guru Ram Das, continued the teachings and practices of his predecessors and also founded the city of Amritsar (de Souza, 1986).

The fifth Guru, Guru Arjan, is remembered for two very important contributions to the Sikh religion and the Sikh community, building the Golden Temple and the compilation of the Granth Sahib (Sikh Holy Book). However, unlike the Mughal emperor Akbar, who was tolerant of other religions, his successor Jahangir felt threatened by the Guru and the Sikhs and tried to convert him to Islam. When Guru Arjun refused he was tortured and executed by the emperor. The martyrdom of the fifth Guru had a profound impact on his successor and led to an important shift in the orientation and methods of the Sikh community of using force if necessary to defend their faith.

The sixth Guru, Hargobind, started the military organization of the Sikhs to fight against religious persecution and started using two swords, Miri and Piri, the former to endow worldly strength and the latter for spiritual might (de Souza, 1986). He also established the throne of religious authority, Siri Akal Takht, at Amritsar.

The seventh and eighth Gurus (Har Rai and Hari Krishen) continued to follow the religious path of their predecessors.

The ninth Guru, Tegh Bahadur, faced both internal and external challenges. Within the Sikh community, some of his relatives questioned the legitimacy of succession. Externally, non-Muslims faced religions persecution by the Mughal emperor Aurangzeb. When some Hindus sought the Guru's help against conversion by force, he told them to tell the Mughal officials that they would convert to Islam if he (the Guru) agreed to such

Box 2.1
Sikh Gurus

Gurus	Date of assumption as Guru	Brief account
1. Guru Nanak Dev Jee 1469–1539	From birth	Founder of Sikh faith: Preached equality, tolerance, peace, unity and truth. Against the caste system and rituals of Hinduism and the fanaticism and intolerance of Islam and Mughal rulers.
2. Guru Angad Dev Jee 1504–1552	7–9–1539	Introduced the Gurumukhi alphabet and taught and wrote in Punjabi. He also compiled the biography of Guru Nanak Dev Jee.
3. Guru Amar Das Jee 1479–1574	26–3–1552	Instituted *langar* (free kitchen) where everyone, regardless of caste, colour, or religion ate together, a practice which promotes equality and egalitarianism.
4. Guru Ram Das Jee 1534–1581	30–8–1574	Founder of Sacred Sarovar (lake of immortality) and founded the present city of Amritsar (pool of immortal nectar).
5. Guru Arjan Dev Jee 1563–1606	1–9–1581	Author–compiler of the Adi-Granth in 1604 and founder of Har-Mandir-Sahib (Golden Temple) at Amritsar. Martyred in 1606.
6. Guru Har Gobind Jee 1595–1644	25–5–1606	Wore two swords of power: Miri for secular authority (worldly power) and Piri for spiritual might. Also built the Akal Takht, seat of Sikh religious authority.

7. Guru Har Rai Jee 1630–1661	8–3–1644	Spent most of his time in propagating the Sikh faith.
8. Guru Har Krishan Jee 1656–1664	6–10–1661	Son of Guru Har Rai Jee whom he succeeded at the age of five. Died after a short life due to smallpox (child Guru).
9. Guru Teg Bahadur Jee 1621–1675	20–3–1665	Fought for freedom of worship for religions and against conversion by force to Islam by Mughal emperor Aurangzeb. Martyred at Delhi on 11 November 1675.
10. Guru Gobind Singh Jee 1666–1708	11–11–1675	Gave the final form to the Sikh faith, instituted baptism and created the Khalsa. All male initiates are given the name Singh (lion) and women Kaur (princess). Completed the Adi Granth and ordained the Khalsa to recognize the Granth Sahib as the manifest body of the Gurus for their guidance.

conversion. When Guru Tegh Bahadur refused to convert, he was beheaded in New Delhi on 11 November 1675. His son, the tenth Guru, later wrote of his father's martyrdom for upholding the rights of Hindus to worship in a manner of their choice:

> To protect their right to wear their
> caste-marks and sacred threads,
> Did he, in the dark age, perform
> the supreme sacrifice.

Guru Gobind Rai, the tenth Guru, was only nine at the time of his father's martyrdom. He was quite clear about his mission, 'to uphold the right in every place, to destroy sin and evil', and was prepared to use force if necessary to defend the rights and faith. He declared:

> When all other means have failed,
> It is permissible to draw the sword.

He gave final form to the Sikh faith, instituted baptism and created the order of baptised Sikhs called the Khalsa.

The Guru founded the Khalsa at Anandpur on Baisakhi day in 1699. On this particular day the Guru appeared before a large public gathering who had come to celebrate this festival with his sword drawn and asked for a volunteer to come forward to be sacrificed in the cause of religion. A man stepped forward and was taken into a tent by the Guru, who later emerged alone with his sword dripping in blood. He repeated this process four more times. In this manner five men were led into the tent and were apparently sacrificed by the Guru. However, the five later emerged from the tent unharmed, accompanied by the Guru. He announced to the gathering that the five would be known as Panj Piara (the five beloved ones). The Guru then baptised the five by using *amrit* (sugar and water stirred by a double-edged sword). They all drank from the same bowl to signify equality, unity, and community. They were all given the one family name of Singh (lion). The Guru then asked the five to baptise him and from then on also assumed the name Singh and became Guru Gobind Singh. The females initiated were given the name Kaur (princess).

Thus, the tenth Guru gave the final form to the Panth (the Sikh community) and the Khalsa (the pure ones, the order of baptised Sikhs). The members of Khalsa were given five emblems: *kes, kangha, kachha, kara,* and *kirpan*, commonly known as the 5Ks (see Box 2.2). All these five emblems and the turban now form an integral part of the distinct identity of the Khalsa, 'even one is recognized in a crowd of a thousand'. The baptised Sikh must keep the five Ks and are forbidden (SGPC, 1945) to:

1. Smoke tobacco or take drugs and intoxicants.
2. Eat meat killed by ritual slow slaughter (halal).
3. Commit adultery.
4. Cut bodily hair.

Guru Gobind Singh's purpose in asking for five volunteers (the Panj Piara) in the dramatic manner he did was to emphasize that the members of the Khalsa must be prepared to sacrifice their lives in defence of their faith. Hence a new fighting community was born who believe in

Raj Karega Khalsa
(The Khalsa Shall Rule)

BOX 2.2

SIKH EMBLEMS: THE TURBAN AND THE 5KS

Kes (hair)	Represents simplicity of life, saintliness, wisdom, and devotion to God.
Kangha (comb)	To keep the hair tidy and clean. It signifies physical and mental cleanliness.
Kara (steel bracelet)	Refers to ethics, a symbol of responsibility. It reminds Sikhs not to misuse their hands and not to commit any sins.
Kachha (shorts)	Refers to sexual morality and is meant as a constant reminder of fidelity.
Kirpan (sword)	Refers to the sovereign power of God, which controls the destiny of all creation.
Turban	In addition to the 5Ks, the Sikh turban is an integral part of the Khalsa identity. '*Sabat surat dastar sira*', only with the turban on is the appearance complete.

---

and

Waheguru ji ka Khalsa siri Waheguru ji ka fateh
(Hail Khalsa of the wonderful Lord who is always Victorious)

After having created a distinct community of the Khalsa, the Guru felt ready to confront and resist persecution by the Mughals. In this struggle his four sons lost their lives (two in battles and two walled-in alive) along with many other Sikhs. Guru Gobind Singh himself died on 7 October 1708, of stab wounds.

The tenth Guru also found time to compose poetry and other writings which subsequently became part of the Dasam Granth. The Granth Sahib, first compiled in 1604 by Guru Arjan, was completed in its final form by Guru Gobind Singh. Before his death in 1708, he also told his followers that the line of Gurus was to end with him and they were to seek guidance from then on from the Granth. He, in essence, invested Guruship in the Granth, frequently referred to thereafter at the Guru Granth Sahib: the symbol and the living voice of the Gurus.

The recognition of Khalsa Panth and 'Granth as Guru' is signified in the following hymns which are sung at the conclusion of every *ardas* which is a short direct prayer to God (SGPC, 1945).

Agya bhai Akal ki tabhi chalaio Panth.
Sabh Sikhan ko Hukam hai Guru Manio Granth.
Guru Granth ji manio paragat Guran ki deh.
Jo Prabh ko milbo chahe khoj Shabad main leh.
Raj karega Khalsa aki rahe na koe.
Khawar hoe sabh milenge bache saran jo hoi.

This is translated as:

Command came from the Timeless God.
And there was established the (Khalsa) Panth.
All Sikhs are commanded to recognize the Granth as the Guru.
Recognize the Granth as the Guru;
It is the visible body of the Masters.
Those who wish to meet the Lord may see Him therein
(in the Granth).
The Khalsa shall rule, no hostile refractories shall exist. Frustrated,
they shall all submit, and those who come in for shelter shall be
saved.

This is followed by a spirited *Sat Sri Akal* (True is the Eternal Lord).

The Guru Granth Sahib begins with *Mool Mantra*, the basic beliefs of the
Sikh faith (SGPC, 1945):

Ik O-Ankaar Satnam,
Karta, Purakh, Nirbhao Nirvair,
Akaal Moorat A Joonee Sarbang,
Gur Parsad.

This translates as:

There is One God; His Name is Truth
The All Pervading Creator,
Without Fear, Without Hatred,
Immortal, Unborn, Self-Existent,
He is realized with Guru's Grace.

Sikhs continued resistance and struggle against persecution, led by Banda
Singh who was named by the Guru as army commander before his death.
Banda Singh was captured by the Mughals and executed in 1716. The
persecution of the Sikhs continued to intensify and often led to massacre,
including the first 'Ghallugahara' (holocaust) in June 1746 when 7,000
Sikhs were massacred around Lahore (now in Pakistan). Lahore is also the

location of Shahid Ganj (place of the martyrs) in remembrance of Sikh martyrs (de Souza, 1986). The Afghan ruler (successor to the Mughals) Abdali, continued atrocities against the Sikhs, and was responsible for the desecration of the Golden Temple several times. He is also infamous for the slaughter of an estimated 30,000 Sikhs, principally old men, women and children, on 5 February 1762. This episode is known and remembered today as 'Vada Ghallugahara' (the big holocaust).

Yet, in spite of all these atrocities the Sikhs survived and flourished, and the Sikh armies captured Lahore in 1765 and later extended their influence and power throughout Punjab and beyond.

THE DEVELOPMENT OF SIKHISM AND SIKH IDENTITY

The Sikh religion originated in particular social, economic, and political conditions. Guru Nanak, the founder, spoke against religious intolerance, caste prejudices, religious rituals, oppression and inequality between men and women. His message was one of equality, religious tolerance, fraternity, and egality. Speaking against the ill-treatment of women, the Guru said: 'How can you condemn her who gives birth to kings or prophets'. He thus promoted change and liberation theology. Following Guru Nanak, as noted earlier, his successors initiated other practices to promote equality, such as *langar*, dissemination of knowledge in common everyday language, baptism available to men and women, and supremacy of the *sangat* (congregation) in decision-making.

These tenets of liberation and equality, and their popularity among the people, were always viewed by the Mughal rulers as a threat to their empire. The Mughal rulers and their Afghan successors, with the exception of Akbar, continued a campaign of religious intolerance and forcible conversion of Hindus to Islam and persecution of the followers of the Gurus. These oppressive policies of the Mughals transformed the Sikhs from a primarily pacifist people under Guru Nanak to a people prepared to use force to defend their faith and religion and the religious practices of the Hindus. For the Sikhs the idea of sacrifice is exemplified in the martyrdom of Gurus Arjan and Teg Bahadur, the willingness of the Panj Piaras to offer their lives in response to the Guru's call, sacrifice of four sons of Guru Gobind Singh, and his own life to resist and fight oppression. The creation of the Khalsa by Guru Gobind Singh gave a final form to this transformation. It gave Sikhs not only a distinct identity in the form of physical appearance, but also as a people prepared to make the ultimate sacrifice to defend themselves by force (militancy) if necessary.

Their sense of persecution as a religious minority, self-sacrifice, and militancy have their roots in the historical–structural conditions of the origin and development of the Sikh religion. More recent struggles and events discussed later, such as the Gurdwara Reform Movement (1920–5), the partition of Punjab in 1947, and Operation Blue Star have only contributed to and reinforced their sense of persecution as a religious and political minority. These events, to a large extent, are also responsible for Sikh demands for autonomy and the resort to militancy to secure these demands.

SIKH ETHICAL VALUES: PERSONAL AND SOCIAL CONDUCT

The Sikh religion is concerned both with a person's life as an individual and his corporate life as a member of the Sikh community (SGPC, 1945). The Sikh religion, like other faiths, prescribes a code of conduct which gives guidance in matters religious, social, and personal (Philauri and Court, 1959; Mansukhani, 1986; SPGC, 1945). In all spheres, the 'Code of the Sikhs' is democratic, egalitarian, and progressive. Sikh ethical values and moral standards are those prescribed by the Gurus. Some of the codes of behaviour have been discussed in previous pages, such as the five Ks, prohibition of consumption of intoxicants, and moral conduct. Sikhism also postulates certain other ethics and values which are applicable to people's daily existence. Sikhism 'rejects asceticism and retreat from normal life' and recommends general ethical values such as 'hard work, honesty, understanding moderation in all things and moral purity' (Mansukhani, 1986:17). Sikhism 'offers a chance for material success and spiritual uplift of all people' (Mansukhani, 1986:17). The Sikhs are expected to 'shun those things which cause either pain or harm to the body or produce evil thoughts in the mind' (Guru Granth Sahib [GGS]:16). In matters of economic pursuit, the Gurus emphasized hard work and honesty. The means used to earn one's living should be moral and legal, and should not involve deceit, cheating, double-dealing, or other underhanded methods. Dishonesty in business or the utterance of lies causes inner sorrow (GGS:1062).

Guru Nanak recommended honest earning and sharing: 'The best course is to use the fruits of one's own labour, and share it with others' (GGS:1245).

Even 'the wealth and worldly goods are permissible for a holy person, since he can use them for charitable purpose and the giving of happiness to others' (GGS:1246).

In social conduct and behaviour, Sikhism promotes equality for all human beings. The Guru particularly focused on equality between men and women and abolished such practices as sex-segregation in worship, veiling (*purdah*) of women, female infanticide, prohibition of widow remarriage, and the practice of *sati* (Mansukhani, 1986). Women may lead the congregation in worship, perform the baptism ceremony, become a Panj Piara, and fight in battles alongside men.

At a more general level, the Gurus had a vision of a society and the state based on 'equality, liberty, justice and one without hunger, poverty or distress' and social harmony and just administration (Mansukhani, 1986). The Guru says:

Now is the gracious Lord's ordinance promulgated: no one should cause another pain or injury: all mankind should live in peace together, under a shield of government benevolence [GGS:74].

Sikhism also emphasizes Five Virtues: chastity, patience, contentment, detachment, and humility (Mansukhani, 1986). Chastity primarily promotes mutual fidelity in family life and prohibits pre-marital and extra-marital sex. Patience implies forbearance and courage in the face of adversity, challenge, and suffering. The Guru declares: 'The contented ones do not tread the path of evil; rather they practice righteousness and good to others ...' (GGS:467). Detachment does not mean renunciation or indifference to the world, but rather, 'the detached individual lives in the world, but is not involved in worldliness, for he has his eyes set on spiritual goals' (Mansukhani, 1986). Humility is a remedy against egoism and pride. Sikh daily prayers ask for humility: 'Be not proud of your virtue, say to God and others, I am virtueless' (GGS:577).

The most authoritative source on the Sikh way of life is *Rehat-Maryada*, published by the Shiromani Gurdwara Parbandhak Committee (SGPC, 1945), Amritsar, which includes detailed guidelines for Sikhs in many areas: study of scriptures; daily prayers; congregational devotion and behaviour; maintenance of the Gurdwara; the norms and prescriptions concerning *kirtan* (singing of hymns); *ardas* (Lord's prayer); religious ceremonies concerning birth, marriage, and death. The relevant section, entitled 'Living According to the Guru's Teaching', is reproduced below (Box 2.3).

CONTRADICTIONS OF EVERYDAY LIVING

As the foregoing discussion indicates, the Sikh religion was born in a particular time in Indian history when the country was engulfed in social, economic, and political turmoil and uncertainty. Political oppression, religious intolerance, caste biases, extreme economic inequality, prejudice and discrimination against women, religious superstitions and idol worship,

---

Box 2.3
LIVING ACCORDING TO THE GURU'S TEACHINGS
(From SGPC, *Rehat-Maryada, 1945*)

A Sikh should live and work according to the principles of Sikhism, and should be guided by the following:

(a) He or she should worship only one God, and should not indulge in any form of idol worship.

(b) Live a life based on the teachings of the ten Gurus, the Guru Granth, and Sikh Scriptures.

(c) Sikhs should believe in the 'oneness' of the ten Gurus, that is, that a single soul or entity pervaded the lives of the ten Gurus.

(d) A Sikh should have no dealings with caste, black magic, superstitious practices such as the seeking of auspicious moments, eclipses, the practice of feeding Brahmins in the belief that the food will go to one's ancestors, ancestor worship, fasting at different phases of the moon, the wearing of sacred threads and similar rituals.

(e) The Gurdwara should serve as the Sikh's central place of worship. Although the Guru Granth is the centre of Sikh belief, non-Sikh books can be studied for general enlightenment.

(f) Sikhism is distinct from other religions, but Sikhs must in no way give offence to other faiths.

(g) Knowledge of Sikhism is highly desirable for a Sikh and this should be acquired in addition to his other education.

(h) It is the duty of Sikhs to teach Sikhism to their children.

(i) Sikhs should not cut their children's hair. Boys are to be given the name Singh and girls the name Kaur.

(j) Sikhs should not partake of alcohol, tobacco, drugs or other intoxicants.

(k) The religion strongly condemns infanticide.

(l) Sikhs should only live on money that has been honestly earned.

(m) No Sikh should gamble or commit theft.

(n) Sikhs must not commit adultery.

(o) A Sikh should respect another man's wife as he would his own mother; and another man's daughter as his own daughter.

(p) A Sikh should enjoy his spouse's companionship and both should be loyal to each other.

(q) A Sikh should live his life from birth to death according to the tenets of his faith.

(r) A Sikh should greet other Sikhs with the salutation 'Waheguru ji ka Khalsa, Siri Waheguru ji ki fateh' (Hail Khalsa of the wonderful Lord who is always victorious).

(s) It is contrary to Sikhism for women to wear *purdah*.

(t) Any clothing may be worn by a Sikh provided it includes a turban (for males) and shorts or similar garment.

and other backward practices such as *sati*, characterized Indian society. Guru Nanak, the founder, spoke against all these ills and his social message was one of equality, fraternity, egality. His religious message was of belief in one God and against superstitions and idol worship, and of religious tolerance. The successors to Guru Nanak continued and promoted the basic religious and social tenets of Sikhism. The Sikhs, in their personal and social behaviour, are expected to live their lives according to Sikhism.

While the message of Sikhism is one of emancipation, liberation, tolerance, and change, Sikhs and Sikh religious institutions have to contend with the prevailing social, cultural, and other societal forces. The prevalent social and cultural practices are in contradiction and conflict with the basic Sikh principles and ethical values. Therefore, in their daily existence, devotees are likely to face the dilemma posed by the contradictions between religious tenets and their own behaviour. For instance, caste prejudices, religious intolerance and conflicts, inequality, and differential treatment of women are dominant characteristics of Indian society. Sikhs, as a minority and part of that society cannot insulate themselves from these practices.

Consequently, caste prejudices, sex discrimination, and other such practices are not any less prevalent among the Sikhs than amongst the other religious groups. Sikhs are not a homogeneous group: contradictions of occupational differentiations, political differences, educational background, different economic interests, struggles for political and economic control of the Gurdwaras contribute to the internal dissension and disunity within the Sikh community. However, within the four walls of Sikh institutions, such as the Gurdwara (the Sikh place of worship Sikh temple), equality and egalitarian practices are easy to attain. Everyone is welcome to enter the Gurdwara (regardless of caste, creed, and religion), men and women can participate as equals in religious activities and services and the institution of *langar* in Gurdwaras promotes equality and service.

The contradictions and conflicts between the 'ideal' and the 'real' are not unique to the Sikh religion. All religions to some extent have to deal with the social, cultural, economic, and political forces in the society. However, rather than in conflict, the religion may also support the status quo and provide supernatural legitimacy to the prevailing structural arrangements. Thus, as noted previously, religion may challenge and pose a threat or lend support to the status quo.

SUMMARY

Since its inception the Sikh religion and the Sikh community have experienced numerous changes. The history of the Sikhs is replete with persecution, oppression, martyrdom, sacrifices, and the genocidal policies of Mughals and Afghans. These experiences led to the transformation of the Sikhs from being a peaceful community to one prepared to defend their faith 'with sword' if necessary. The last Guru, Gobind Singh, gave birth to the Khalsa Panth in 1699 and gave the Sikhs a distinct physical identity, the 5Ks and turban, and the Granth Sahib became the embodiment of the Gurus and the pre-eminent source of religious guidance. The Sikh identity of self-sacrifice, bravado, and valour is rooted in their historical experiences, the Panj Piaras, and the exemplary conduct of the Gurus, especially Gurus Arjan Dev, Teg Bahadur, and Gobind Singh.

The Sikh religious message is of belief in one God, and of respect and tolerance for other religions. Sikh principles promote equality, egality, fraternity, and service; and the Sikhs are expected to live their lives according to the Gurus' teachings. Sikhs are not, however, insulated from the dominant social and cultural forces and other prevailing societal institutions. This may lead to potential contradictions between one's religious tenets and everyday living experiences. These contradictions are, however, not unique to any one particular religious group.

Religion is an important source of community identity, internal solidarity, and cohesion. At the same time, religion is often the source of intra-group conflict and may form the basis of political division and struggles. As the discussion in the following pages indicates, religious affiliation and identity continue to play an important role in Indian politics. Religionization of politics is intertwined with the 'politics of language', caste, and regional loyalties. There appears to be a weakening of secular forces, and increasing importance of religion based political parties at the regional and national levels. These developments have contributed to the political instability in India, in particular at the federal level (central government), which is manifested in the inability of any one party to win a parliamentary majority in recent elections (since the nineties), leading to fragile and unstable coalition governments. Strong electoral showing by the Hindu nationalist Bharatiya Janata Party (BJP) at the central level is seen by the religious minorities (Muslims, Christians, Sikhs and others) as a threat to their religion and religious institutions. These trends in Indian politics are likely to heighten religious consciousness and sensitivities, increase religious conflicts, and pose a threat not only to the secular foundation of the Indian state, but also to its very survival.

REFERENCES

Bannerjee, S. (1984): 'Divide and Rule Tactics', *South*, The Third World Magazine (London: South Publications Ltd. May).

Cole, W. Owen and P.S. Sambhi (1978): *The Sikhs: Their Religious Beliefs and Practices* (London: Routledge & Kegan Paul).

Dawson, Lorne L. (1993): 'Religion and Legitimacy', pp. 311–27 in Peter Li and B. Singh Bolaria (eds), *Contemporary Sociology: Critical Perspectives* (Toronto: Copp Clark Pitman Ltd.).

de Souza, Allan (1986): *The Sikhs in Britain* (London: B.T. Batsford Ltd.).

Howard, Michael (1995): Address of the House Secretary, The Wembley Conference Centre Celebration. *Sikh Messenger* (London), Summer–Autumn.

Mansukhani, G.S. (1986): 'Sikhism and the Ethical Values', *Sikh Messenger* vol. no. 1, 21–3 (London).

McLeod, W.H. (1993): 'Sikhs: History, Religion and Society', *Pacific Affairs*, vol. 66, no. 2, Summer.

Ministry of Planning, Government of India (1990): Statistical Abstract—India, Central Statistical Organization, Department of Statistics.

Philauri, Sharadha Rama, and Henry Court (1959): *History of the Sikhs* (Calcutta, India: Susil Gupta Printer Ltd.).

Puri, Gopal Singh (1992): *Multicultural Society and Sikh Faith* (New Delhi: Falcon Books).

Shiromani Gurdwara Parbandhak Committee (SGPC) (1945): *Rehat-Maryada: A Guide to the Sikh Way of Life* (Amristar).

Shiromani Gurdwara Parbandhak Committee (1982): 'The Golden Temple', Amritsar.

Sikh Society (1984): 'Khalsa', Newsletter of the Sikh Society, University of Cambridge, June.

Singh, Khushwant (1963): *History of the Sikhs*, vol. I, 1469–1839 (Princeton, New Jersey: Princeton University Press).

Singh, Harbans (1983): *Heritage of the Sikhs* (Columbia, Missouri: South Asia Books).

State, Religion, Language, and Politics

❦

INTRODUCTION

The distinct identity and the formation of Khalsa Panth is rooted in particular structural conditions of the origin of the Sikh religion and the prolonged historical struggles of the Sikhs against oppressive state policies of the Mughal–Afghan rulers. With the weakening of the Mughal–Afghan state and the progressive military strength of the Sikhs, they were able to consolidate their state power under Maharaja Ranjit Singh. It seems that it was only during this short time period that the Sikhs enjoyed a certain level of political, economic, and social stability. After the death of Maharaja Ranjit Singh, dissension and political conflicts among his successors created the opportunity for the British to annex Punjab and extend and consolidate their colonial rule throughout India.

Around this time there were also internal conflicts within the Sikh community over religious practices and principles, and over the control of Sikh institutions. The Sikhs had to engage in a long five-year struggle (1920–5) to secure control and governance of their Gurdwaras and religious affairs.

The rise and fall of the Sikh state; colonial state policies toward Sikhs; Indian anti-colonial politics, and the role of the Sikhs, all need to be considered to fully appreciate the current political, economic, and geographical demands of the Sikhs.

Of course, independence and partition of India in which religion played a decisive role in the creation of the separate state of Pakistan, and the partition of Punjab and the resettlement of Sikhs are important events in post-Independence politics in India. The actions of the Congress party and the Indian state, the Indian constitution and the federal–provincial jurisdictional conflicts sharpened political contradictions and conflicts in India. Regional and tribal movements to form provincial and territorial boundaries based on linguistic and cultural bases sprang up in various parts of India. Punjab's post-Independence politics since 1947 is deeply rooted in the linguistic and cultural distinctiveness of the area in conjunction with economic and political demands.

Over the years, 'Punjabi demands' have come to be increasingly identified as 'Sikh demands' leading inexorably to communalization/religionization of politics. The growing militancy of a segment of the Sikh community, and political opportunism of the central government, finally culminated in extremely oppressive state policies in Punjab in the 1980s. Events such as Operation Blue Star in Punjab and anti-Sikh riots in various parts of India following the assassination of Indira Gandhi heightened religious consciousness and sense of alienation among the Sikhs. The Sikh community is by no means monolithic in its political strategy to secure and safeguard their rights.

The self-perception of the Sikhs as an oppressed minority discriminated against and their desire to create political and economic conditions and a geographical entity to safeguard their religious and linguistic rights can only be fully appreciated in the context of the pre- and post-Independence politics and events.

This chapter is an attempt to provide the social, economic, political, and communal (religious) context of the historical and contemporary dimensions of the 'Punjab problem'.

THE SIKH STATE PRIOR TO BRITISH COLONIALISM: THE SIKH RAJ

After Guru Gobind Singh died there was a period of turmoil and uncertainty for the Sikhs. The Sikhs continued their resistance against persecution under Banda Singh (Banda Bahadur) who was named by the tenth Guru as army commander before his death and commissioned to go to Punjab and fight to protect the Sikh religion and the interests of the Sikh community. He was able to establish rule in the Sirhind area of Punjab for a short time but was later arrested by the forces of Bahadur Shah and executed in Delhi.

During this time period, Muslim rule began to weaken due to internal conflicts and Sikhs were able to establish small independent principalities, called *misls*. Each of these 12 *misls* was headed by a *sardar* who exercised sovereignty over a certain geographical area (see Box 3.1). The descendant of the rulers of one of these *misls* (Sukkarchakkia), Ranjit Singh, was eventually able to bring under his control most of the *misls*. Ranjit Singh was born on 13 November 1780 in Gujranwala. At the age of 19 he took control and power, and was proclaimed Maharaja of Punjab. Over the years he

---

Box 3.1
Sikh *Misls*
(Confederacies–Principalities)

Misls	Area
Ahluwalias	Held territory in the neighbourhood of Kapurthala in the Jullundur *doab*, and some villages in the Majha such as Sarhali, Jandiala, Bundala, Vairowal, and Fatehabad.
Bhangis	Owned Sialkot, Gujrat, Multan, Amritsar, Taran Taran, and Lahore.
Ramgarhias	Quadian, Batala, Sri Hargobindpur in the Bari *doab*, Miani, Sarih and Urmur Tanda in Jullundur *doab*.
Singhpurias	Jullundur and the villages of Banur, Ghanauli, Manauli, and Bharatgarh in Malwa.
Sukkarchakkias	Controlled Gujranwala and parts of Pothohar.
Kanhaiyas	Controlled the *parganna* of Batala.
Shahids	Had their possessions in the present districts of Ambala (*parganna* of Shahsadpur) and Saharanpur.
Nakais	Ruled over the country south of Lahore, between the Ravi and the Sutlej.
Dallewalias	Under Tara Singh Ghaiba held Rahon, Mahatpur, Nawanshahar, and Phillaur, in the Jullundur *doab*.
Nishanwala	Standard-bearers of the Khalsa army, had their centre at Ambala.
Karorsinghias	Adopting the name of the leader, Karora Singh, took Hoshiarpur and the surrounding district.
Phulkians	Embraced the territories of Patiala, Sirhind, Nabhia, and Jind.

Source: Compiled from Harbans Singh, *Heritage of the Sikhs* (Columbia, Mo.: South Asian Books, 1983), p. 142.

consolidated his empire in various stages by negotiating with the various *sardars* (heads) of the *misls* and by conquest.

Ranjit Singh remained very popular with the masses after he became Maharaja because of his humility and rejection of traditional symbols of superior status. For instance, he refused to wear the emblem of royalty on his turban and preferred to sit cross-legged on the floor, rather than sit on a throne when meeting other people. Neither the emblem nor the coins of the government bore any reference to him.

During his rule he demonstrated his political shrewdness and leadership qualities. He recruited capable and competent persons into his government, irrespective of their religion, ethnicity, or nationality. His army had officers from the UK, France, the US, and other foreign countries, with the objective of learning from the experience of foreigners and create discipline and order in his kingdom. He himself was trained in martial arts and hand-to-hand combat.

Ranjit Singh believed that, 'it was the destiny of the Sikhs to rule, and that perhaps he had been chosen by the Gurus to be the instrument of their inscrutable design' (Singh, K., 1963:202). His goal was to form a Punjabi state rather than a Sikh kingdom. True to the teachings of Sikhism, his policies were of religious tolerance and religious freedoms. Hindus, Muslims, and others were all free to practice their religion and maintain their customs.

Ranjit Singh had a formidable army which was well trained and well equipped. It is estimated that he had an army of 123,800 men: 60 regiments of regular infantry (42,000), Akali fanatics (5,000), irregular levies and garrison troops (45,000). With respect to resources, the cavalry had 31,800 horses, 337 field artillery and heavy guns, and 228 light artillery (Hasrat, 1968:186). Ranjit Singh controlled the area between the 28th and 36th parallels of the north latitude and between the 71st and 77th meridians of the east longitude (Cunningham, 1853:1).

By 1800 the British had established their rule in all of the other parts of India except Punjab. A Friendship Treaty was signed between the British rulers of India and Maharaja Ranjit Singh in 1809. The relationship between the British and the Maharaja was cordial. Ranjit Singh had an understanding with the British that embodied two basic agreements: not to expand south of the Sutlej River and not to intervene in the affairs of the other *misls* which fell under the area of British rule. He respected this agreement with the British and did not therefore violate the Friendship Treaty.

After a short illness, Ranjit Singh died on 27 June 1839. The Sikh state disintegrated after his death due to internal struggles among his descendants and external threat from the British. The internal conflicts weakened the state, and in the absence of a strong leader like Ranjit Singh there were mutinies within the army. Ranjit Singh's sons and relatives, his ministers and others continued to struggle against one another to control the state power. The British took advantage of these divisions which corresponded to their 'divide and rule' strategy in India (Singh, H., 1983:209). This struggle often took the form of betrayal, conspiracies, and murder (Singh, H., 1983:187–193).

Recognizing this progressive worsening of internal conflicts among the Sikhs and weakening of their power, the British declared war on the Sikhs. The Sikhs fought bravely and engaged the British in battle for over a year, often referred to as the First Anglo–Sikh War. They were defeated by the British primarily due to traitors within their own ranks. General Lal Singh and Tej Singh betrayed the Sikhs in exchange for favours from the British (Singh, K., 1963:48). The Sikhs surrendered on 29 February 1846, and in March 1848 Punjab was annexed by the British (Singh,. H., 1983:205–10). There were small rebellions in 1848, but eventually in March 1849, the Sikh flag was lowered in Lahore and replaced by the Union Jack. Thus the British succeeded in extending their rule throughout India, where they remained until 1947. The last ruler, Maharaja Dalip Singh, was exiled to England and was forced to convert to Christianity. Never allowed to return to India, he died in Paris on 22 October 1893.

GURDWARA REFORM MOVEMENT

During Maharaja Ranjit Singh's reign the Sikh religion and the Sikh community flourished and prospered. Many more gurdwaras and shrines were built, restored, and renovated under Ranjit Singh's patronage. The dream of the Khalsa had been realized. The collapse of the Sikh state and colonial rule led to the decline of the Khalsa Panth, and weakening of the Sikh religion. Internal conflicts and factionalism among the Sikhs gave rise to groups with competing religious beliefs and practices. Some Sikhs were even reverting to Hindu traditions, and they also basically lost control of their gurdwaras, at least temporarily. The struggle to revitalize the basic Sikh principles and regain control of the Sikh institutions were important factors in the formation of Sikh identity.

One of the challenges faced by the Sikhs was posed by the 'Nirankaris'. The founder (Baba Dyal Singh, 1783–1855) and the followers of this movement believed in a 'living Guru' rather than the Guru Granth Sahib. This, of course, is contrary to the teachings of Guru Gobind Singh who before his death told his followers that the line of Gurus was to end with him and in essence invested Guruship in the Granth Sahib.

Numerous organizations and movements emerged to restore the basic principles of Sikhism, including the Kuka movement by Bhai Balik Singh and the Singh Sabha and Guru Singh Sabha movements. The Singh Sabha movement, established on 1 October 1873, was formed in response to a number of events and trends which threatened Sikhism in India: the conversion of Sikhs to Christianity; attacks on the Sikh religion by some European and Indian writers; and the tendency on the part of the Sikhs to follow Hindu rituals and superstitions. Therefore, the primary objective of the Singh Sabha movement was to counter these trends and revitalize Sikh principles, practices, and ideals.

Other organizations and institutions were formed to coordinate the activities of sundry groups and promote Sikh studies and religion. For instance, the Khalsa Diwan was formed in 1883 to coordinate the work and efforts of various Singh Sabha chapters and the Khalsa Diwan Society on 19 August 1902 with the objective of promoting the Sikh religion. The prominent educational institution, the Khalsa College in Amritsar was established on 5 March 1892 to encourage Sikh studies and higher education for Sikhs. This institution has been primarily supported by the Sikh princely states and the Sikh community and continues to be an important symbol of Sikh identity in Punjab.

One of the most important and protracted struggles waged by the Sikhs in the 1920s was for the control of the Sikh gurdwaras. This struggle was to expel the *mahants* (priests) from the Sikh shrines. The *mahants* were using the gurdwaras for personal material gains and power and were engaged in anti-Sikh activities and often desecration of the Sikh shrines. These *mahants* were supported by the British. In this struggle, nearly forty thousand Sikhs were jailed and approximately four hundred lost their lives (Singh, H., 1983:279). Finally, after much violence and loss of life, the British government capitulated to the Sikh demands to control their own gurdwaras by passing the Gurdwara Act on 25 July 1925.

Two important Sikh organizations were also formed during this period. The Shiromani Gurdwara Parbandhak Committee (SGPC) was formed on

15 November 1920 to administer the operation of the gurdwaras. The Shiromani Akali Dal (Sikh political party) was formed on 14 December 1920 to work for reforms in the gurdwaras under the direction of the SGPC (Singh, H., 1982:34).

The British colonial policy of 'divide and rule' also contributed to the distinct political and religious identity of the Sikhs. The British electoral policies, such as the Morley–Minto 'reforms' of 1909 and the 'communal awards' of 1932, encouraged communal conflict among various religious groups (Singh, H., 1983:291). Under the Morley–Minto reforms of 1909, 50 per cent of the legislative seats in Punjab were designated for Muslims and the others for Sikhs and Hindus. In the 1932 'communal awards', representation was also extended to other religious groups. Despite opposition, the Government of India Act was passed by the British Parliament in 1935 to implement the 'communal awards'. This institutionalization of religious politics has had a profound impact on relations among various ethno–religious groups and pre- and post-independence politics in Punjab and indeed in India as a whole.

SIKHS AND THE ANTI-COLONIAL STRUGGLE

The Sikhs, both in India and Canada, were actively involved in anti-colonial politics to free India from British rule and played an important role in the freedom movement both in India and in North America. The participation and contributions of the Sikhs to the independence struggle is sometimes denigrated and misrepresented (Arun Shourie, 1985). However, historical evidence does not support this portrayal of the Sikhs. To the contrary, Sikhs were indeed actively involved in the movement in India as well as in other countries. They were active in the organization of the Indian National Army (INA), as 60 per cent of the 20,000 persons in the INA were Sikhs. Moreover, they also actively participated in the mutiny of the Indian Navy and the Delhi Police strike of 1946.

The Sikh passengers of the *Komagata Maru* (340 of 376 passengers were Sikhs) who were forced to return to India from Canada, also played an important role in the anti-colonial struggle. In North America, the Sikhs were also active in the formation of the Gadar Party to assist in India's freedom from British colonial rule. Baba Sohan Singh Bhakana (a Sikh) was the first president of the party. Indeed, it can be argued that the Sikhs' participation and sacrifices were disproportionately high in relation to their numbers in the Indian population (*Spokesman*, 1984:2). The figures below indicate that while the Sikhs constituted only 1.5 per cent of the Indian population, they made significantly more sacrifices than their numbers warranted prior to 1947 (*Spokesman*, 1984:2).

Punishment Suffered	Sikhs	Non-Sikhs	Total
Hanged	93	28	121
Imprisoned for life	2,147	499	2,646
Killed at Jallianwala Bagh	799	501	1,300
Killed at Budge Ghat	67	46	113
Killed in Kooka movement	91	–	91
Killed in Akali movement	500	–	500
Total	3,697	1,047	4,771

The importance of the Sikh community in pre- and post-Independence India was well recognized by the All India Congress Party and the Muslim League. This is reflected in a number of meetings and consultations between the Congress, Muslim League, and Sikh leaders to determine Sikhs' geographical and political options in independent India. M.A. Jinnah, the leader of the Muslim League and Sikh leaders had a number of formal and informal meetings to discuss the possibility of the Sikhs joining the new Muslim state of Pakistan. To persuade the Sikhs, they were promised limited independence and recognition, and promotion of their religion and culture in the new Pakistani nation. On the other hand, the Congress Party sought to persuade the Sikhs to stay with the new state of India. Various promises were made by Mahatma Gandhi and Jawaharlal Nehru on behalf of the Congress Party to convince the Sikhs that it would be in their best interest to stay in India and not join Pakistan. The Congress Party at its Lahore session in 1929 incorporated the Sikh national colour, *kesri*, in the Indian National Flag and adopted the following resolution:

The Congress assures the Sikhs ... that no solution thereof in any future Constitution will be acceptable to the Congress that does not give them [Sikhs] full satisfaction [Sikh Ex-Servicemen and Intellectual Forum, n.d:5].

Mahatma Gandhi, who played a dominant role in India's independence movement, supported the just aspirations and rights of Sikhs as a distinct group when he made the following statement in 1931 in Delhi:

Sikh friends have no reason to fear that we [the Congress party] will betray them. For, the moment it does so, the Congress would not only thereby seal its own doom but that of the country too. Moreover, the Sikhs are a great people. They know how to safeguard their rights by the exercise of arms if it should ever come to that [Sikh Ex-Servicemen and Intellectual Forum, n.d.:5].

Nehru stated his position on 4 April 1946 with the following statement:

I stand for semi-autonomous units ... I would like them [Sikhs] to have a semi-autonomous unit within the Province [Punjab] so that they may experience the glow of freedom [Singh, Harbans, 1983:351].

In June 1947, Hindu and Sikh members of the Punjab Legislative Assembly unanimously passed the following resolution: 'In the divided Punjab, special constitutional means are imperative to meet the just aspirations and rights of the Sikhs' (Sikh Ex-Serviceman and Intellectual Forum, n.d.:6).

It is apparent that prior to Independence, the political importance of the Sikh community was recognized both by the Muslim League and the Congress party leadership who both made every effort to woo the Sikhs. However, while the Congress leaders put forth some concrete political incentives for the Sikhs to remain in India, the Muslim leaders were generally vague in their promises to the Sikhs. Thus, with this consideration along with cultural, religious, and social affinities with the Hindus and historical hostilities and conflict between the Sikhs and the Muslim rulers, the Sikhs decided to join India. A large segment of the Sikh community paid a very heavy price in lives, land, and property when Punjab was partitioned between India and Pakistan. While every ethnic and religious community suffered due to communal riots and violence, the Sikhs in Punjab, mostly agriculturists (Jat Sikhs), because of loss of land feel that they made the greatest sacrifices for India's Independence.

POLITICS OF LANGUAGE

The differences on political and constitutional issues between the Indian government and Sikhs started almost immediately after Independence. Based on pre-Independence statements by the Congress leaders, Sikhs expected special status and an important role in constitutional and administrative matters. Mahatma Gandhi died in 1948 and Jawaharlal Nehru changed his position on the Sikhs. For example, in the Indian Constitution,

Sikhs, unlike Muslims, Christians, and other minority groups, were not considered a separate religious group. Instead, they were lumped together with Hindus. The Sikhs were dissatisfied with this article in the Constitution and accordingly registered their complaint with the Indian government. Both the Sikh nominees of the Shiromani Akali Dal, Hukam Singh and Bhopinder Singh Mann, protested by not signing the Constitution.

As early as 1951, the linguistic and communal/religious policies also began to raise their heads in Punjab province. The Punjabi speaking Hindu residents in Punjab began to 'disown' their mother tongue Punjabi. This decision was primarily based upon political considerations and fear amongst Hindus that the Sikhs would ask for a separate linguistic state on the basis of the Punjabi language, and as a result, many Punjabi Hindus 'disown[ed] Punjabi as a mother tongue in the 1951 census' (Singh, Harbans, 1983:342).

Starting around 1956, various states (provinces) in India were being organized on linguistic basis, reflecting the mother tongue of those residing in that area. The Indian government was favourably inclined to this policy in various parts of India with the exception of the formation of a state on the basis of the Punjabi language. This request for a 'Punjabi speaking state' was misinterpreted by the Indian government as a demand for a separate Sikh state (Khalistan) even though neither the SGPC nor the Akali Dal Party ever asked for a separate state. The only exception was the demand for an autonomous Sikh state made by Master Tara Singh in 1965 when he lost the leadership of SGPC to Fateh Singh (Grewal, 1990:203). While in other parts of India the Indian government showed its receptiveness to the formation of state boundaries on a linguistic basis, the Sikhs in Punjab had to struggle for over ten years before receiving the same consideration. In essence, the Sikh 'demand' was a basic one: the Sikhs wanted a state within the federation in which Punjabi would be the principal language of instruction in schools and would be used in the administration of the state government. On 31 November 1966 a Punjabi speaking state finally became a reality. It is important to note that the Punjabi-speaking Hindus in Punjab did not lend much support to this, contributing thereby to the communal antagonism in Punjab and also fostered resentment among the Sikhs against the Indian government.

As the Sikhs are only a small majority in Punjab (about 52 per cent of the total population), and as Sikhs are by no means monolithic in their political support of a single party, it is difficult for the Akali Dal party to come to power on their own at the provincial level. For this to occur, a coalition with other parties is often necessary. Punjab politics continues to be rooted in communal antagonism, opportunistic alliances, political and communal violence, nepotism, and political corruption.

THE ANANDPUR SAHIB RESOLUTION

After Independence in 1947, the Indian state was faced with a number of constitutional, political, and economic issues often rooted in the unique linguistic, religious, and cultural identities of specific geographic regions of the country. The regional issues and demands largely centred on centre–state relations and the distribution of political power and relative control of economic and natural resources by various levels of government. Other issues involved the linguistic, religious, and cultural rights and traditions of the minorities. In this context, the political–economic–regional issues and religious, linguistic, and cultural demands of the Sikh minority in India were not particularly unique in their content. Nevertheless, the 'Punjab problem' over the years has received considerable attention by the central government and the mass media. While political and economic issues arose almost immediately after Independence, these issues became crystallized and the contradictions and conflicts sharpened in the 1970s and 1980s, between the Sikhs and the central government, as well as the other ethnic/religious communities in Punjab. This period also saw a progressive deterioration of state–centre relations and increasing antagonism among religious communities and ethnicization of politics. Contentions remain between various interested groups and levels of government about the nature and content of Sikh demands and regional political issues.

The 'Anandpur Sahib Resolution', an important document passed by over a hundred thousand persons at the general session of the Akali Dal on 28–9 December 1978 very clearly illustrates this. This document, in fact, contains a number of resolutions which have over the years received considerable attention and divergent interpretations. One of the most detailed, and often considered the most authoritative legal and constitutional analysis of these resolutions is by former Chief Justice of High Court, Justice R.S. Narula. His article is reproduced in its entirety in the boxed pages of this chapter.

THE ANANDPUR SAHIB RESOLUTION*

R. S. Narula

IDENTITY OF RESOLUTION

The authenticated final Anandpur Sahib Resolution is no longer in dispute. The Akali Dal's case has all along been that the final Resolution is the one approved by the General House of the Akali Dal attended by over a hundred thousand persons at its general session in Ludhiana on October 28–29, 1978. The copy authenticated by the late Sant Harchand Singh Longowal, then President, Shiromani Akali Dal, forms Annexure III (page 67–90) to the 'Government of India, White Paper on the Punjab Agitation'.

Page 72 of the Government of India version of the Punjab agitation contained in the said White Paper also specifies that, 'it was after the passing of this Resolution (dated October 28–29, 1978) that the Shiromani Akali Dal started the struggle for the achievement thereof'.

I have been asked to put the record straight by presenting the legal aspects of the Anandpur Sahib Resolution and its possible constitutional implications. I was asked particularly to discuss those resolutions, which might be interpreted in any manner as being secessionist or endangering the unity or integrity of the country by the formation of an independent Sikh State. I have, therefore, examined each of these Resolutions in detail.

Resolution No. 1

The Shiromani Akali Dal realizes that India is a federal and republican geographical entity of different languages, religious and linguistic minorities, to fulfil the demands of the democratic traditions and to pave the way for economic progress, it has become imperative that the Indian constitutional infrastructure should be given a real federal shape *by redefining the central and state relations* and rights on the lines of the aforesaid principles and objectives.

The concept of total revolution given by Lok Naik, Sh. Jaya Prakash Narain is also based upon the progressive *decentralization of powers*. The climax of the process of centralization of powers of the States through amendments to the Constitution during the Congress regime came before the people in the form of the Emergency, when all fundamental rights of all citizens were usurped. It was then that the *programme of*

---

* Reprinted with the permission of Justice R.S. Narula. Emphasis by the author.

decentralization of powers ever advocated by Shiromani Akali Dal was openly accepted and adopted by other political parties including Janata Party, CPI (M), ADMK etc.

Shiromani Akali Dal has ever stood firm on this principle and that is why after very careful consideration it unanimously adopted a resolution to this effect first at the all India Akali Conference, Batala, then at Sri Anandpur Sahib which has endorsed the *principle of State autonomy in keeping with the concept of Federalism.*

As such, the Shiromani Akali Dal empathetically urges upon the Janata Government to take cognizance of the different linguistic and cultural sections, religious minorities as also the voice of millions of people and *recast the constitutional structure* of the country on real and meaningful *federal principles* to obviate the possibility of any danger to *national unity and the integrity of the country* and further, to enable the states to play a useful role for *the progress and prosperity of the Indian people* in their respective areas by the meaningful exercise of their powers.

None of the following operative parts can be called 'outside the framework of the Constitution' or 'Secessionist' or a threat to the unity and integrity of the country. Nor are they in any manner contrary to the interests of the country:

(i) 'The Akali Dal realizes that India is a federal and republican geographical entity of different languages, religions and cultures'.

Is this statement in any way untrue or illegal? Can anyone state that India is not a federal republic? Can anyone argue that India is not a geographical entity comprised of different languages, religions and cultures?

(ii)'To safeguard the fundamental rights of the religious and linguistic minorities, to fulfil the demands of the democratic traditions, to pave the way for economic progress ... '

The above quotation from the first resolution says nothing more than what is stated in the Constitution Articles 25(1) of Part III (Fundamental Rights), Article 38, 39(b) contained in Part VI (Directive Principles of State Policy) and Article 51–(A)(F)(Part IV A) which are reproduced below:

Article 25(1): 'Subject to public order, morality and health and to the other provisions of this Part, all persons are equally entitled to freedom of conscience and the right freely to process, practise and propagate religion'.

Article 51–A(f): 'to value and preserve the rich heritage of our people by securing and protecting as effectively as it may a social order in which justice, social, economic and political, shall inform all the institutions of the national life'.

Article 51–A(f): 'to value and preserve the rich heritage of our composite culture'.

Article 39(B): 'That the ownership and control of the material resources of the community are so distributed as best to subserve the common good'.

The resolution goes on ... 'it has become imperative that the Indian constitutional infrastructure should be given a real federal shape by redefining the central and state relations and rights on the lines of the aforesaid principles and objectives'.

This part of the resolution only reaffirms principles stated by various jurist members of the Constituent Assembly including Jawaharlal Nehru and more recently in the terms of reference of the Sarkaria Commission.

As is specifically mentioned in the Anandpur Sahib Resolution, the Akali Dal's desire for a real federal shape to the Constitution and the redefinition of centre–state relations in accordance with the objective spelt out in their first and second Resolutions is shared by other political parties, including the Janta Party, the CPI(M) and ADMK and others.

The next part of the resolution refers to, 'the climax of the process of centralization of powers of the States through repeated amendments of the Constitution during the Congress regime'. The resolution refers to two historical facts: 'the concept of total revolution given by Lok Naik, Sh. Jaya[prakash] Narain which was based upon the progressive de-centralization of powers,' the 'repeated amendments of the Constitution during the Congress regime' and the Emergency with the attendent suspension of fundamental rights.

The third part of the first resolution again refers to the unanimous adoption of the resolution at the Akali Conference at Batala and at Anandpur Sahib and states that the Akali Dal has always '*endorsed the principle of state autonomy in keeping with the concept of federalism*'.

The concept of federalism is inconsistent and irreconcilable with the concept of a separate state (Khalistan). Federalism can only refer to different states within the composite whole of the country, as envisaged in the federal structure legislated by the British Parliament in the 1935 Constitution Act and carried over in a somewhat hybrid form in our present Constitution.

Finally the operative part of the first resolution addresses itself to the Government in power at the Centre in October 1978 and empathetically urges the Janata Government, 'to take cognizance of the different linguistic and cultural selections, religious minorities as the voice of millions of people'. It also urges the Central Government to 'recast *the constitutional structure of the country* on real and meaningful federal principles to obviate the possibility of any danger to national unity and integrity of the country and, further, to enable the States to play a useful role for the *progress and prosperity of the Indian people* in their respective areas by the meaningful exercise of their powers'.

The very demand for recasting the constitutional structure of the country, as envisaged in the Constitution itself and as upheld by the Supreme Court in Keshvananda Bharati's case, and that stated objective of preserving the 'National Unity and Integrity' of the country contains the Akali Dal's implicit commitment against secession. In fact the resolution expressly demands such a structure 'to obviate the possibility of any danger to national unity and integrity of the country'.

During the recent [1985] Lok Sabha elections the Congress Party adopted this slogan of the Alkali Dal (most probably borrowed from Article 51–A(C) of the Constitution) for maintaining the 'national unity and integrity of the country' and it proclaimed it loudly during its own election meetings, as if the Anandpur Sahib Resolution, in contrast, stood for the 'disunity' and 'disintegration' of the motherland. This is a travesty of facts. *Either those who maligned and condemned the Resolution as secessionist during the elections had not read the Resolution published in the Government's own White Paper. Or they deliberately misrepresented the facts.*

Resolution No. 2

'The momentous meeting of the Shiromani Akali Dal calls upon the Government of India to examine carefully the long tale of the excesses, wrongs, illegal actions committed by the previous Congress governments, more particularly during the Emergency [1970–77] and try to find *an early solution to the following problems*:

(a) *Chandigarh* originally raised as a Capital for Punjab should be handed over to Punjab.

(b) The long standing demand of the Shiromani Akali Dal for the merger in Punjab of the *Punjabi speaking areas*, to be identified by linguistic experts with the *village as a unit*, should be conceded.

(c) The control of *Head Works* should continue to be vested in Punjab and, if need be, Reorganization Act should be amended.

(d) The arbitrary and unjust Award given by Mrs Indira Gandhi during the Emergency on the *distribution of Ravi–Beas waters* should be revised on the universally accepted norms and principles, thereby justice be done to Punjab.

(e) Keeping in view the special aptitude and martial qualities of the Sikhs the present *ratio* of their *strength in the Army* should be maintained.

(f) The excesses being committed on the *settlers in the Terai region* of UP in the name of Land Reforms should be vacated by making suitable amendments in the Ceiling Law on the Central guidelines.

Through the second resolution the Akali Dal calls on the then Government of India 'to examine carefully the long tale of excesses, wrongs and illegal actions' committed by the previous Congress Government, particularly during the Emergency and to try to find an early solution to the problems enumerated (a) to (f) in that resolution. It is the legal and constitutional rights of every citizen and of every lawful body of citizens, particularly of recognized political parties, to make claims on their own Central Government for whatever such citizen, body or party thinks is in the interest of the country as a whole, or of any part of the country, and/or for the Indian nation as a whole, or for the benefit of any unit which forms part of the whole. None of the demands made by the Akali Dal in the second resolution are either secessionist or opposed to the interests of the country or the nation or in any manner inconsistent with the 'unity or integrity of the country'.

Demand (a) is the request for Chandigarh to be allocated to the State of Punjab as it was originally 'raised as a capital' for that State. Demand (b), is described as 'the long standing demand of the Akali Dal for the merger with Punjab of Punjabi speaking areas, 'to be identified by linguistic experts with the village as a unit'. Both demands are for readjustment of territories of different states within the country, for which express provision is made in Article 3 of the Constitution. This Article provides that Parliament may, by law, form a new state by separation of territory from any state, or by uniting two or more states or parts of states, or by uniting any territory to a part of any state, to increase the area of any state, to diminish the area of any state, to alter the boundary of any state and to alter the name of any state. The States Reorganization Act establishing linguistic states and other legislation have previously been passed under the authority of Article 3. Demands for readjustment have been made by and conceded to other States. For example, the Akali Dal demand for creation of a Punjabi speaking state on a linguistic basis was conceded when the present Punjab was carved out and Haryana was created. What is unconstitutional in asking for the redress of any injustice felt to be done during that reorganization?

Both demands, (a) and (b), had been repeatedly conceded *in principle* by the late Prime Minister Indira Gandhi but the matters remained unresolved for political or other reasons. Prime Minister, Mr Rajiv Gandhi, had conceded both demands in the Rajiv Gandhi–Longowal Accord of July 24, 1985. The appointment of the Mathew Commission and the Centre's undertaking to appoint another Commission for the merger with Punjab of the Punjabi speaking areas which may be with Haryana, and vice versa, are the follow-up action. The proceedings of both Commissions and the handing over of Chandigarh to Punjab have been made time bound.

Demand (c) in the second resolution claims for the State of Punjab, and not for the Akalis or any community, the continued control of all Head Works situated in the Punjab territory and suggests amendment of the States Reorganisation Act, if necessary, to implement this.

The specific reference to amendment of a Parliamentary Act, if necessary, to achieve the objective of the demand makes it clear that the propagators of the Resolution want the demand to be met in a demo-cratic, legal manner. Prime Minister Rajiv Gandhi has accepted the demand and the Accord provides that the present set-up regarding supply of water in Punjab—(whether legal or illegal, justified or unjus-tified) as on July 1, 1985—shall continue till the Commission ap-pointed for the purpose makes its recommendation, to be binding on the Central Government as well as on the representatives of all con-cerned parties.

Demand (d) of the resolution asks for revision of the executive Award given by the late Mrs Indira Gandhi during the Emergency on the distribution of the Ravi–Beas waters. Again, this is a legal demand in the interest of the entire State of Punjab, and not for any particular political party or community's interest. It is a fact that the river water dispute, which was pending before the Supreme Court by the Congress-run Governments of Punjab and Haryana during the Emergency and what the Resolution describes as a 'arbitrary and unjust Award' was given by Prime Minister Indira Gandhi. Whether the Award was 'arbitrary' or 'unjust' or fair or just, is a matter of opinion based on certain data. The Constitution (Article 19(1)(a) expressly guarantees 'freedom of speech and expression' to every citizen of the country. Making the demand is not unconstitutional.

Significantly, this demand too has been accepted by the Rajiv–Longowal Accord. It has also been accepted both by the Central Govern-ment and the Akalis that a Tribunal presided over by a sitting Supreme Court judge shall adjudicate the river water dispute between the riparian State of Punjab and the States of Haryana and Rajasthan, and that until then the status quo which existed on July 1, 1985 shall continue.

Demand (e) is for maintenance of the present ratio of the Sikh strength in the Army. The Centre can accept or reject the demand. But asking for maintenance of the ratio of any particular community in the Army is neither unconstitutional nor illegal. On the contrary it is consistent with the provision made in Article 46 of the Constitution and with the assurance given by the Central Government from time to time about giving special consideration to the minorities.

Recruitment to the Army was originally based on merit in different recruiting centres without reference to any community or place of residence. It is true that on the basis of such recruitment the number of Sikhs, who were recruited as sepoys (the lowest rank in the Army), was proportionally higher than their population in the country. The demand asks that recruitment on merit be continued and that no one who is fit on merit should be excluded from recruitment to the Army merely because the quota of a particular community or State, arbitrarily or logically fixed by the Government, has already been filled. Recruitment of commissioned officers is done on the basis of all-India open competitive examinations, without consideration of caste, community, religion or place of residence. Therefore the demand made for the lowest rung in the Army is in keeping with the Government practice for recruitment to the higher ranks. This demand also appears to have been fully conceded in the Rajiv–Longowal Accord which states that recruitment to the Army will henceforth be on merit.

The last demand, demand (f) in the second resolution, complains of excesses which were being committed at the time of passing of the Resolution, i.e. in 1978 during the Janata regime, on the Punjabi settlers in the Terai settlement in Uttar Pradesh in the name of land reforms. In order to give redress to those settlers the resolution suggests that 'suitable amendments in the Ceiling Law on Central Guidelines' be made.

That unjust excesses were committed on the Punjabi settlers of the Terai region is a fact. Most of the Terai lands were originally impregnable jungles, and allotted free to the tribals in the hope that they would bring them under the plough. The experiment failed and not one acre of land was made arable by the tribals. The Punjabi agriculturalists who had brought about the green revolution in what was desert area in the Punjab before partition of the subcontinent, were then encouraged by the authorities to settle in the Terai. The Government made allotments to them for limited periods of 10 to 30 years. Braving the jungles, nearly half of these pioneer settlers died due to diseases like Malaria etc. but the rest succeeded in converting the Terai jungle into fertile agricultural lands. Some other enthusiastic Punjabi farmers took *Pattas* from the tribals, to whom the remaining land had been allotted, and similarly, brought it under the plough.

After 30 years of hard labour and sacrifice, when the Punjabi farmers (mostly Sikhs) had brought about a green revolution in that inhospitable and non-productive area, the UP Government wanted to take back the fertile land and turn out the Punjabi settlers. A Tribal Minister in the State Government raised a hue and cry, purportedly in the interests of the tribals and succeeded in having draconian laws enacted. As a result of these, the Sikh farmers who had earlier been uprooted by partition from their place of origin were again uprooted.

The legislation was questioned in the Allahabad High Court. I myself argued one of those Writ Petitions at the Motion stage before a Divisional Bench of the Allahabad High Court. Their Lordships admitted the petition and granted a stay order. Some of those petitions were still pending. It is for the legislature to see that justice is done, but since the matter falls within the Concurrent List in the Constitution, the Centre can certainly intervene to save the innocent Punjabis from gross injustice, and from the trauma of being uprooted a second time. Again, there is nothing secessionist or unconstitutional in the demand.

Resolution No. 3

Resolution 3 is an economic policy Resolution which states—'The chief source of inspiration of the economic policies and programme of the Shiromani Akali Dal are the secular, democratic and socialist concepts of Sri Guru Nanak Dev and Sri Guru Gobind Singh Ji. Our Economic programme is based on three basic principles:

(a) Dignity of labour.

(b) An economic and social structure which provides for the uplift of the poor and depressed sections of society.

(c) Unabated opposition to concentration of economic and political power in the hands of the capitalists.

To call this basis of the third resolution objectionable, is to be against secularism, against democratic institutions, or the socialistic concepts of the Sikh Gurus or against Articles 39(c). 41, etc. of the Constitution. Our constitution itself is based on the resolve, 'to constitute India into a sovereign, socialist, secular, democratic republic and to secure to all its citizens social, economic, political justice'. By laws such as the Industrial Disputes Act, the Minimum Wages Act etc., we are committed to the dignity of labour. The Constitution is expressly armed for the uplift of the poor and depressed sections of society. Part IV (Directive Principles of State Policy) aims at avoiding concentration of economic and political power in the hands of the capitalists. In the circumstances any objection to the basis of the third resolution is an objection to the basic policies enshrined in the Constitution.

The resolution goes on to state that the Akali Dal lays great stress on the need to break the monopolistic hold of capitalists foisted on the Indian economy by 30 years of Congress rule in India and reiterates the socialist Sikh way of life as propounded by Guru Nanak in the *Shabad* (translated into English), 'He alone realizes the True Path who labours honestly and shares the fruits of that labour'

After referring to the three principles enunciated in the above *Shabad*, viz., (i) honest labour, (ii) sharing the fruits of labour, and (iii) mediation in the Lord's name, the Akali Dal appeals to the Central and State Governments to eradicate unemployment during the next 10 years, ameliorating the lot of the weaker sections. Concrete suggestions are then given for achieving those objectives. These include a demand for rapid diversification of farming and for the removal of shortcomings in the land reform laws. Committed to the freedom of conscience under the Human Rights Charter, as India is, can there be any objection to the principles, suggestions and demands which form the third resolution?

Resolution No. 4

The Resolution complains of discrimination against the Punjabi language in the adjoining States of Himachal Pradesh, Haryana, Delhi and Jammu and Kashmir. It is a fact that next to the spoken language in these 4 States, the mother-tongue of the majority of the people settled there is Punjabi. Punjabi should therefore be the second language. Is it fair to Punjabi or the Punjabi-speaking people living in Haryana that the official second language declared by that State was Tamil in spite of the fact that there are hardly any Tamil-speaking permanent residents in that state? Delhi has in fact already accepted Punjabi as one of its official languages. The demand of the Punjabi speaking people for giving the Punjabi language its appropriate status in the four states is neither secessionist nor unconstitutional. One may agree or disagree with it but there can be no objection to the demand being made, nor any suggestion that such a demand will lead to the country's disintegration.

Resolution No. 5

The resolution asks the State of Jammu and Kashmir to rehabilitate the refugees from West Pakistan who migrated to that state at the time of partition of the country (1947). The suggestion that Parliament amend

Article 370 of the Constitution, if necessary, to achieve that objective is no different from many other suggestions made by individuals and parties year after year for amendment of the Constitution.

Resolution No. 6

Through this resolution the Akali Dal Conference takes strong exception to the discrimination to which the minorities (not only the Sikhs) in other states are subjected. The complaint is that their interests are ignored. The resolution demands redress of injustices against the Sikhs in those states and asks for appropriate representation for them in the services of the Government of local bodies and in State legislatures through nomination, consistent with the declared policy of the Central Government. The Government, by appointing official bodies such as the Minorities Commission and Minorities Panel, recognizes that discrimination still exists. To object to the demand and/or to disagree with the arguments is one thing. To complain about, and doubt the nationalism of those making the demand, is another.

Resolution No. 7

After noting with satisfaction the increase in farm yields, as a result of which 'the country is heading towards self-sufficiency', the resolution regrets that poor farmers are unable to take to mechanization because of the enormous costs involved. The resolution asks the Government of India to abolish the excise duty on tractors so that ordinary farmers may also be able to avail themselves of farm machinery and contribute to the growth of the gross agricultural produce of the country.

Can any fault be found with either the statement or the demands made in the resolution?

Resolution No. 8

The resolution merely appeals to the Central and State Governments 'to pay particular attention to the poor and labouring classes' to make suitable amendments in the Minimum Wages Act and take other legal steps 'to improve the economic lot of the labouring classes to enable them to lead a respectable life and play a useful role in the rapid industrialization of the country'. It contains nothing anti-national.

Resolution No. 9

In the Resolution the Akali Dal seeks permission from the Government of India to install a broadcasting station at the Golden Temple, 'for the relay of *Gurbani Kirtan* for the spiritual satisfaction of those Sikhs who are living in foreign lands'. There is nothing illegal in the demand. Demands for autonomous broadcasting stations and TV stations can be declined, if it is not consistent with the policy of the Central Government. However, should one read into this demand a non-existent threat of separation from the country? This demand has already been granted in principle by the Government itself putting up a broadcasting station in the Golden Temple from which *Kirtan* is relayed every morning.

Resolution No. 10

This resolution asks the Government to make necessary amendments in the relevant clause of the Hindu Succession Act to give a woman the rights of inheritance in the property of her father-in-law instead of her father, and to exempt agricultural lands from wealth-tax and estate duty.

This is a matter of policy for the Central/State legislatures. Again one need not agree with the demands but that does not make them secessionist.

Resolution No. 11

This resolution impresses upon the Government of India the desirability of providing for the welfare of the economically backward scheduled and non-scheduled castes, and for setting up a special *Ministry at the Centre* as a practical measure to render justice to them on the basis of reservation. Some people may be opposed to reservation for the backward classes, but the demand of the Akalis is consistent with the declared and proclaimed policy of the Congress party since the Independence of the country. The last part of this resolution asks the Central Government to create safeguards, etc. for the backward, scheduled and other castes and to ensure that no discrimination is made between a Sikh *Harijan* and a Hindu *Harijan* in any part of the country. This is in keeping with the Constitution (Article 14), and there is nothing secessionist in the demand.

Resolution No. 12

The last resolution asks the Congress Government in the Punjab to 'vacate the gross injustice' done to the state (not to the Sikhs alone) in the distribution of the Ravi–Beas waters. This matter has since been accepted by the Central Government, which has directed that a special Tribunal headed by a judge of the Supreme Court deal with it. The only other demand made in this resolution is for approval of the immediate establishment of six sugar and four textile mills in Punjab to allow the state to implement its agro–industrial policy. There is nothing unconstitutional or secessionist in this demand. The necessity of implementing the state's agro–industry policy has since been recognized by Prime Minister Rajiv Gandhi, who has already taken the first bold step in implementing this policy through setting up the prestigious Railway Coach Factory near Kapurthala in Punjab. The Centre should have no objection in permitting the establishment of as many sugar mills and textile mills in the Punjab as is found viable on the basis of detailed blueprints submitted to it by the Punjab Government.

CONCLUSION

These are the contents of the much maligned Anandpur Sahib Resolution as authenticated by Sant Longowal. Can the critics of that Resolution in all honesty show in what way the Shiromani Akali Dal, which passed the Resolution at the General Meeting at Ludhiana, was aiming at breaking up the country or creating a separate state?

History records that even when the British, who wanted to break up the country into as many parts as possible at the time of Independence, urged the Sikhs to form a separate state, the Akali leaders rejected the suggestion point blank and asserted that the Sikhs were as much integral members of India as any other citizens of the country. It is a matter of regret that certain motivated political leaders have complained that whereas they received the Sikhs with open arms when they came from Pakistan, the Sikhs now want to live as equals but maintaining their separate identity; a wish that these politicians interpret as an act of ingratitude of the highest order! Aberrations like this alienate the Sikhs. Sikhs were responsible for saving a large number of Hindus by bringing them into the Gurdwaras in Pakistan during the July/August 1947 riots, looking after them as part of their natural duty as real brothers, and for escorting them in convoys to what is now India, without ever suggesting that they were doing any favour to anyone. At that time this was recognized and eulogized by the leaders of the country.

But memories are short. The only way to save the country from disintegration is to accept and adopt the Anandpur Sahib Resolution for the entire country and for every state unit of India.

Resolution 1 is the most contentious because it is often interpreted as being secessionist and damaging to the unity of the country seeking the formation of an independent Sikh state. This resolution recognizes the linguistic, religious, and cultural diversity of India and acknowledges it too as a federal and republican geographical entity, and seeks to safeguard the fundamental rights of the religious and linguistic minorities and a redefinition of central and state relations. Justice Narula argues that these statements are consistent with the articles in the Indian Constitution relating to Fundamental Rights and Directive Principles of State Policy. He concludes; 'that those who consider the resolution as secessionist either have not read it or deliberately misinterpret and misrepresent the facts'.

The second resolution asks the central government to examine the illegal acts of the previous Congress governments and address the issue of the capital city Chandigarh, linguistic and water rights, administrative control of headworks, and the percentage of Sikhs in the armed forces. Justice Narula argues that none of the demands in this resolution are secessionist or endanger the unity and integrity of the country.

Resolution 3 is an economic policy resolution and resolution 4 in particular complains of the discrimination against the Punjabi language in the states adjoining Punjab. Resolution 5 asks the state of Jammu & Kashmir to take steps to rehabilitate refugees who migrated from Pakistan to that state after India's partition, and Resolution 6 demands redress of injuries against Sikhs and other minorities in other states. Resolutions 7 and 8 are primarily economic resolutions to improve the economic conditions of working people by amending the Minimum Wages Act and elimination of excise duty on farm machinery to enable poor farmers to buy such machinery. Resolution 9 seeks permission from the government of India to install broadcasting facilities in the Golden Temple 'for the relay of *Gurbani Kirtan* for the spiritual satisfaction of those Sikhs living in foreign lands'. Resolution 10 asks for the extension of women's rights in property inheritance and Resolution 11 asks the central government to safeguard the interests of the economically backward minorities and scheduled castes. Resolution 12 asks the (then) Punjab Congress government to 'vacate the gross injustice' done to the state in the distribution of irrigation waters.

As the above presentation indicates, none of these resolutions are secessionist or in any way a threat to the national unity. These 'demands' are primarily oriented towards political and economic reforms to create and improve economic conditions for the workers and farmers, and to safeguard and protect the rights of the minorities. Furthermore, these 'demands' address the regional and provincial issues of importance to all the citizens of this region rather than to the Sikhs alone, perhaps with the exception of a broadcasting radio station. However, as a large number of Punjabi Hindus did not support these resolutions, they have come to be perceived as Sikh 'demands' rather than Punjabi and regional issues. That these resolutions originated within the Akali Dal, contributed to this perception. As Bhatanagar notes (1984:54):

It is tragic that some of our Punjabi Hindus should be betraying their own State's [Punjab's] welfare by not supporting the common cause of Chandigarh and river water, etc., and thus alienating themselves from the Sikhs.

The opponents of the Anandpur Sahib Resolution continue to characterize it as secessionist and a threat to national unity and the Indian state. On the contrary, Justice Narula concludes that, 'the only way to save the country from disintegration is to accept and adopt the Anandpur Sahib Resolution for the entire country and for every state unit of India'.

Akali leaders never preached secession from India. Longowal clearly enunciated the Akali position on this matter on 11 October 1982:

Let me make it clear once for all that the Sikhs have no designs to get away from India in any manner. What they simply want is that they should be allowed to live within India as Sikhs, free from all direct and indirect interference and tampering with their religious way of life. Undoubtedly the Sikhs have the same nationality as other Indians [cited in Noorani, 1985:151].

To throw additional light on the economics and politics of the 'Punjab problem' we discuss below the regional economic development policy and its contradictions and the political interests of and conflicts among various interested groups at the provincial and central levels.

ECONOMIC DEVELOPMENT AND ITS CONTRADICTIONS

Economic development in Punjab, particularly the Green Revolution, while leading to considerable prosperity and improvement in overall standards of living and health of the population, also increased economic disparities and inequality in the region.

The relative prosperity of Punjab is apparent on a number of indicators, such as food consumption, access to financial institutions, and availablity of health facilities and other services. For instance, Punjabis consume 3000 calories a day as against the national average of 2100 calories. Punjab has the most bank branches per capita of any Indian state and the most health facilities. Every village is electrified and television sets are becoming increasingly common (New York Times, 1 October 1982). The farmers of Punjab produce 25 per cent of the country's wheat. By providing two-thirds of the nation's central reserves of wheat and nearly 45 per cent of its rice reserves, Punjab is primarily responsible for India's self-sufficiency in food, which has been widely viewed as modern and independent India's greatest accomplishment (*New York Times*, 1 October 1982; also see Kaur, 1990:44). The financial prosperity in Punjab is also helped by remittances from oversees Punjabis.

As the Green Revolution in Punjab was a great success story in the area of agricultural growth, Punjabi farmers were given due credit for their hard work, progressive attitude, and sense of entrepreneurship. New varieties of wheat were introduced in the 1960s. By 1972, farm income had doubled and savings had grown even faster. The savings that occrued were then primarily invested in productive assets resulting in a sixfold and fourfold increase in tube wells and tractors respectively. Land that had previously lain fallow in the dry season could now be cultivated, resulting in a 50 per cent increase in the acreage under wheat cultivation. Fertilizer use increased sixfold and local research led to continuing improvements in varieties of wheat, rice, potatoes, and other crops (*World Development Report*, 1982:70).

However, this overall prosperity and increase in agricultural production was not without its economic contradictions and personal costs for many farmers. It also had political implications for the SGPC and the Akali Dal, whose leadership and political base is in rural areas, predominantly the agricultural community. Many farmers in Punjab are experiencing the same problems as farmers in the rest of the world. They are caught in the cost–price squeeze, namely the price of the agricultural commodities is not increasing in proportion to the increase in prices of farm inputs. This predicament creates serious economic problems for the farmers. Likewise, river water is very important as it is essential for intensive farming. The use of new varieties of wheat, rice, corn, and other crops requires a regular and adequate irrigation system.

While the Green Revolution increased agricultural production in Punjab, it also displaced many small farmers who did not have large landholdings or a large cash flow to buy farm inputs and farm machinery. Thus, they have either moved to cities to become part of the urban slums or have joined the increasing numbers of the unemployed and underemployed in the rural areas.

Thus, along with considerable agricultural prosperity, there are major economic problems in the state of Punjab. The Sikh youth with an education have a difficult time finding jobs. The rural unemployment rate is estimated to be close to 30 per cent. Principal Gurbax Singh Shergill of Amritsar Khalsa College states that:

This lack of jobs for the rural youth increases tension in the countryside. Both yield and income have peaked but the costs of agricultural inputs keeps rising. As a result, 70–80 per cent of all landowners are in debt and cannot pay back their loans. Only 10 out of 100 graduates from this college could secure jobs [Singh, Ramindar, 1985:45.]

Access to bank loans for investments in Punjab are limited, as about 70 per cent of Punjab's bank deposits are invested outside the state. This frustrates the educated younger generation of Sikhs who want to invest in new businesses (Gujral, 1985:119–20). Sikhs living outside the state of Punjab face social and economic discrimination.

Other economic opportunities for Sikhs are decreasing. As the Punjab state shares a border with Pakistan, and in view of continuing conflict between the two countries, the central government doesn't want to set up heavy industry of any nature in Punjab as it will be susceptible to an attack from Pakistan. Also, for Sikhs, the employment opportunities in the army are gradually being closed. They still constitute about 12 per cent of the armed forces but their comparative numbers are decreasing. Such economic realities are paramount when analysing the Sikh agitation in India. This statement is supported by Bannerjee (1984:11) who argues:

The growing assertions of ethno–regional identities must be seen in the economic context. Intense competition exists for scarce jobs, contracts, loans, licences, as well as access to limited education and health facilities. Those frustrated in the process tend to seek refuge in their communal or cultural exclusivity.

In other words, the analysis of ethno–religious conflicts embodies broader economic issues, and economic forces of displacement and unemployment have contributed to the Sikh agitation in Punjab.

THE POLITICS OF THE 'PUNJAB PROBLEM'

Provincial and central political interests have played an important part in shaping the political process and forces in Punjab and in the social construction of the 'Punjab Problem'. The Congress party which held power in India since 1947 with few exceptions (1977–9;1990–91; 1997 to the present), as would be expected, is predominantly composed of Hindus, who constitute about 82 per cent of the population. It is absolutely essential for any national party to appease the Hindu majority in order to gain and stay in power. The secular political rhetoric of the Congress party also secured electoral support of religious minorities and disadvantaged castes.

When confronted with loss of power, Indira Gandhi resorted to 'divide and rule' tactics (Bannerjee, 1984:9). Indira Gandhi and her party actively engaged in the communalization of Punjabi politics and generated conflict and contradictions among the Sikhs. For instance, it was in the best political interests of Indira Gandhi to create divisions in the Akali Party. Therefore, she supported Jarnail Singh Bhindranwale against the Harchand Singh Longowal group in the 1979 SGPC election. Indira Gandhi also provided legitimacy to Bhindranwale's leadership by sharing a dais with him while campaigning for the Lok Sabha election in Gurdaspur. Indira Gandhi's principal objective was to win the 1985 general election in Punjab and in other parts of India (Kothari, 1985:78).

These external events and internal contradictions among the Sikhs contributed to increasing polarization of politics in Punjab. In the Sikh community, these divisions came to be identified as 'moderate' and 'extremist' elements. 'Moderates', under Longowal and 'extremists', under Bhindranwale were considered to be two main contending groups. Lack of progress on negotiations between Sikh leaders and the stalling tactics of Indira Gandhi contributed to the feeling that she was not negotiating in good faith. On 6 May 1984, as Gujral stated, 'It is ironical but true that each time the final approval [of the accord] was denied in the name of the Prime Minister [Indira Gandhi]' (cited in Noorani, 1985:159). This political opportunism, policy and tactics of Indira Gandhi's Congress party encouraged the 'extremist' element among the Sikhs and demands for a separate Sikh state. The principal Sikh leaders went out of their way to dissociate themselves from these demands, but the mass media and the Indian governments highlighted only the demands made by the 'extremists' among the Sikhs.

The consequences of such political opportunism and misrepresentation of Sikh demands were costly for the Sikhs and for the nation as a whole. Conflict between the 'moderates' and the 'extremists' intensified within the Sikh community. Imprisonment of many Sikhs further contributed to dissatisfaction and alienation amongst the Sikhs and support for the 'extremists'.

Subsequently, Bhindranwale and his supporters occupied the Golden Temple and armed themselves. Crimes against and murders of moderate and clean shaven Sikhs, leftists, and Hindus are often attributed to these 'extremists'. Over 80 per cent of the several hundred persons killed between 1982–4 in Punjab during the 20 months were Sikhs (*Economist*, 1984:38).

The law and order situation deteriorated further in Punjab. Presidential rule was imposed in Punjab in October 1983. The Hindus in Punjab and elsewhere in India exerted pressure on the central government to take action against the Sikh extremists in the Golden Temple and other parts of India. The Indian government launched Operation Blue Star on 5 June 1984 and attacked the Golden Temple in Amritsar with full military force. The Golden Temple was attacked on the day when thousands of people were in the temple as it was a day of martyrdom of Guru Arjan Devji. It was alleged that about 400 Sikh extremists were present in the Golden Temple at the time. The military not only desecrated the Golden Temple, the most sacred holy place of the Sikhs, but also killed about a thousand innocent men, women, and children who were worshipping in the Golden Temple. They also killed all of the extremists and burned their bodies without providing any identity or information to the relatives of the dead (Chauhan, 1984:4). Thirty-eight other gurdwaras in Punjab were besieged by the Indian armed forces and several thousand persons were arrested. While some of them were released, about 365 people were kept in detention in Jodhpur (Rajasthan, India) for about four years without any charges being framed against them. Some of these individuals were detained in solitary confinement and many of them have died or suffered mental breakdowns.

Justice Ajit Singh Bains, the chairman of the Punjab Human Rights Commission, investigated thousands of cases of youth who were arrested after the attack on the Golden Temple. The Bains Commission reached the conclusion that most of the youth were innocent and there were no grounds for their arrest or detention. Even though the Bains Commission report was submitted to the Punjab government, as late as 1988, many of these Sikh youths remained in detention in Jodhpur jail. Justice Bains states: 'there are no basic rights. ... There is in fact no law in the land'. (Wangar, 1987:23).

The Sikh community in India and abroad never imagined that the Gandhi government would ever attack the Golden Temple. The Golden Temple to Sikhs is as important and sacred as the Vatican is to the Catholics, Mecca to the Muslims, and Jerusalem to the Jews and Christians. This action of the government alienated the entire Sikh community. Punjab state was sealed from all sides. When a state of emergency was declared, journalists were not allowed into Punjab for several months. No inquiry was made to determine the reasons for the death of the innocent people, no compensation was paid to the victims and relatives, and no effort was made to negotiate with the Sikhs after the attack.

On 31 October 1984, two Sikh security guards of Indira Gandhi murdered her in New Delhi. The assassination sparked off the Delhi riots, resulting in the murder of about 3,000 Sikhs in Delhi alone. Another 5,000 Sikhs were left destitute in Delhi (Gonick, 1985:23). Various independent commission reports, inquiries, and press reports have clearly established the active involvement of influential members of the Congress party in instigating and supporting riots in Delhi. Innocent Sikh men, women, and children were murdered by Hindu mobs and politicians. The police generally looked the other way. At the height of the riots, the police in Delhi were either totally absent, passive spectators, or direct participants in killing Sikhs. Discussing the Delhi Riots, Cy. Gonick comments on the premeditated nature of the Delhi riots. He states:

Spontaneous grief does not arrive with iron rods and firearms and a seemingly endless supply of petrol, in vans, scooter, motorcycles, trucks and buses. Men in mourning do not take up strategic positions, block escape routes and embark on loot, rape and murder with the cool confidence of those who have plenty of time, knowing that the police would not disturb them. [Gonick, 1985:23.]

After two days of indiscriminate butchery of Sikhs in the capital city of India, army control was imposed. Sikhs were also murdered in other parts of India. Khushwant Singh, in his speech in the parliament concerning the Delhi riots stated:

In these two days [1 and 2 Nov. 1984] good innocent Sikhs were massacred in different parts of the country; at least 900 women were widowed, 50,000 Sikhs were rendered homeless and were removed to refugee camps; thousands of crores worth of property of Sikhs was destroyed [Singh, K., 1985:63].

Other documents and sources substantially support the allegations of murder, rape, destruction of homes and properties of the Sikhs (Shourie, 1985; Amnesty Report on Human Rights Abuses 1986; People's Union for Democratic Right and People's Union for Civil Liberties, 1984; Singh, K., 1985; Menon, 1985; Singh and Malik, 1985).

After Indira Gandhi's death, Rajiv Gandhi, her son, became prime minister of India. Despite the allegations of Rajiv's Congress party's role in the Delhi riots, the Indian government for about five months refused to establish an inquiry to investigate the murder of 3,000 innocent Sikhs. This is not only disturbing when one considers that India claimed to be the world's largest democracy, but it is equally tragic that the Indian government called itself secular. As Menon, discussing the carnage in Delhi in 1984, states (Menon, 1985:65): 'Secularism, which is at best a patronising concept in the Indian Constitution, is revealed today to be the con-game it is'. The Sikh leaders (Harchand Singh Longowal, Surjit Singh Barnala, and Balwant Singh) eventually forced the Indian government in mid-April 1985 to set up a judicial inquiry to investigate the carnage in New Delhi. The Misra Mission hearings were held on camera and the terms of reference of the one-man commission were somewhat limited.

The government of India issued a presidential order in May 1986 which enabled it to suppress the Misra report. The report was submitted to the Indian government which did suppress it initially and then released it in 1987. The commission ruled that 19 low level Congress party functionaries were involved in the 1984 Delhi riots and should be punished. At the same time, however, it rejected the position of other independent commissions and groups that the riots were organized by Congress cabinet ministers or senior party officials. The Misra Commission and the Indian government did not fully investigate these allegations or provide an explanation of why some Cabinet ministers and senior party officials in the Congress party were not implicated.

It was not until January, 1996, that one Congress minister was charged for his role in the Delhi riots that took place in 1984, and even he was released in March 1996 on bail. Only three individuals in the last 10 years have been convicted of committing murder in the riots. It is important to note that the government of India is appealing all three cases. The government of India paid Rs 20,000 (less than $1,000) to families who lost a breadwinner and another Rs 20,000 to those whose homes were destroyed.

Rajiv Gandhi signed a memorandum of settlement with the Sikh leadership on 24 July 1985. The then Akali Dal leader H.S. Longowal negotiated the settlement with the Federal government, which had broad support of 'moderate' Sikhs in Punjab. The principal areas covered in the memorandum were as follows (Kapur, 1987:1219–20).

The memorandum of settlement was aimed at beginning the process of negotiation. It conceded the basis of some of the demands which the Akali Dal deemed essential prerequisites for discussions, and set the parameters for addressing other demands. Thus, the agreement stipulated that the central government would pay compensation to the families of innocent people killed in agitations or actions which had taken place since August 1982, as well as compensation for damage to property. However, the modalities for determining the extent of the compensation and to whom it was to be paid were not spelt out. It was further agreed that the city of Chandigarh, the shared capital of Punjab and Haryana, would be transferred to the Punjab; however a commission would be established to determine what territory Punjab would transfer to Haryana in return. Other territorial claims between Punjab and Haryana states would be referred to a boundary commission whose decision would be binding. The Akali Dal's demand for a reapportionment of river waters was similarly addressed. In addition, the central government reiterated its commitment to consider the formulation of legislation for the management of all Sikh shrines in consultation with the Akali Dal.

The question of greater autonomy for the Punjab and the controversial Anandpur Sahib resolution were dealt with in a similar spirit of compromise. The memorandum declared that the Akali Dal states that the Anandpur Sahib resolution is entirely within the framework of the Indian Constitution, and 'that the purpose of the resolution is to provide greater autonomy to the states with a view to strengthening the unity and integrity of the country' ... The portion dealing with centre-state relations in the resolution would be referred to an independent commission which was to make recommendations to the central government.

However, the 'extremist' Sikhs were dissatisfied with this settlement as it did not address the question of Khalistan, a separate Sikh state. H.S. Longowal was murdered on 20 August 1985. However, Rajiv Gandhi benefited politically and won the 1985 elections with a huge majority. With this mandate it was expected he would implement the accord, but, it soon became evident that Rajiv Gandhi's involvement, as the subsequent events show, was also political opportunism.

The Akali Dal formed the government in Punjab after the 25 September 1985 elections under the leadership of Surjit Singh Barnala. The Akali Dal leadership was divided into different factions or groups, as Sikhs were and continue to be divided on the basis of their religious and political interests. As of August 1986, Barnala was supported by Congress members, whereas some of the MLAs of his own party had joined another Akali Dal group headed by Parkash Singh Badal. Meanwhile, violent crimes, including murder, continued to occur in Punjab. After the death of H.S. Longowala, the Federal government did not fulfil the conditions of the Accord which it signed on 24 July 1985. This passivity of the Rajiv government served as a further setback to 'moderate' Sikhs and the Akali Dal dominated government led by Chief Minister Barnala. However, he did not receive much support from the central government to resolve the conflict in Punjab or from the Akali party which was not united in supporting him. In consequence, his ministry was dismissed by the central government in May 1987 (Grewal, 1990:230–4).

A number of direct control tactics over Sikhs were initiated by the central government of Rajiv Gandhi. In 1986 the Indian army invaded the Golden Temple again to expel the Sikh 'militants' who were occupying it. In May of 1987 Prime Minister Rajiv Gandhi dissolved the Punjab government and introduced direct rule from the centre. In 1988 the Indian government had started building a 160 km fence to prevent the infiltration of arms and terrorists from Pakistan into India as Punjab shares an approximately a 553 km long border with Pakistan.

Finally, on 9 May 1988 the police took action in Golden Temple again. About 100 'extremist' Sikhs barricaded themselves in the Golden Temple by building brick and mortar bunkers to protect themselves. Some 47 Sikh 'militants' were killed in the attack and the rest surrendered to the police.

There were a number of differences between the 1984 and 1988 attack on the Golden Temple. In 1988, Sikh 'extremists' who were barricaded in the Golden Temple had no prominent leaders as was the case when Bhindernawale led the Sikh extremists in the Golden Temple in 1984. Moreover, broad opposition has also emerged in the Sikh community against the use of the Golden Temple for political, terrorist, and criminal activities. This was evident in their muted reaction to the 1988 attack or action in comparison to the 1984 attack. The Indian government invited the Indian and foreign media into Amritsar in 1988 at the time of the action and during the aftermath without any restrictions, though foreign reporters have to clear their reports with the Indian government before sending them to foreign countries. In 1984, Punjab's borders were sealed completely to foreign and Indian reporters. In Operation Black Thunder 1988, the damage to the Golden Temple was not nearly as extensive as in Operation Blue Star in 1984 and there were far fewer casualties. The Indian army and police did not suffer any casualties and it is estimatedd that 47 Sikhs were killed or committed suicide during the operations. The loss of lives on both sides in 1984 was significant. After 1984, the government also cleared a 2 km corridor around the Golden Temple in Amritsar. That displaced about 10,000 people. Some 1,281 shops and business units and 900 houses were demolished to carve out the corridor. The estimated cost was about Rs 136 crores. (*India Today*, 15 June 1988:47). In addition to houses and business units, there were 111 religious places which had to be demolished under the scheme. Out of 111 religious places, 47 were owned by the SGPC, even though religious places are protected under the Land Acquisition Act. Thus, in spite of the resistance by of the home owners, business operators, and religious groups to the 2 km corridor around the Golden Temple, the Indian government went ahead.

Since 1988, the situation in Punjab has changed and some argue that it has improved. It is however important to note that the Congress government at the central level and the then Prime Minister Narasimha Rao failed to resolve the 'Punjab problem' and did not act on the Longowal–Gandhi accord, nor did he try to utilize any of the mechanisms to deal with reasonable Sikh demands or resolutions of the Anandpur Sahib resolution. Moreover, Rao's government ignored the recommendations of the Sarkaria Commission which had argued that the Central government decentralize its powers and give greater fiscal, executive and administrative powers to the states. These recommendations, if implemented, would have satisfied some Sikh demands.

The central government imposed its own rule over Punjab until February 1992. It is important to note that the Indian government amended the constitution in March 1988, permitting it to proclaim a state of emergency in Punjab on the ground that disturbance in that state threatened the integrity of India. The new law allowed direct rule of Punjab by the central government for up to three years without parliamentary approval. These changes gave the federal government unlimited powers to arrest, detain, or shoot people. After the election in 1992 in Punjab (the Akali Dal party did not participate in these elections) the Congress party came to power and Beant Singh became the chief minister. He extended unlimited powers to the police to eliminate 'terrorism' in Punjab and several other state agencies were also given extensive powers to aid in this effort.

At the central level, the Rao government was replaced by a coalition Janata Dal government in 1997, and the election in 1998 led to the formation of a coalition government headed by Bharatiya Janata Party (BJP), often referred to as a Hindu nationalist party. At the provincial level, the Akali Dal and BJP alliance in Punjab won all the parliamentary seats except one. The Akali Dal is an important ally of the BJP government at the national level.

The BJP led coalition at the central level may not be in a position to develop a coherent and unified approach towards the 'Punjab problem' which is acceptable to all the parties that provide its parliamentary majority. Punjab politics appears to be fragmented and the Sikh community divided on religious and political grounds. The Punjab government, because of its alliance with BJP, on the one hand, and the political and economic demands of the Sikh community, on the other, appears to be caught in the midst of the contradictory demands of its various constituents. Increasing communalization of politics in India, particularly at the central level, may make it difficult for the BJP led government to resolve the regional and state issues which are often perceived or construed as 'demands' of particular religious, cultural, and ethnic groups. For instance, if in Punjab the central government responds favourably to 'Sikh demands' it faces the potential risk of losing the 'Hindu vote', if this is characterized as capitulation to the Sikhs.

On the surface, at least, the 'situation' in Punjab appears to be stable. Various levels of government take credit for restoring peace and law and order, and elimination of 'terrorists' in the region. However, the basic political issues, articulated in the Anandpur Sahib Resolution remain unresolved. Rising communalism and religionization of politics and political opportunism of the BJP and the Congress party remain an impediment to the resolution of minority issues. Rajni Kothari (1985:98) in conclusion to the article 'Electoral Politics and the Rise of Communalism' states:

Communalism in India, especially of recent vintage, is a direct outcome of the decline in democratic politics, in participation, in effective citizen action. It is only by rejuvenating citizen initiatives and forcing the state to concede to the just demands of the minorities that a long-term strategy of combating communalism can evolve.

To compete for 'Hindu votes' even the Congress party forsook the secularism and ethnicized regional demands in Punjab. Gupta (1985:221) states:

The Hindu communalism is no backlash. The raw material of popular Hindu perceptions was carefully worked upon by the Congress (I) such that in Punjab today one has two completely distinct views, one Sikh and one Hindu, on almost everything. In the years 1980 to 1984 the government portrayed the Anandpur Sahib Resolution principally as a religiously inspired secessionist document, when in reality it was far from that.

However, ethnicization and religionization of politics creates its own contradictions. This is evident in the dilemma faced by the BJP led coalition government. Its anti-minority political rhetoric comes into conflict with the parliamentary support it needs from religious and parties with an ethnic base to remain in power. The Babri Mosque issue in Ayodhya is a case in point. The BJP is finding it increasingly difficult to satisfy the Hindus (Vishwa Hindu Parishad [VHP]) who are bent on constructing Rama temple at the site of the Babari Masjid which was destroyed in 1992 while at the same time not alienating the Muslims, and in the process other minorities. Muslims constitute about 12 per cent of the population. In some crucial states, in electoral terms, such as Uttar Pradesh, Bihar, West Bengal, and Assam, their concentration varies from 15 to 20 per cent. Thus, Muslim support is not only necessary in the immediate context, but crucial in the future for any national political party interested in state power at the centre and in states with a concentration of Muslim votes. This communal politics may secure state power for some political parties in the short run, but in the long run such a strategy will only perpetuate hatred and violence in the country and undermine its democratic and secular institutions.

Those who control the state and its institutions can use state power and the vast state machinery against political opponents to maintain the status quo. The role of the state is therefore important in any discussion of the 'Punjab problem'.

STATE CRIMES AND CRIMINALIZATION OF POLITICAL DISSENT

Much of the literature on the 'Punjab problem' has focused on the activities and political and economic demands of various groups and political parties opposed to the status quo in Punjab. The nature and role of the state have received relatively little attention. Most journalists, academics, political analysts and others have uncritically accepted the popular and official state definition of the 'problem'. There is also uncritical acceptance of concepts such as 'extremists' and 'terrorists' in their description of certain groups and their activities. Such studies which examine the issues and problems within officially pre-established limits, constraints, definitions, and conceptual frameworks produce an impoverished product. Rather than take the official and popular conceptions as given, a thorough scholarly analysis must subject to scrutiny the very conceptualization and social construction of the problem. At a minimal level, this requires an analysis of the nature of the state and state power and its role in protecting the status quo.

The state has monopoly over the legitimate use of power, and its coercive force is embodied in law and legal institutions. The few who control state power exercise control over the many and protect the status quo through various forms of domination. In the process, to secure and maintain the existing class structure and order, the state may often engage in extra-legal criminal acts, such as denial of human rights and due process, illegal detentions, manufactured evidence, unlawful police acts, and state-sponsored terrorism, illegal abuse of prisoners and torture, mutilation and rapes by law enforcement agents. However, these activities are not considered crimes because of the legitimization of the state's use of force and are often masked under the name of public interest and security, and the need to restore law, order and safety (Corrado, 1996, 1991; Schafer, 1974; Clinard and Meier, 1998; Chambliss, 1976; Reasons, 1973; Spitzer, 1983; Bolaria, 1986; Quinney, 1977, 1979; Turk, 1982; Proal, 1973).

The state also uses its ideological hegemony and control over the means of communication to discredit and oppress those who pose a serious threat to its power by labelling them as extremists, terrorists, funded and supported by foreign agents and enemies. This allows the state to criminalize all political dissent and rationalize the suppression of even legal activities by further extending extraordinary powers to the police, the army, and law enforcement agencies. The official response to crimes of conspiracy and treason is more severe than conventional criminality. The primary objective is not simply to regulate and deter but, rather, to eliminate all opponents and foreign enemies and destroy any threat to the state. An analysis of the nature of state and state power and its ideological hegemony and control over the legitimate use of force provides a framework within which its social construction of and response to political demands and dissent in Punjab need to be discussed.

The state will go to any lengths to protect the existing order and discredit serious political threats to its authority (Turk, 1982). However, in order to secure the existing order 'crimes of domination' are committed (Quinney, 1977). Quinney characterizes these crimes as crimes of control, crimes of government, and crimes of economic domination. Crimes of control are the crimes committed by law enforcement agencies and agents in the name of the law. Crimes of government are the crimes committed by the elected representatives of the capitalist state. Crimes of economic domination include crimes committed by individual entrepreneurs, business executives, professionals, and by corporations (price-fixing, pollution of the environment, marketing of hazardous drugs) to protect and further capital accumulation. Thus many social injuries are committed by the capitalist class and the capitalist state that are not considered crimes by the state. The denial of human rights, sexism, racism, and economic exploitation are an integral part of capitalism and are important to its survival (Quinney, 1979; Platt, 1974). Quinney emphasizes that underlying all capitalist crimes is the appropriation of surplus value created by labour. Quinney(1979:328) states that, 'domination and repression are a basic part of class struggle in the development of capitalism... Crime control and the crimes of domination are thus necessary features and the natural products of capitalist political economy'. Proal's definition of political crimes includes, 'crimes perpetrated by government for alleged reasons of state and by politicians for alleged reasons of expediency or political advantage' (Proal, 1973, cited in Corrado, 1996:460).

Political crimes involve issues of power and authority. In response to minority demands seen as a threat to the state power, the state may use a criminal label against individuals, groups and organizations to protect its interests and authority. The state's ability to define what constitutes crime enables it to use criminal laws to deal with political opposition and dissent (Turk, 1982). Crimes against the state may include attempts to change unjust and discriminatory laws, legitimate peaceful civil rights protests, and attempts to alter social and political structures. In the face of increasing threat to the status quo, the state may resort to more oppressive legislation in the name of peace and security and increasingly limit and restrict the boundaries of 'legitimate' political dissent. In addition to a criminal label, the opposition may also be discredited by such labels as fanatics, extremists, fundamentalists, agents of foreign powers, and terrorists, or characterize their activities as mentally disordered behaviours or acts of mentally disturbed individuals. The state uses its ideological hegemony and domination over the mass media to project a particular official definition of events and circumstances surrounding these events. This virtual monopoly over social construction of events portrays state activities in a favourable light and use of force and strong measures are almost always justified in public interest and common good and control of criminals and criminality. This portrayal and characterization of opponents as criminals tends to undermine the political and economic grievances underlying their activities (Corrado, 1991:451).

In this process of control the state may extensively violate its own laws, such as obstruction of justice, illegal confinements, faked encounters, bribing or intimidating individuals to prevent testimony and misuse of government agencies. Chambliss (1976) and Reasons (1973) contend that governments are overwhelmingly the most serious political criminals. However, these crimes seldom draw strong public reaction and opposition primarily because of the legitimacy of the state and the public's general acceptance of government authority.

As we have discussed in the previous pages, the state's (state and central governments) actions and response played an important role in the communalization of politics in Punjab. The promotion and support of Bhindranwale by the Congress party contributed not only to his 'build-up' but also to conflict and the polarization of politics within the Sikh community. Political opportunism also encouraged extremism and random acts of violence attributed to the terrorists. The state also proceeded to 'demonize' Bhindranwale and the Golden Temple as a fortress with a well-stocked arsenal of weapons.

The breakdown in public security and law and order created conditions for the Indian state to institute extreme measures and oppressive state policies. Denial of human rights and due process, extra-legal activities of police, army, and other law enforcement agencies were all justified in the name of national security and national unity. The allegations of involvement and support of foreign governments and agents in Punjab provided further rationale for the state to take all necessary steps to eliminate foreign enemies. The public is more likely to accept strong measures and extreme state controls when the activities and actions of political opponents are labelled as conspiratorial and treasonous, and a threat to national integrity and unity, and even the survival of the nation.

In this process, the state passed laws to strengthen its law enforcement machinery, imposed central rule, and arrested and detained many people without trial. The 'military action' caused deaths of hundreds of innocent pilgrims during Operation Blue Star. State crimes have become increasingly evident in various inquiries and reports, and current trials and criminal charges against law enforcement agents and politicians. State-sponsored terrorism and crimes include criminal negligence of its duty to protect its citizens from mob and communal violence. This was particularly the case after Indira Gandhi's assassination by two Sikh bodyguards. The whole Sikh community was held responsible (collective responsibility) for the criminal act of two Sikhs and thousands of innocent Sikhs lost their lives and property in the aftermath (collective punishment). The complicity of ruling party leaders and workers, police inaction and even encouragement, organized mob killings, rapes and arson, and sharing the loot are all now coming to light (see Malik, 1985; other chapters in Singh and Malik, 1985).

State control of mass media, selective reporting, misinformation and disinformation helped the state in social construction of the 'Punjab problem' and 'black out' of news on everyday life in Punjab, harassment, arrests, killings and torture of innocent and ordinary citizens (Gupta, 1985; Singh, 1985; Malik, 1985).

Our central point in this discussion is that the state played an important role in the social construction of the 'Punjab problem' and in the characterization of political opponents and their activities to justify strong and coercive responses by it.

The politics of random violence and terror by a small minority provided the state further justification for its actions. Any coercion, abuse, and violence against the civilian population to secure mass support in pursuit of political goals becomes counterproductive because, on the one hand, it allows the state to use extraordinary power to criminalize and suppress the opposition (state-organized and legalized terrorism is used to control terrorism and threats to public safety) and, on the other, it discredits legitimate political demands and weakens mass support for change. Death threats, blackmail, extortions and killings of 'moderate' elements in the Sikh community weakened political support among the Sikhs for 'radicals' and 'extremists'. Also, their similar activities against non-Sikhs contributed to an increase in the communal and sectarian conflict in Punjab and helped to define regional political and economic issues as 'Sikh demands'. These conditions discredited even the legitimate political and economic regional demands and weakened democratic and mass support for change. As noted above, this also allowed the state to criminalize all political activities.

While in the short run, it sustains the existing social, economic and political structures, in the long run, it also generates cynicism and undermines the legitimacy of the state, the political process, and democratic institutions.

SUMMARY AND CONCLUSIONS

A full appreciation of the current situation in Punjab requires a historical–structural analysis of a number of forces and events both internal and external to the Sikh community. The discussion and analysis above covers the social, economic, political, and communal context of historical and contemporary dimensions of the 'Punjab problem'. It should be noted that our discussion is by no means exhaustive but is limited to what we consider to be some of the most salient factors relevant to the subject.

The prolonged historical struggles of the Sikhs against the often oppressive state policies of Mughal–Afghan rulers ended with the formation of the 'Sikh Raj'. During this period the Sikhs enjoyed a certain level of political, economic, and social stability, and the Sikh community prospered. Under state patronage, many more new shrines were built and old historical places important to Sikhs were restored and renovated. However, the death of Maharaja Ranjit Singh and political intrigues and conflicts among his successors created an opportunity for the British to extend and consolidate their colonial rule over Punjab and hence throughout India. Subsequent to the collapse of the 'Sikh Raj', and internal political power conflicts, the Sikh community also had to contend with internal contradictions and conflicts over religious principles and practices and control of religious institutions. The struggles to revitalize the basic Sikh principles and regain control of gurdwaras from *mahants* (priests) are not only historically important factors in the formation of the Sikh religious and political identity but also have profound bearing on contemporary politics and governance of their gurdwaras and religious affairs. As discussed above, two important organizations emerged during this period: the Shiromani Gurdwara Parbandhak Committee (SGPC) and Akali Dal (Sikh political party). Since their formation these two organizations continue to be important sites of political and religious struggles among various factions in the Sikh community and hence a forum for political debates and crystallization of political strategy and demands. The Akali Dal, in particular, has also been an important political force in provincial and federal politics. The democratization of governance of Sikh institutions by the elected SGPC and the close links between the SGPC and the Akali Dal often make it difficult to clearly distinguish between the religious and political activities of the community (separation of religion and politics). Sikh gurdwaras have always been sites of Sikh political gatherings and launching of political agitations (*morchas*).

The 'religious factor' was important in British 'communal awards' of proportionate allocation of legislative seats in Punjab; anti-colonial politics by the Muslim League and the Congress party vis-à-vis the Sikhs; the partition of India and the creation of a separate state of Pakistan. Notwithstanding independent India's constitutional commitment to secularism, religion in conjunction with other factors has been an important political force in electoral politics. Punjab politics is deeply rooted in religious, linguistic, and cultural distinctiveness of the area in conjunction with regional and provincial political economy. While most of the 'Punjab issues' are not particularly unique in the context of other regional/territorial demands, Punjab being a border state with Pakistan has received considerable attention and contentions remain between various interested parties and levels of government about the nature and content of these issues and demands. The discussion of the 'Anandpur Sahib Resolution' clearly illustrates this. This official document of the Akali Dal contains a number of resolutions primarily oriented towards political, territorial, and economic demands and reforms to improve the living conditions of workers and farmers and safeguard the rights of the minorities within the framework of the Indian constitution. Moreover, these resolutions address regional/state issues of importance and benefit all the Punjabis rather than Sikhs alone. In spite of evidence to the contrary, manifested in legal–constitutional analysis of the content of the resolutions, and Longowal's statement 'that the Sikhs have no desire to get away from India in any manner' and the recognition in the Gandhi–Longowal accord that this resolution is entirely within the framework of the Indian constitution, and, 'that the purpose of the resolution is to provide greater autonomy to the states with a view to strengthening the unity and integrity of the country ...', the opponents of the resolution continue to characterize is as secessionist and damaging to the unity of the country. The political interests of contending parties to enhance their electoral success have contributed to communalization of politics both at the provincial and central levels. The 'politics of violence' by a segment of the Sikh community and the state response helped to reinforce the sectarian and secessionist perception of the 'Punjab problem'. This characterization also helps to divert attention away from the underlying material conditions of the region. Political issues and agitation are rooted in economic development policies and its contradictions in Punjab, and embody broader economic forces of displacement, unemployment, and underemployment, and increasing economic disparity and inequality.

Political interests and attempts to secure and maintain power at any cost played an important role in the social construction of the Punjab problem. When faced with threat of loss of power, even the Congress party abandoned its secular political rhetoric and contributed to the communalization of Punjab politics. It actively encouraged contradictions, conflicts, and polarization of politics in the Sikh community for electoral gains. This political opportunism encouraged the 'extremists' among the Sikhs and demand for independent Sikh leaders and the center further weakened the moderate forces and strengthened those who preached politics of violence and armed struggle.

Conflicts within the Sikh community between the 'moderates' and the 'extremists' intensified. External political interests and internal politics and contradictions among the Sikhs contributed to increasing polarization of politics in Punjab. Thus, state and central politics not only played an important role in shaping the political process and forces in Punjab and in social construction of the 'Punjab problem' but also the state response and 'solution' to this problem. Oppressive state policies in Punjab, the assault on the Golden Temple to 'root out' the 'extremists', and other actions of the military and security forces were justified on grounds of restoration of peace, law and order. The military assault on the Golden Temple and other state activities led to the subsequent assassination of Prime Minister Indira Gandhi and the anti-Sikh riots in Delhi and other parts of India. These and other events have contributed to giving an increasingly ethnic, religious and regional bias to political and economic issues in India.

While on the surface the 'Punjab problem' appears to have stabilized, the basic political and economic issues articulated in the Anandpur Sahib Resolution remain unresolved. The growing communalism and political opportunism of various national and regional parties remain an impediment to the resolution not only of the 'Punjab problem' but also to the solution of regional, minority, and central provincial issues in the rest of India.

The chapter concludes with a discussion of the role of the state in protecting the status quo through various forms of domination. In the process of securing and maintaining the existing class structure and social order the state may engage in extra-legal criminal acts. However, because of the legitimacy of the state's use of force these acts are not considered crimes and are often masked in the name of public safety and national security. The state's power to define what constitutes crime enables it to use criminal laws to deal with political opposition and dissent and discredit them by the use of such labels as extremists and terrorists. This portrayal of opponents as criminals and terrorists tends to undermine the political and economic grievances underlying their activities and justify strong and coercive response by the state. The politics of random violence by a small minority provides the state further rationalization for its actions. The use of coercion and intimidation against the civilian population to secure political support also discredits legitimate political demands and weakens democratic and mass support for change. Under these circumstances the state through coercive force in the short run may sustain the existing social, economic, and political structures but in the long run it also generates cynicism and undermines the secular and democratic institutions and polity.

REFERENCES

Amnesty International (1986): *Amnesty International, Annual Report* (London: Amnesty International Publications).

Bannerjee, Sumanta (1984): 'Divide and Rule Tactics', *South: Third World Magazine*. London, May, p. 9.

Bannerjee, S. and M. Lodhi (1984): 'Questioning the Temple Rage', *South: Third World Magazine*. London, July.

Bhatnagar, Asaha (1984): 'The Language and Culture of the Punjabis', *Sikh Review*, Calcutta, May, 1984, p. 54.

Bolaria, B. Singh (1986): 'Capital, Labour and Criminalized Workers', pp. 295–312, *in* Brian D. MacLean (ed.), *The Political Economy of Crime* (Scarborough, Ont.: Prentice Hall).

Butani, D.H. (1986): *The Third Sikh War? Towards or Away from Khalistan* (New Delhi: Promilla & Co. Publishers).

Cambridge University (1984): 'Khalsa', Newsletter of the Sikh Society, University of Cambridge, June.

Chambliss, W. (1976): 'Functional and Conflict Theories of Crime: The Heritage of Emile Durkheim and Karl Marx', pp. 1–28, *in* W. Chambliss and M. Markoff (eds), *Whose Law? What Order? A Conflict Approach to Criminology* (New York: Wiley).

Chauhan, Malook S. (1984): 'The Genocide of Sikhs in Punjab, Where Do You Stand?' (London Sikh Missionary Society), p. 4.

Clinard, Marshall B. and Robert F. Meier (1998): *Sociology of Deviant Behaviour* (Toronto: Harcourt Brace College Publishers).

Cole, W.O. (1984): *Sikhism and Its Indian Context: 1469–1708* (London: Darton, Longman & Todd).

Corrado, Raymond R. (1996): 'Political Crime in Canada', pp. 459–493 in Rick Linden (ed.), *Criminology: A Canadian Perspective* (Toronto: Harcourt Brace).

Corrado, Raymond R. (1991): 'Contemporary Political Crime: National and International Terrorism', pp. 451–70, *in* Margaret A. Jackson and Curt T. Griffiths (eds), *Canadian Criminology* (Toronto: Harcourt Brace Javonovich).

Cunningham, J.D. (1853): *History of Sikhs* (London. John Murray).

Economist (1984): 'Dogs Eat Dogs in Punjab', *The Economist*, London, 21 April, pp. 37–8.

Economist (1986): *Economist*, London, 5 April, p. 41.

Globe and Mail (1986): 'New Chief in Punjab to Take Four Lives for Each Slain Officer', Toronto, 10 April, p. 3A.

Gonick, Cy. (1985): 'The Delhi Riots', *Canadian Dimensions*, Winnipeg, vol. 19, no. 4, Sept.–Oct. p. 23.

Grewal, J.S. (1990): *The Sikhs of the Punjab* (Cambridge: Cambridge University Press).

Gujral, I.K. (1985): 'The Sequence', pp. 111–21, *in* Patwant Singh and Harji Malik (eds), *Punjab: The Fatal Miscalculation* (New Delhi: Published by Patwant Singh, Crescent Printing Works).

Gupta, Dipankar (1985): 'The Communalising of Punjab, 1980–1985', pp. 209–29, *in* Patwant Singh and Harji Malik (eds), *Punjab: The Fatal Miscalculation* (New Delhi: Published by Patwant Singh, Crescent Printing Works).

Hasrat, Bikrama Jit (1968): *Anglo–Sikh Relations, 1799–1849: A Reappraisal of the Rise and Fall of the Sikhs* (Hoshiarpur, Punjab: V.V. Research Institute Book Agency).

India Today (1988): 'Punjab: The Problems Ahead', Delhi, 15 June.

Kapur, Rajiv, A. (1987): 'Khalistan: India's Punjab Problem', *Third World Quarterly*, London. vol. 9, no. 4, Oct.

Kaur, Upinderjit (1990): *Sikh Religion and Economic Development* (New Delhi: National Book Organization).

Kothari, Rajni (1985): 'Electoral Politics and the Rise of Communalism', in P. Singh and H. Malik (eds), *Punjab: The Fatal Miscalculation* (New Delhi: Published by Patwant Singh, Crescent Printing Works).

Malik, Baljit (1984): 'The Politics of Religion', *The Illustrated Weekly of India*, New Delhi, 22 June, p. 27.

Malik, Harji (1985): 'The Politics of Alienation', pp. 33–62, *in* Patwant Singh and Harji Malik (eds), *Punjab: The Fatal Miscalculation* (New Delhi. Published by Patwant Singh, Crescent Printing Works).

Menon, Sadanand (1985): 'The November Carnage: Lifetime of Uncertainty, Terror, Paranoia, Humiliation and Distrust', *Sikh Review*, Calcutta, June, p. 65.

Nayar Kuldip and Khuswant Singh (1984): *Tragedy of Punjab: Operation Bluestar and After* (New Delhi: Vision Books).

New York Times (1982): 'Prosperity in Punjab', *New York Times*, 1 October.

People's Union for Democratic Rights and People's Union for Civil Liberties (1984): 'Sikh Holocaust: Who are the Guilty? Report of a Joint Inquiry into the causes and impact of the Riots in Delhi from October 31–November 10, 1984' (New Westminster, B.C.: Khalsa Diwan Society).

Noorani, A.G. (1985): 'A White Paper on A Black Record', pp. 145–161, *in* Patwant Singh and Harji Malik (eds), *Punjab: The Fatal Miscalculation* (New Delhi. Published by Patwant Singh, Crescent Printing Works).

Philauri, Sharadha Rama, and Henry Court (1959): *History of the Sikhs* (Calcutta: Susil Gupta Printer Ltd, Amiya Rao, et al.)

—— (1985): *A Citizens for Democracy Report to the Nation: Truth About Delhi Violence* (New Delhi: Citizens for Democracy).

Platt, Tony (1974): 'Prospects for a Radical Criminology in the United States', *Crime and Social Justice* (Spring-Summer), 2–10.

Proal, Louis (1973): *Political Crime* (Montclair, N.J.: Patterson Smith).

Quinney, Richard (1979): 'Crimes and the Development of Capitalism', pp. 319–33, *in* R. Quinney (ed.), *Capitalist Society* (Homewood, Ill.: Dorsey Press).

—— (1977): *Class, State and Crime: On the Theory and Practice of Criminal Justice* (New York: Longman).

Reasons, Charles (1973): 'The Politicization of Crime, the Criminal, and the Criminologist', *Journal of Criminal Law and Criminology* 64, 471–7.

Sathananthan, S.M. et al. (1983): *Hindu Sikh Conflict in Punjab: Cause and Cure* (Houston, Texas: Sikh Council of North America and Sikh Centre of the Gulf Coast Area. Inc.), p. 15.

Schafer, Stephen (1974): *The Political Criminal: The Problem of Morality and Crime* (New York: The Free Press).

Shourie, Arun (1985): 'Can India Survive?', *Illustrated Weekly of India*, New Delhi, Jan. 1985.

—— (1982): *Indian Express*, 12–14 May

Sikh Ex-Servicemen and Intellectual Forum (nd): *The Betrayal of the Sikhs* (Chandigarh, Akal Printmatics).

Singh, Hakam (1982): *Sikh Studies: A Classified Bibliography of Printed Books in English* (Patiala: Punjab Publishing House).

Singh, Harbans (1983): *Heritage of the Sikhs* (Columbia, Mo: South Asia Books).

Singh, Indarjit (1984): 'Gandhi Speak and the Murderous Truth', *Manchester Guardian*, London, 24 June.

Singh, Khushwant (1963): *A History of the Sikhs, Vol. 2. 1839–1964* (Princeton, N.J.: Princeton University Press).

—— (1985): 'Speech in the Parliament', *Sikh Review*, Calcutta, Feb. 1985., p. 63.

Singh, Milkha (1984): 'Law and Order—Whose Baby?', *Sikh Review*, Calcutta, May, pp. 59–62.

Singh, Patwant (1985): 'The Distorting Mirror', pp. 9–32, *in* Patwant Singh and Harji Malik (eds), *Punjab: The Fatal Miscalculation* (New Delhi: Published by Patwant Singh, Crescent Printing Works).

Singh, Patwant and Harji Malik (1985): *Punjab: The Fatal Miscalculation* (New Delhi: Published by Patwant Singh, Crescent Printing Works).

Singh, Ramindar (1985): 'Sikh Youth: Wounded Psyche', *India Today*, New Delhi. June 30, 1985 pp 42, 45.

Singh, Saran (1985): 'The Numbers Games', *Sikh Review*, Calcutta, March, p. 4.

Spokesman (1984): *Spokesman: A Weekly Newspaper*, Toronto, no. 1008, 26 Aug.

Spitzer, Stephen (1983): 'The Rationalization of Crime Control in the Capitalist Society', pp. 312–33, *in* Stanley Cohen and Andrew Skull (eds), *Social Control and the State* (Oxford: Martin Robinson).

Subramanian, Swamy (1984): 'Three Days in the Darbar Sahib', *Illustrated Weekly of India*, New Delhi, 13 May, pp. 2, 4.

Turk, Austin T. (1982): *Political Criminality: The Defiance and Defense of Authority* (Beverly Hills: Sage).

Wangar (1987): A Publication of the Indian People's Association in North America (IPANA). vol. 8, no. 2. Vancouver,(Nov-Dec.).

World Bank (1980): *World Bank Report, Migration and Money* (New York: Oxford University Press).

World Bank (1982): *World Development Report* (New York: Oxford University Press), p. 70.

World Bank (1984): *Punjab Tangle, The Different Perspective* (New Delhi: World Sikh Peace Organization).

Migration, Labour, and Racism

❀

INTRODUCTION

To fully appreciate the migration patterns and characteristics of immigrants to Canada it is important to consider some of the salient aspects of the theoretical and conceptual debates in migration studies and perspectives on racism and racial inequality. Such a discussion is important to understand the reasons for migration, the volume and characteristics of migrants, and their social, economic, and political location in the Canadian mosaic. Those interested in the study of migration and racism approach and examine such issues from various theoretical perspectives and paradigms and use varying levels of analysis. In the area of migration, explanations range from individual motivation and economic self-interest to migrate, to an analysis of structural determinants involved in patterned migration movements determined by the dynamics of capitalist development and the interface between the needs of the capital and characteristics of labour. Similarly, in the study of racism and racial inequality, explanations range from individual racism which refers to the attitudes and actions of individuals to institutional racism which refers to the normal daily social practices of legal, political, and economic institutions that systematically exclude racial minorities from equal participation and treatment in society.

This chapter discusses various perspectives and paradigms used in studies of migrations and racism with a view to providing a broader context within which the migratory flows and social inequality can be fruitfully analysed. More specifically, the following topics are discussed: international migrations; capital and foreign labour; state and labour procurement; and institutional racism and exploitation.

INTERNATIONAL MIGRATIONS

The history of migrations is the history of a succession of labour reservoirs. The migration of labour across national boundaries has been part of the global relations between the colonial and advanced capitalist and the colonized or neo-colonial underdeveloped countries. Historically, it took the form of the slave trade from Africa (Williams, 1964); indentured and 'coolie' labour from India and China (Tinker, 1974; Huttenback, 1976; Gangulee, 1947; Saha, 1970). Currently, foreign workers constitute a significant part of the workforce in many Western European countries, Australia, North America, and some Middle-Eastern countries (see Bolaria and Bolaria, 1997).

The conditions and mechanisms of transfer and use of slave and unfree labour were, of course, different from the current voluntary and free-labour movements from one country to the other. The slave trade involved overt violence and forced transfer of labour. The present-day migrations take place under different conditions and are caused by a different set of forces, though not necessarily less coercive. In the following pages we discuss some perspectives on migration.

The international circulation of workers has traditionally been understood as resulting from mechanical demographic forces rather than as a consequence of international inequality between rich and poor nations. The primary focus of demographic studies is to compile the demographic characteristics of migrants and to search for individualist reasons or motives for migration. The tendency of this type of inquiry is to produce a so-called theory of migration that amounts to identifying a list of 'push' and 'pull' factors (Bolaria and Li, 1988). The assumption here is that, because of self-interest and economic rationality, individuals decide to migrate to maximize their opportunities for better employment, higher wages, a better quality of life, and other favourable conditions. This perspective has been criticized for its focus on individual interests and motivation, and assumptions of a uniform international labour market and freedom of mobility across national boundaries without adequate recognition of the social, economic, and political contexts of decision-making (Gardezi, 1995). It is argued that demographic studies with their focus on migrations as movements of people not only distract attention from the economic role migrants play in the receiving countries but also do not explain the structural determinants involved in patterned migration movements. In essence, these studies obscure and devalue the essential role of migrants as labour resource and reservoirs.

Contrary to the assertions of demographers, an aggregate flow of migrants is not a random collection of 'individual choices' to migrate (Cockcroft, 1982). Patterned migration movement and migratory flows are determined by conditions of differential development between countries. Migratory flows will be produced and reproduced so long as such unequal conditions persist. As Sassen-Koob (1978:514–15) notes: 'The nature of migratory flow depends on the nature of these conditions, not on those of the migrants themselves, these being a consequence of those conditions.' Thus, 'migrants can be viewed as stepping or falling into a migratory flow, rather than initiating or constituting such a flow through their individual decisions and actions' (Sassen-Koob, 1978:515).

Recent studies of international circulation of labour and resources have begun to pay greater attention to capitalism as a world-system characterized by gross disparities and unequal accumulation of capital between core and peripheral countries (Elling, 1981; Jonas and Dixon, 1979). The political and economic forces that produce wealth in core capitalist countries simultaneously produce and sustain underdevelopment, unemployment and poverty in peripheral countries. The transfer of labour is one aspect of the unequal and exploitative relations between labour-importing and labour-exporting countries. Blocked development and underdevelopment create high unemployment and hence surplus labour, thus forcing many workers to migrate. As Bonacich and Cheng (1984:2) state: 'migration is a product not of discrete and unconnected factors in the sending and receiving countries, but of historical connections between the countries. It is not fortuitous; it is systematic.'

As capitalism becomes increasingly global in character, the internationalization of capital is accompanied by the internationalization of labour (Navarro, 1986; Elling, 1981; Barnet and Muller, 1974; Turner, 1973). Global disparities allow core countries to have access to an international labour pool. The core countries play an important role in regulating the flow of labour and capital. The poor economic conditions of many Third World countries facilitate both the transfer of workers from these countries to advanced capitalist ones and the direct penetration by multinational firms of the cheap overseas market.

Workers of poor nations face exploitation both in their own countries and in foreign lands. To service large foreign debts many Third World nation states are dependent upon remittances from abroad. To ensure this, some labour-exporting countries are involved in enforcement of labour contracts to provide a stable workforce to employers and to require these workers to remit a certain percentage of their earnings to the 'home' state (Arnold and Shah, 1984; Choucri, 1983; World Bank, 1980; Gardezi and Rashid, 1983). These funds, however, have little impact on economic development in the labour-exporting countries (Whyte, 1984; Satzewich, 1995a or b; Gardezi, 1995). On the contrary, these funds often disrupt local economies, create inflationary pressures in some sectors, and increase consumption of goods from countries where those workers are employed. In reality, the presence of contract labour allows employers to super-exploit their labour power and increase capital accumulation in those countries. Ironically, this process further increases inequalities between the countries and sustains structured conditions for continued exploitation. Globalization of production, enhanced mobility of capital across national boundaries, and capital's enhanced structural power have created a new despotism of capital over labour. This mobility of capital has strengthened its power and position over the workers and weakened labour in any one community, region, state, or country. Workers are compelled to make concessions to keep their jobs and compete for investments.

CAPITAL AND FOREIGN LABOUR

Material production requires labour power. For a capitalist economy to function, its labour force must be produced, maintained, and renewed. In the process of consuming labour power, the capitalist is able to realize a gain in value beyond that required to purchase the labourer. Capitalists seek every means to reduce the labour cost and to increase the output of workers so that an even larger surplus is realized. Among the strategies used to reduce labour costs are the export of capital to areas of low-cost labour or procurement and use of ready-made labour, immigrant and migrant workers (Bolaria, 1984a, 1984b, 1986).

What specifically are the attractions of foreign-born labour? What are the specific characteristics of this labour that make it so attractive even when there might be a pool of unused domestic labour? The answer lies in the political, legal, and social status of this labour.

Immigrant labour is advantageous to capital in many respects (Satzewich, 1995a; Bolaria and Li, 1988; Trumper and Wong, 1997). As noted earlier, for a capitalist economy to function its labour force must be maintained and renewed. In the case of imported labour, the costs of labour force renewal are externalized to an alternate economy and/or site (Burawoy, 1976). The circulation of workers across the borders helps to reduce the cost of renewing labour at the point of production (Burawoy, 1976; Bach, 1978; Sassen-Koob, 1978).

Migration involves the transfer of valuable human resources from one country to the other. This transfer represents a very large economic cost to the countries of emigration. Emigration is considered by some economists as 'capital export' similar to the export of other factors of production (Berger and Mohr, 1975). Considerable sums are invested in the reproduction, creation and upbringing of workers (Gorz, 1970). The use of labour, already produced and paid for elsewhere, means a considerable saving for the receiving countries (Berger and Mohr, 1975). Generally, as migrant workers enter the country at the beginning of their working lives, they make an important contribution to the workforce, to production, and to capital accumulation (Jones and Smith, 1970).

The purpose of allowing immigration is not only to increase the supply of labour but to increase the supply of a particular form of labour: cheap labour (Portes, 1977; 1978a; 1978b). This low-cost labour is often used to replace high-cost labour and to counteract and weaken the organizational efforts and bargaining position of the domestic workforce (Portes, 1978a).

For capital, immigrant workers represent a labour force that is stateless, deprived of legal and political rights, and therefore vulnerable and defenceless, and isolated from the indigenous working class (Dixon et al., 1982). These workers can be easily deported if they 'cause trouble' or are no longer needed. The immigrant workers from Mexico, Central America, and the Caribbean represent a labour force that 'because of the historical workings of colonialism and racism, can be submitted to levels of degradation which are socially unacceptable for other sectors of society' (Dixon et al., 1982:108).

The newly-arrived workers are often used as scabs and, whenever necessary, as scapegoats, particularly when the labour pool is overflowing and capital faces an accumulation crisis. Cockcroft states: '... capital seeks more immigration labour to build up the pool and yet intensifies the pace of scapegoating and deportations, as part of its general anti-labour and racist offensive, to extricate itself from its crisis in accumulation' (1982:58). Because of their legal and political vulnerability (aliens), migrants become easy targets of blame for social and economic ills (Bustamonte, 1972; 1976).

Immigrant workers are not only a source of cheap labour; they also regulate class conflict, '... directly by undercutting the collective actions launched by domestic worker organizations and indirectly by diverting the class hostilities rooted in the economy onto alien scapegoats' (Jenkins, 1978:324–5).

These workers are used in specific sectors of the economy, particularly in agribusiness and the garment industries. Capitalists in all of these sectors are seeking to combat the tendency of the rate of profit to fall by saving on wages. The immigrant workers are used as one 'way out' of the structured periodic crises in capital accumulation. The employers benefit from immigrant labour both economically, as a temporary resolution to crises in accumulation, and politically, because of the divisions and many social contradictions between migrant workers and indigenous workers. The migrant and immigrant labour force is now a permanent part of the economic structure of many countries and their labour cannot be relinquished.

These workers also form the basis of the modern industrial reserve army (Castles and Kosack, 1972). Other groups which might serve the same function—men thrown out of work by rationalization and capitalist crisis, non-working women, members of the *lumpen-proletariat*—have already been integrated into the production process to the extent to which it is profitable. The use of further reserves of this type would require costly social measures, such as kindergartens and day-care services (Castles and Kosack; 1972).

Castells (1975) also argues that this labour force is a fundamental element in the economic structure of many capitalist countries and is not simply an extra source of labour during times of rapid economic expansion. The immigrant and migrant labour help to maintain the rate of surplus value (profits) and capital accumulation by, 'paying a proportionately smaller value for the reproduction of the labour force, and increasing the duration and intensity of work' (Castells, 1975:46). As far as these conditions are concerned, immigrant and migrant workers usually receive the lowest wages; these workers are generally young and healthy (health screening examinations for immigrants ensure this), and they are likely to be working in the worst safety and health conditions, which permits considerable savings in the organization of work (Bolaria, 1988a; 1991). Racial minority and women workers face extreme exploitation in the labour market and often end up in low-paying and dead-end jobs and unhealthy work environments (Bolaria, 1991).

A foreign workforce is viewed as a production factor that can be repatri-ated when no longer needed (Sassen-Koob, 1981). Cockcroft points out that, 'because of the intensity of their exploitation, the migrants themselves have their productive capacities "used up" relatively early in life and are then discarded to the margins of society, to be replaced by new waves of younger migrants' (1982:56). Access to offshore workers assures an almost infinite supply of labour.

In summary, the circulation of workers across borders helps to reduce the cost of renewal of labour at the point of production. Obviously, immigrant workers do supplement the supply of domestic labour. Their importance and usefulness is that they increase the supply of a particular type of labour: docile and cheap. Many economic and political advantages accrue to capital from this situation.

STATE AND LABOUR PROCUREMENT

The state uses immigration laws to regulate the quantity and composition of immigrants and control their legal–political status. Canadian immigra-tion policy regulations have been changed periodically to accommodate its labour force and demographic needs (Bolaria, 1984a; 1984b; Bolaria and Li, 1988). For instance, during the 1960s and 1970s, many Western countries, including Canada, were in need of a highly specialized and technical labour force to accommodate the demands of rapid industrial development, especially when the domestic educational system was unable to generate a professional–skilled work force. To facilitate the recruitment of professional–scientific labour, a change in 1967 immigration regulations eliminated racial and nationality quotas and stressed linguistic, educational, and occupational qualifications of immigrants (Bolaria, 1992; Li, 1992). More recently, another important change has been to allow business immi-grants to Canada to facilitate capital import as well (Wong and Netting, 1992).

Immigration laws often create the flexibility to allow foreign labour to be admitted without granting the workers the legal status of regular immi-grants. In this way the state has the maximum benefit of importing cheap labour from all over the world without having to finance the overhead costs of labour reproduction. For instance, in addition to regular immigrant-settler labour, Canada also relies upon transient migrant workers to meet the labour force needs in various sectors (Bolaria, 1984a; 1992). In 1973,

Canada introduced Employment Authorization Regulations to allow the admission of non-residents for temporary employment. Thousands of workers have been admitted under this programme. Through the use of entry regulations, the Canadian state has been successful in converting what might otherwise have been permanent settlers into a lower-cost migrant–contract labour force. This labour procurement strategy, which was initially used in the case of domestic servants and agricultural sectors, has also been extended to the professional–scientific workforce (Bolaria, 1992).

The state through other immigration controls helps to reduce the labour costs, such as, single male or female workers without their families. The social cost of maintenance of workers without families is quite low. The recipients of this labour force save on a whole range of social costs: housing, schooling, and so forth. The absence of 'normal' married family life also delayed the growth of the native-born population of non-white immigrants, such as Indo-Canadians. The denial of legal–political rights and legal protection makes foreign workers vulnerable to extreme-exploitation by their employers. Various state-administered labour contracts also determine whether the foreign-born nationals are free to sell their labour power (free labour) or are confined and restricted to particular jobs and are not free to circulate in the labour market (Bolaria, 1992; Trumper and Wong, 1997). The state, of course, also has to manage the contradictions and political and ideological constraints in using immigration to solve demographic and fiscal problems associated with the declining fertility and aging of the Canadian population (Satzewich, 1995a).

The state, by regulating the migratory flows, admissibility and entry status of foreign-born nationals and workers, and denial of legal and political rights, provides capital with the cheapest, most submissive, docile, and exploitable workforce.

INSTITUTIONAL RACISM AND EXPLOITATION

Racial and ethnic inequality is a basic feature of the Canadian mosaic. Racial privileges, like class privileges, reach far back into the Canadian past. The colonization of the native population, racist immigration policies directed against South Asians and Chinese, the internment of the Japanese, all attest to the racist policies and practices of the Canadian state (Bolaria and Li, 1988). These policies and practices are present in the other institutions of this society, and continue to affect the current status of racial minorities in Canada. While patterns and practices of discrimination have changed over time, racial domination and racial inequality remain permanent features.

With a few exceptions, sociological studies of racial minorities are guided by the traditional 'race relations cycle' perspective and its many present-day variations of assimilation theories. It is barely possible to escape the literature dealing with cultural distinctiveness, cultural patterns and orientations, adaptation, integration, accommodation, identity, assimilation, and the like. In addition, the tendency has been to examine the 'problems' of non-Europeans. Studies of racial minorities, for the most part, tend to degenerate into more or less socio-psychological examinations of 'ethnic problems', or 'identity crises', or 'adaptation problems' or 'assimilation problems' or 'race problems' or 'family problems'. In short, they highlight the personal and social pathologies of racial minorities and their institutions (Bolaria, 1983; Basran, 1983; Bolaria and Li, 1988). The disadvantaged position of the racial minorities is often explained by biological and cultural deficiency theories in which the organization of the society along racial lines, institutional racism, and differential power relations are typically overlooked (Eitzen and Zinn, 1989).

The biological and cultural deficiency theories in fact argue that some groups are 'inferior because they are inferior' (Eitzen and Zinn, 1989:213). The inferiority of the groups is attributed to 'flawed genetics' or 'flaws' within their way of life which impedes their success. These theories tend to, '... blame the victim and ignore the structural constraints that deny certain groups the same opportunities that others have' (Eitzen and Zinn, 1989:215). While deficiency theories focus on minorities, some other theories, which Eitzen and Zinn refer to as bias theories, focus on the prejudicial attitudes and bigotry of the majority members. The focus on individual attitudes overlooks the importance of 'racial organization of the society that is the cause of people's racial beliefs', and that the determining feature of racial inequality is not prejudicial attitudes but rather the differential power relations and institutional and structural arrangements that maintain these inequalities (Eitzen and Zinn, 1989).

In contrast to the biological and cultural deficiency theories that put the blame on racial minorities, and others that blame individual racism for the disadvantaged position of the minorities, the structural theories focus on institutional patterns and structural inequalities that perpetuate racial inequality and exploitation. Carmichael and Hamilton (1967:4–5) discuss both types of racism. Individual racism 'consists of overt acts by individuals, which cause death and injury, or the violent destruction of property', and institutional racism 'originates in the operations of established and respected forces in the society'. Institutional racism entails both a racist theory and a social practice embodied in institutions that systematically exclude racial minorities from equal treatment and participation in society. Wilson (1973:34) describes it as follows:

When ideology of racial exploitation gives rise to normative proscriptions designed to prevent the subordinate racial group from equal participation in associations or procedures that are stable, organized, systematized ... institutional racism exists. Institutional racism therefore represents the structural aspect of racist ideology.

Institutions and social arrangements provide differential opportunities for groups: advantage some and disadvantage others. As Knowles and Prewitt state, societal institutions 'have great power to reward and penalize. They reward by providing career opportunities for some people and foreclosing them for others. They reward as well by the way social goods and services are distributed . . . (1965:5).

Racial categorization of a segment of the working class, which Miles (1982:151) calls 'the racialized fraction of the working class' provides a pretext for extreme exploitation of coloured labour. The process of racial categorization, 'can then be viewed as affecting the allocation of persons to different positions in the production process and the allocation of material and other rewards and disadvantages to groups so categorized within the class boundaries established by the dominant mode of production' (Miles, 1982:159).

Racial categorization provides a convenient basis for generating low-cost labour, and racial discrimination serves as an effective barrier in preventing non-white workers from moving away from undesirable jobs. For instance, labour market profiles of white workers are often different from those of racial minority workers. The latter group is more likely to be concentrated in the secondary labour markets characterized by low-paying jobs: arduous, dangerous, and seasonal work (Collins, 1997; Trumper and Wong, 1997).

Racist ideology provides justification for differential treatment and exploitation of racial minorities. It has been argued that this ideology flourished concomitantly with colonialism and justified the control in the political, economic and social spheres and exploitation of the coloured people the world over (Blauner, 1972; Baran and Sweezy, 1966). Due to conquest and colonial expansion and domination, the people of colour not only came to be exploited in Asia and Africa but also when they were brought to work in various parts of the colonial empires. Justification for exploitation was provided by racial stereotypes and colonial heritage. Racial minority workers find themselves 'branded with the stigma of colour and racial inferiority (Moore, 1977:146).

There are various examples and dimensions of institutional racism in Canada (Basran, 1983; Bolaria, 1983; Bolaria and Li, 1988; Satzewich, 1995b; Trumper and Wong, 1997). Institutional racism has been most explicit in the immigration legislation in the form of restricted entry and quotas for racial minorities. Historically, it is also evident in the denial of legal–political rights and racial labour policy. For instance, the Chinese residing in British Columbia were denied the right to vote as early as 1875, and twenty years later this was extended to other Asians living in British Columbia. The disfranchisement had a wider impact in terms of occupations and employment opportunities. Chinese and Japanese were denied practice of law and pharmacy because eligibility to these fields was limited to those on the voters' list. East Indians could not enter certain occupations for the same reasons (Basran, 1983; Bolaria, 1983).

There were other laws and practices that were discriminatory. As soon as the Canadian Pacific Railway (CPR) construction was completed in 1885, and Chinese labour started entering into other occupations, institutional racism began in various forms (Li, 1979; Munro, 1974; Palmer, 1970). A head tax of $50 was imposed on the Chinese in 1885, later increasing to $100 in 1900, and $500 in 1903. Other Orientals were also subjected to a head tax, while passage assistance was available to the British immigrants. As the Chinese and East Indians had to pay a head tax in Canada, their immigration was virtually brought to a halt after 1907. Other laws and regulations were intended to control immigration from non-white countries. In the 1906 Immigration Act, important discretionary powers were given to immigration officers, who used them to deny entry to non-white immigrants (Krotki and Matejko, 1977). The continuous journey requirement from India to Canada was intended to control immigration from India. In 1914 there was the *Komagata Maru* incident, where Sikh immigrants were refused entry to Canada after following the requirements of the continuous journey stipulation. This is one of the few incidents when the Canadian navy was employed to uphold the exclusionary racist laws of the land. In another case in 1923, the Chinese were squeezed out of fishing. The

Canadians had a gentlemen's agreement with the Japanese, limiting Japanese immigration to Canada. In 1907, immigrants from Asia were required to have a minimum of $200 and in 1919, this amount was increased to $250. In 1930, Section 38 of the Immigration Act prohibited the landing in Canada of immigrants of any Asiatic race. The wartime relocation of the Japanese (many of them Canadian citizens) from the British Columbia coastal areas and virtual confiscation of their property is another instance of racial confinement and differential treatment (Sunahara, 1980; Broadfoot, 1977). In 1946, nearly 4,000 Japanese returned to Japan, many of them disenchanted and disillusioned after their wartime experiences in Canada. According to 1912 legislation, Saskatchewan made it an offense for an Oriental businessman to hire a white woman. Until 1952, a city ordinance prohibited Japanese immigrants to live in Lethbridge, a city in the province of Alberta.

A racialized hierarchy of acceptability has been part of the Canadian immigration policy. In 1923, defined by order-in-council 183, British and American immigrants were the most-favoured, northern Europeans were relatively well-received, and other Europeans were accepted if none of the other preferred categories were available. Non-whites were not welcomed and were actively barred from entering Canada through various pieces of legislation. This policy was partly justified by immigration and government officials on the basis of the inability of immigrants from certain countries to assimilate into Canadian society and adapt to the Canadian climate.

However, discriminatory policies were changed because of international and domestic reasons. After the Second World War, a large number of colonized countries became independent and started playing an important role in the United Nations and in world politics. International political considerations and rapid economic growth in Canada and its labour force needs led to changes in the immigration regulations. However, immigrants from Third-World countries were still limited to an annual numerical quota. In 1962 (P.C. 86), for the first time in the history of Canadian immigration policy, any explicit reference to race, ethnicity, and nationality for admissibility to Canada was removed. Canada moved away from institutional racism and started the process of receiving immigrants on the basis of individual qualifications and characteristics regardless of race and nationality. Characteristics like educational qualifications, occupational training, and language proficiency and their correspondence to the labour force needs became the important considerations in admissibility to Canada.

Eventually this system was replaced by the 1967 changes in the immigration policies (P.C. 1616). These new regulations have three elements: 1) they clarified the principles governing the selection and admission of immigrants; 2) established a distinction between dependent and close relatives of Canadian citizen or permanent residents of Canada, and 3) created an assessment system for the admission of immigrants. The point system, based on a person's qualifications, ability, training in the two official languages (English and French), age, prospects of getting a job, education, occupational skills, and occupational demands, was introduced to admit independent immigrants.

The 1967 regulation was a fundamental departure from the explicitly racist immigration policy. There have been other changes since then to accommodate the demographic and labour force needs of Canada. These changes are manifested in the increasing diversity of the Canadian population.

SUMMARY

This chapter provides an overview of various perspectives and paradigms used in the studies of migrations and racism. Migration studies range from focus on individual motivation and economic self-interest to migrate, to an analysis of structural determinants of migratory movements of people. Similarly, in the study of racism and racial inequality explanations range from individual attitude and prejudicial behaviour and actions, to institutional and structural factors and practices which perpetuate racial inequality and exploitation of racial minorities.

The individual level and demographic studies of migration tend to obscure and devalue the economic role of migrants as labour resource and reservoirs and do not focus on structural determinants involved in patterned migration movements. Recent studies, however, have begun to focus on structural factors and global disparities and unequal accumulation of capital between core and peripheral countries. Global disparities and internationalization of capital is accompanied by internationalization of labour. Workers of poor countries face exploitation both in their own countries and in foreign lands. Globalization of capital and production has enhanced capital's structural power over workers and has weakened labour in any one country or region. Circulation of workers across national boundaries helps to reduce labour costs and provide capital an increased access to cheap and docile labour. The state, by regulating the migratory flows and by controlling the political and legal status of migrants, creates labour flexibility and provides capital with the cheapest and most easily exploitable work force.

Racialization of a segment of the working class provides a pretext for extreme exploitation of racial minority workers. Institutional and social arrangements create differential opportunity structures for various groups. This is also manifested in allocation of workers in the labour market and labour profiles of different groups. Racial minority workers are more likely to be concentrated in secondary labour markets characterized by low paying jobs and unhealthy, dangerous and seasonal work.

Racial inequality is a basic feature of Canadian society. While patterns and practices of discrimination have changed over time, racial inequality remains a permanent feature of the Canadian mosaic.

References

Arnold, Fred and Nasra M. Shah (1884): 'Asian Labour Migration to the Middle East', *International Migration Review* 18:294.

Bach, Robert L. (1978): 'Mexican Immigration and the Canadian State', *International Migration Review* 12:536–58.

Baran, Paul and Paul Sweezy (1966): *Monopoly Capital: An Essay on the American Economic and Social Order* (New York: Monthly Review Press).

Barnet, R.J. and R.E. Muller (1974): *Global Reach: The Power of the Multinational Corporations.* New York: Simon and Schuster.

Basran, G.S. (1983): 'Canadian Immigration and Theories', pp. 3–14, *in* Peter S. Li and B. Singh Bolaria (eds), *Racial Minorities in Multicultural Canada* (Toronto: Garamond Press).

Berger, John and Jean Mohr (1975): *A Seventh Man: Migrant Workers in Europe* (New York: The Viking Press).

Blauner, Robert (1972): *Racial Oppression in America* (New York: Harper & Row Publishers).

Bolaria, B. Singh (1983): 'Dominant Perspectives and Non-White Minorities', pp. 157–69, *in* Peter S. Li and B. Singh Bolaria (eds), *Racial Minorities in Multicultural Canada* (Toronto: Garamond Press).

—— (1984a): 'Migrants, Immigrants and the Canadian Labour Force' in John A. Fry (ed.), *Contradictions in Canadian Society* (Toronto: John Wiley and Sons), pp. 130–9.

—— (1984b): 'On the Study of Race Relations', pp. 219–47, *in* John A. Fry (ed.), *Contradictions in Canadian Society* (Toronto: John Wiley and Sons).

—— (1986): 'Capital, Labour and Criminalized Workers', pp. 295–312, *in*

Brian D. MacLean (ed.), *The Political Economy of Crime* (Scarborough, Ontario: Prentice Hall).

Bolaria, B. Singh (1988a): 'The Health Effects of Powerlessness: Women and Racial Minority Immigrant Workers', pp. 439–59, *in* B. Singh Bolaria and Harley D. Dickinson (eds), *Sociology of Health Care in Canada* (Toronto: Harcourt Brace Jovanovich).

—— (1988b): 'Profits and Illness: Exporting Health Hazards to the Third World', pp. 477–96, *in* B. Singh Bolaria and Harley D. Dickinson (eds), *Sociology of Health Care in Canada* (Toronto: Harcourt Brace Jovanovich).

—— (1991): 'Environment, Work and Illness', pp. 222–46, *in* B. Singh Bolaria (ed.), *Social Issues and Contradictions in Canadian Society* (Toronto: Harcourt Brace Jovanovich).

—— (1992): 'From Immigrant Settlers to Migrant Transients: Foreign Professionals in Canada', pp. 211–28, *in* Vic Satzewich (ed.), *Deconstructing A Nation: Immigration, Multiculturalism and Racism in 90s Canada* (Halifax: Fernwood Publishing).

Bolaria, B. Singh and Peter S. Li (1988): *Racial Oppression in Canada* (Toronto: Garamond Press).

Bolaria, B. Singh and Rosemary von Elling Bolaria (eds)(1997): *International Labour Migrations* (New Delhi: Oxford University Press).

Bonacich, Edna and Lucie Cheng (1984): 'Introduction: A Theoretical Orientation to International Labour Migration', *in* Lucie Cheng and Edna Bonacich (eds), pp. 1–56, in *Labour Immigration Under Capitalism: Asian Workers in the United States Before WWI* (Berkeley, California: University of California Press).

Broadfoot, Barry (1977): *Years of Sorrow, Years of Shame: The Study of the Japanese Canadians in World War II* (Toronto: Doubleday Canada).

Burawoy, Michael (1976): 'The Functions and Reproduction of Migrant Labour: Comparative Material from Southern Africa and the United States', *American Journal of Sociology* 81(March): 1050–87.

Bustamonte, Jorge A. (1972): 'The Historical Context of Undocumented Mexican Immigration to the United States', *Chicago Journal of the Social Sciences* 3:257–82.

—— (1976): 'Structural and Ideological Conditions of Undocumented Mexican Immigration to the United States', pp. 145–57, *in* W.J. Littrel and G.P. Sjoberg (eds), *Current Issues in Social Policy* (Beverley Hills, California: Sage).

Carmichael, S. and C.W. Hamilton (1967): *Black Power: The Politics of Liberation in America* (New York: Vintage).

Castells, Manuel (1975): 'Immigrant Workers and Class Struggles in Advanced

Capitalism: The Western European Experience', *Politics and Society* 5:33–66.

Castles, Stephen and Godula Kosack (1972): 'The Function of Labour Immigration in Western European capitalism', *New Left Review* 72:3–21.

Choucri, Nazli (1983): 'Asians in the Arab World: Migration Processes and Policies', Paper Presented at Conference on Asian Labour Migration to the Middle East (East-West Centre, Hawaii).

Cockcroft, James D. (1982): 'Mexican Migration, Crises, and the Internationalization of Labour Struggle', pp. 48–61 in M. Dixon and S. Jonas (eds), *The New Nomads: From Immigrant Labour to Transnational Working Class* (San Francisco: Synthesis Publications).

Collins, Jock (1997): 'Immigrant Labour, Racism and Class: The Australian Experience', pp. 67–98, *in* B. Singh Bolaria and Rosemary von Elling Bolaria (eds), *International Labour Migrations* (New Delhi: Oxford University Press).

Dixon, Marlene, Susan Jonas, and Ed McCoughan (1982): 'Reindustrialization and the Transnational Labour Force in the United States Today', pp. 101–15, *in* Marlene Dixon and Susan Jonas (eds) *The New Nomads: From Immigrant Labour to Transnational Working Class* (San Francisco: Synthesis Publications).

Eitzen, D. Stanley and Maxine Baca Zinn (1989): *Social Problems*, 4th edn (Boston: Allyn & Bacon).

Elling, Ray (1977): 'Industrialization and Occupational Health in Underdeveloped countries', *International Journal of Health Services* 7:209–35.

—— (1981): 'The Capitalist World System and International Health', *International Journal of Health Services* 11:21–51.

Gangulee, N. (1947): *Indians in the Empire Overseas* (London: The New India Publishing House Ltd).

Gardezi, Hassan N. (1995): *The Political Economy of International Labour Migrations* (Montreal: Black Rose Books).

Gardezi, H. and Jamil Rashid (eds) (1983): *Pakistan, The Roots of Dictatorship: The Political Economy of a Praetorian State* (London: Zed Press), p. 209.

Gorz, Andre (1970): 'Immigrant Labour', *The New Left Review* 61:28–31.

Huttenback, Robert A. (1976): *Racism and Empire* (Ithaca: Cornell University Press).

Jenkins, Craig J. (1978): 'The Demand for Immigrant Workers: Labour Scarcity or Social Control?', *International Migration Review* 12:514–35.

Jonas, S. and M. Dixon (1979): 'Proletarianization and Class Alliances in the Americas', *Synthesis* 3:1–13.

Jones, K. and A.D. Smith (1970): *The Economic Impact of Commonwealth Immigration* (Cambridge: Cambridge University Press).

Knowles, Louis L. and Kenneth Prewitt (eds) (1965): *Institutional Racism in America* (Englewood Cliffs, N.J.: Prentice Hall).

Krotki, Karol J. and Joanna Matejko (1977): 'Chronology in the Development of Canadian Immigration and Ethnic Policies', An Unpublished Report, University of Alberta.

Li, Peter S. (1979): 'A Historical Approach to Ethnic Stratification: The Case of the Chinese in Canada, 1858–1920', *Canadian Review of Sociology and Anthropology* 16:320–32.

—— (1992): 'The Economics of Brain Drain: Recruitment of Skilled Labour to Canada, 1954–1986', pp. 145–,62 *in* Vic Satzewich (ed.), *Deconstructing A Nation: Immigration, Multiculturalism and Racism in 90s Canada* (Halifax: Fernwood Publishing).

Miles, Robert (1982): *Caste, Class and Race: A Study in Social Dynamics* (New York: Monthly Review Press).

Munro, John A. (1974): 'British Columbia and the Chinese Evil: Canada's First Anti-Asiatic Immigration Law', *Journal of Canadian Studies* 6:42–51.

Moore, Robert (1977): 'Migration and the Class Structure of Western Europe', pp. 136–49, *in* Richard Scase (ed.), *Industrial Society: Class, Cleavage and Control* (London: George Allen and Unwin Ltd.)

Navarro, Vincente (1986): *Crisis, Health and Medicine: A Social Critique* (New York: Tavistock Publications).

Palmer, Howard D. (1970): 'Anti-Oriental sentiments in Alberta, 1890–1920', *Canadian Ethnic Studies*, Bulletin of Research, Centre for Canadian Ethnic Studies at the University of Calgary, vol. 11 (Dec.).

Portes, Alejandro (1977): 'Labour Functions of Illegal Aliens', *Society* 14:31–7.

—— (1978a): 'Migration and Underdevelopment', *Politics and Society 8:1048.*

—— (1978b): 'Toward a Structural Analysis of Illegal (Undocumented) Immigration', *International Migration Review* 12:469–84.

Saha, P. (1970): *Emigration of Indian Labour (1834–1900)* (Delhi: People's Publishing House).

Sassen-Koob, Saskia (1978): 'The International Circulation of Resources and Development: The Case of Migrant Labour', *Development and Change* 9:509–45.

—— (1980): 'Immigrant and Minority Workers in the Organization of the Labour Process', *The Journal of Ethnic studies* 8:1–34.

—— (1981): 'Toward a Conceptualization of Immigrant Labour' *Social Problems* 29:68–85.

Satzewich, Vic (1995a): 'Capital Accumulation and State Formation: The Contradictions of International Migration', pp. 318–35, *in* B. Singh Bolaria (ed.), *Social Issues and Contradictions in Canadian Society*, 2nd edn (Toronto: Harcourt Brace).

Satzewich, Vic (1995b): 'Social Stratification: Class and Racial Inequality', pp. 98–121, in B. Singh Bolaria (ed.), Social Issues and Contradictions in Canadian Society, 2nd edn (Toronto: Harcourt Brace).

Sunahara, Ann Gomer (1980): The Politics of Racism: The Uprooting of Japanese Canadians During the Second World War (Toronto: Lorimer).

Tinker, Hugh (1974): A New System of Slavery (Oxford: Oxford University Press).

Trumper, L. and Lloyd Wong (1997): 'Racialization and Genderization: The Canadian State, Immigrants and Temporary Workers', pp. 153–91, in B. Singh Bolaria and Rosemary von Elling Bolaria (eds), International Labour Migrations (New Delhi: Oxford University Press).

Turner, L. (1973): Multicultural Companies and the Third World (New York: Hill and Wong).

Whyte, A. (1984): The Experience of New Immigrants and Seasonal Far— Workers from the Eastern Caribbean in Canada (Toronto: Institute of Environmental Studies).

Williams, André (1964): Capitalism and Slavery (London: Andre Deutsch Ltd).

Wilson, William J. (1973): Power, Racism, and Privilege (London: Collier-McMillan Publishers).

Wong, Lloyd and Nancy S. Netting (1992): 'Business Immigration to Canada: Social Impact and Racism', pp. 93–122, in Vic Satzewich (ed.), Deconstructing A Nation: Immigration, Multiculturalism and Racism in 90s Canada (Halifax: Fernwood Publishing).

World Bank (1980): World Bank Report, Migration and Money (New York: Oxford University Press).

From India to Canada
Immigration Policy and Migration Patterns

❀

INTRODUCTION

The history of immigration from India to Canada dates back to the early 1900s. Entry of Indian immigrants has been regulated through various immigration regulations and laws, which ranged from total exclusion based upon a racialized hierarchy of acceptability, and later racial quota systems, to universal entry regulations tempered with labour force needs and other demographic and political considerations. This is reflected in the volume and characteristics of immigrants, their entry status, and settlement patterns (Bolaria and Li, 1988).

This chapter provides an overview of the migrations from India to Canada. The discussion and analysis is divided into four time periods, each characterized by a more or less distinct policy regulation(s), context of immigrant reception and volume and the characteristics of the immigrants. The chapter concludes with a brief discussion of response and resistance to institutional racism and discrimination.

INDIAN IMMIGRATION: 1900–1908

East Indians started arriving in Canada around 1900.[1] The impetus for early immigrants came from a visit in 1897 when Sikh soldiers visited British Columbia (BC) in the course of their return journey to India after participating in Queen Victoria Jubilee celebrations. Some of these Sikh soldiers resigned from the British armys in India and migrated to Canada. Other immigrants were relatives of these soldiers. Yet other Sikh immigrants during this time came from the British colonies of Hong Kong, Malaysia, and Singapore (Kurian and Srivastava, 1983:31). The passage from India to

Canada at that time cost about three hundred Indian rupees (approximately $65). The usual mode of transportation was by a merchant ship from Calcutta to Hong Kong and then a passenger ship from there to Canada. The passage took about 12 days from Calcutta to Hong Kong and about 18 days from there to Vancouver (Helweg and Helweg, 1990:47).

Early immigrants were predominantly single males,[2] largely employed as manual workers in lumber mills, railroad construction, and in the transportation industry, who faced employment discrimination and exploitation.

By the end of 1908, about 5,000 East Indians had entered Canada, of which 2,124 arrived in 1907 and 2,623 in 1908 (Table 5.1). Though still few in number, East Indians and other Asians found a growing hostility against them. This took the form of serious anti-Oriental riots in Vancouver in 1907 and a number of legislative measures to restrict and control Asian immigration. (Ward, 1978; Bolaria and Li, 1988).

TABLE 5.1

IMMIGRATION OF EAST INDIANS TO CANADA 1900–91

Number	Year	Number	Year	Number	Year
1900	0	1931	80	1962	584
1901	0	1932	47	1963	858
1902	0	1933	63	1964	1,463
1903	0	1934	33	1965	2,664
1904	0	1935	21	1966	2,799
1905	45	1936	10	1967	4,614
1906	387	1937	13	1968	3,858
1907	2,124	1938	14	1969	6,400
1908	2,623	1939	14	1970	6,680
1909	6	1940	11	1971	6,281
1910	10	1941	6	1972	6,239
1911	5	1942	3	1973	11,488
1912	3	1943	0	1974	15,183
1913	5	1944	0	1975	12,309
1914	88	1945	0	1976	3,906
1915	0	1946	1	1977	7,130

Number	Year	Number	Year	Number	Year
1916	1	1947	7	1978	6,269
1917	0	1948	130	1979	5,634
1918	0	1949	63	1980	9,364
1919	0	1950	52	1981	8,989
1920	0	1951	93	1982	8,544
1921	10	1952	81	1983	7,041
1922	13	1953	173	1984	5,502
1923	21	1954	170	1985	4,028
1924	40	1955	245	1986	6,940
1925	46	1956	330	1987	9,692
1926	62	1957	324	1988	10,409
1927	60	1958	451	1989	8,819
1928	56	1959	716	1990	10,624
1929	52	1960	673	1991	12,848
1930	58	1961	744		

Sources: Figures for 1900–36 from *Canada Yearbook*, Adrian Mayer, 1959; 1937–82,
Annual Reports of Department of Mines and Resources (1946–9), Department of
Citizenship and Immigration (1960–6); Department of Manpower and Immi-
gration (1967–76); Department of Employment and Immigration (1977–88);
Citizenship and Immigration Canada (1989–91). 1962–82 figures also include
immigrants from Pakistan.

Most of the provincial political leaders, members of parliament from
British Columbia, labour leaders, church representatives, business groups,
and various racist and right-wing political parties opposed Oriental immigration into B.C. The justifications for these exclusionist policies and
programmes were based on economic, cultural ('Orientals cannot and will
not assimilate'), racist ('Orientals are inferior to whites'), social, and political
arguments. However, these exclusionary and racist policies posed contradictions and conflicts for the Canadian state. State policies and programmes
have to take into consideration domestic political and international diplomatic demands, the political and economic interests of the empire, the
interests of the steamship companies, and need for cheap Asian labour. On

the one hand, many politicians and other Canadian people were opposed to immigration from Asia (Japan, China, and India) into Canada. On the other hand, there were foreign pressures and diplomatic considerations that the Canadian state could not ignore. For example, Prime Minister Sir Wilfrid Laurier of the then Liberal government expressed his views in regard to Asiatic immigrants by saying, 'I have very little hope of any good coming to this country from Asiatic immigration of any kind' (Ward, 1978:59). However, in 1902, with Japan developing political and business alliances with the UK, Joseph Chamberlain, Colonial Office of the UK, did not want to alienate the Japanese government. Moreover, India was still ruled by the British, making it difficult to exclude East Indians (British subjects) from Canada. Furthermore, steamship companies from Canada were against the exclusionist policies of the Canadian government as it was profitable for them to transport immigrants to Canada. In addition, some lumber and railroad companies wanted to have access to cheap Asian labour.

Provincial legislatures in B.C. passed various legislations in order to exclude Orientals from there by depriving them of their rights to own property, to enter certain professions, to start businesses, and to attend schools. However, the federal Canadian government was not always supportive of these discriminatory laws, programmes and policies, as it wanted to 'manage' the East Indian 'problem' in a more 'diplomatic' manner. For example, on 25 October 1908, the government sponsored a delegation to go to British Honduras (now Belize) with two Sikh representatives, Bhai Nagin Singh and Bhai Sham Singh, and a number of government functionaries. The primary purpose was to convince the Sikhs to 'voluntarily' migrate to Honduras permanently. However, the Sikh representatives were not impressed by the wages, living conditions, or with the socio–economic and political situation in Honduras. Even attempts by the Canadian immigration officers to bribe the Sikh representatives to give a positive report on Honduras did not succeed (Muthana, 1975:88). Instead, the Sikh representatives recommended that Sikhs should not accept the proposal to migrate to Honduras. In spite of various discriminatory legislations and personal and social hostilities against early immigrants, they were able to establish their religious institutions.[3] They were also actively involved in various social and political activities and made substantial financial contributions to various groups and causes (Jagpal, 1994:118). For instance, the Khalsa Diwan Society, prior to 1921 contributed nearly $300,000 for various religious, educational, political, and immigration related issues. The major contributions were made to the following: religious and educational causes ($148,000); *Komagata Maru* case ($50,000); sufferers from political causes ($30,000); and $30,000 to immigration cases (Jagpal, 1994). When one considers the level of wages of these immigrants in that period, these are indeed large sums of money.

INDIAN IMMIGRATION:
1909 TO THE SECOND WORLD WAR

The second period of immigration extends roughly from 1909 to the Second World War. During this period many measures were taken to control and restrict entry of potential immigrants from India. The most notable of these was the continuous journey stipulation as well as the requirement to possess $200 upon entry into Canada. Regarding the continuous journey stipulation is the Order in Council of 9 May 1910 which reads as follows:

From and after the date here of the landing in Canada shall be, and the same is hereby prohibited of any immigrants who have come to Canada otherwise than by continuous journey from the country of which they are natives or citizens and only through tickets purchased in that country or prepaid in Canada [*British Columbia Magazine*, 1919:665].

This measure meant that immigrants who came to Canada, 'otherwise than by continuous journey from the countries of which they were natives or citizens, may be refused entry'. Also, the steamship companies stopped issuing tickets to East Indians via Hong Kong, which was the only way to come to Canada. There were no direct lines of steamships from India to Canada at that time (*British Columbia Magazine*, 1912: 665). Another means used by immigration authorities to control immigration from India was to deny proper documents to Indian residents, which were required for re-entry to Canada after travel abroad (Jagpal, 1994:27). As Table 1 indicates, these regulations proved to be quite effective in barring Indian immigrants after 1908. Canada experienced a sharp decline in immigrants from India, with only 29 immigrants admitted between 1909 and 1913, and only 88 in 1914. This trend persisted from 1908 to 1920, when 118 immigrants entered Canada. After this period, few East Indians were admitted until after the Second World War. The number of Canadians who objected to this discriminatory treatment was quite small (Grace, 1913:10–13; see also Johnston, 1989, 1992).

In November 1913, the Order in Council of May 1910 was declared null and void by the Supreme Court. The Canadian government passed another Order in Council which prohibited the immigration of 'artisans or labourers whether skilled or unskilled' from other countries. While apparently universal in intent, in practice these rules and regulations were primarily used against Oriental immigrants.

In 1914, an attempt was made to test the continuous journey regulations. A Sikh businessman, Gurdit Singh, chartered a Japanese ship, *Komagata Maru*, in Hong Kong along with 376 passengers. Of the 376 East Indians on the *Komagata Maru*, 340 were Sikhs, 24 were Muslims, and 12 were Hindus. The ship left Hong Kong on 4 April 1914 and arrived in Vancouver on 23 May 1914 after short halts at Shanghai (China), Moji, Yokohama (Japan) and Victoria (B.C.). With the exception of a few (approximately 22), mainly dependants of earlier settlers, all the other passengers were prevented from landing in Canada.

Sikhs in Vancouver made every effort to convince the provincial, federal, and local politicians to reject the racist continuous journey legislation. These Sikhs collected $18,000 to assist the passengers of the *Komagata Maru*. They appealed to various organizations and groups, but were refused assistance or support from all of them. The *Komagata Maru* left Vancouver for Calcutta, India on 23 July 1914. According to some reports, Sohan Singh Bhakana, president of the Ghadar Party, met the *Komagata Maru* leader Gurdit Singh at Yokohama, Japan. S.S. Bhakana allegedly gave Gurdit Singh 200 automatic pistols and 2,000 rounds of ammunition. Gurdit Singh distributed these weapons to some passengers before they arrived in Calcutta on 29 September 1914. The British army and police were waiting for the *Komagata Maru* in Calcutta. Some passengers were supportive of the anti-colonial Ghadar Party in North America and the British colonial power was very aware of the potential disruptive and destabilizing impact of the *Komagata Maru* passengers on British rule in India. These passengers wanted to immediately go to Punjab but the government of the day wanted to detain them temporarily in Calcutta to delay their departure. When the passengers did not comply with this plan the police opened fire on these innocent passengers. About 193 passengers were arrested, 20 died, several were injured, about 28 remained at large, and 62 were sent to Punjab (Muthana, 1975:321). Gurdit Singh escaped and remained at large for several years. He later returned to Punjab in 1921 and joined the Congress party, which was fighting against British colonialism.

He was arrested several times by the British government for his anti-colonial activities. He died in 1954, at the age of 95, and has never received adequate recognition for his anti-colonial struggles.

Some of the other passengers were arrested in Punjab and were labelled as German spies. It is disturbing to note that Sikh leaders in Amritsar, rather than providing support to the passengers of the *Komagata Maru*, declared their loyalty to the British crown on 6 October 1914. On 15 October 1914, the Government of India (British) appointed a committee to investigate the *Komagata Maru* incident, but the members of the committee were supporters and sympathizers of the government.[4] The report, which was released in the second week of January 1915, was not supportive of the *Komagata Maru* passengers, some of whom were sent to prisons, a few hanged, others were restricted to their villages, and the remainder discharged.

The *Komagata Maru* incident is an important episode in Canadian history and immigration policy. It brought into sharp focus the contradictions between democratic and egalitarian ethos, on the one hand, and discriminatory and racist policies of the state towards racial minority and colonized immigrants, on the other hand. Two plaques in Vancouver dedicated on the 75th anniversary of this incident underscore its significance for the Sikh minority and the Canadian state. The plaque at the Gateway to the Pacific set up by the state describes it as, '... that unfortunate incident of racial discrimination and reminds Canadians of our commitment to an open society in which mutual respect and understanding are honoured, differences are respected, and traditions are cherished'. The plaque in Vancouver at Ross Street Gurdwara, dedicated on 23 July 1989 to the memory of 376 passengers, states that, 'due to the racist immigration policy of the dominion of Canada, they were forced to leave on 23 July 1914. Khalsa Diwan Society, Vancouver, pays respect to those passengers by commemorating the reprehensible incident.' The difference in language used in describing this incident in these two plaques is quite significant (see Box 5.1).

Due to various restrictions on immigration, as well as the discrimination they faced, the number of East Indians in Canada steadily declined. Several thousand Sikhs went to India around 1914 to join the fight against British colonialism at the time of the First World War. In 1921, there were 1,016 East Indians in Canada, while the 1931 census indicated a population of 1,400.

Immigrants from India were also denied family life. The immigrants

---

BOX 5.1

PLAQUES COMMEMORATING *KOMAGATA MARU*

(Plaque at the Gateway to the Pacific, Downtown Vancouver)
On May 23, 1914, 376 British Subjects (12 Hindus, 24 Muslims and 340 Sikhs) of Indian origin arrived in Vancouver harbour aboard the *Komagata Maru*, seeking to enter Canada, 352 of the passengers were denied entry and forced to depart on July 23, 1914. This plaque commemorates the 75th anniversary of that unfortunate incident of racial discrimination and reminds Canadians of our commitment to an open society in which mutual respect and understanding are honoured, differences are respected, and traditions are cherished.

(Plaque in the Vancouver Gurdwara dedicated July 23, 1989)
Komagata Maru Incident 75th Anniversary. Dedicated to the memory of the 376 passengers (340 Sikhs, 24 Muslims, 12 Hindus) who arrived at Burrard Inlet, Vancouver on May 23, 1914, from the Indian subcontinent on the ship *Komagata Maru* (Guru Nanak Jahaz). Due to the racist immigration policy of the Dominion of Canada, they were forced to leave on July 23, 1914. Khalsa Diwan Society, Vancouver, pays respect to those passengers by commemorating the reprehensible incident.

---

were primarily males because of various restrictions concerning immigration of spouses and children. The principal argument advanced by those who opposed the entry of wives and children of Sikh immigrants in Canada was that Sikhs and their families would not assimilate into mainstream Canadian culture and were 'unassimilable in the Canadian civilization' (*British Columbia Magazine*, 22–8; McKay, 1914). They were considered 'unsuitable', and incapable of adaptation and adjustment to this country. MacKenzie King's report on Indian immigration in 1908 states:

It was clearly recognized in regard to emigration from India to Canada that the native of India is not a person suited to this country, that accustomed as many of them are to the conditions of a tropical climate, and possessing manners and customs so unlike our own people, their inability to readily adapt themselves to surroundings entirely different could not do other than entail an amount of privation and suffering which renders a discontinuance of such immigration most desirable in the interests of the Indians themselves. [House of Commons, Sessional Paper No. 360, 1908:7–8].

Moreover, there was a pervasive desire to keep Canada white and exclusively for Europeans. On the other hand, the Sikhs were British subjects and made representation in Canada, Britain, and India to be allowed to bring their wives and children to Canada. By basing the argument for exclusion on assimilation and absorption, the government attempted to avoid any accusation of being racist.

The Imperial Conference of 1918 passed a resolution which allowed domiciled Indians in other countries of the British Empire to bring their wives and children. The Canadian government approved this resolution by an Order in Council the following year. However, not many women and children entered Canada. At the time, few of the East Indian male residents in Canada had enough resources to bring their dependants to this country (Mayer, 1959). Prior to the Second World War, 5,000 men migrated to Canada, as compared to only 400 Indian women and 423 children (Smith, 1944; see Bolaria and Li, 1988). The lack of any normal family life also meant considerable delay in the development of a native-born Indian community. For example, it is estimated that at the outbreak of the Second World War, the 1,100 East Indians in B.C. were composed almost entirely of single males residing in logging camps or apartments in Vancouver, and not more than 15 conjugal families (Mayer, 1959:2). Because of denial of other legal–political rights these immigrants remained alien residents subject to deportation. They also bore the brunt of racial stereotypes, facing considerable discrimination in housing and other matters.

INDIAN IMMIGRATION: POST-WAR PERIOD, 1966

The treatment of East Indians within the Empire continued to be a subject of much discussion between the Colonial and Dominion governments. There were concerns about the incongruity between the differential treatment of domiciled Indians in some parts of the Empire and the position of India as an equal member within the Empire (Holland, 1943). In spite of the recognition, '... that in the interest of the solidarity of the British Commonwealth it is desirable that the rights of such [domiciled] Indians to citizenship be recognized' (Holland, 1943:169), no concrete steps were taken by the Canadian government to grant franchise to East Indians until 1947. In that year, Indians were given the right to vote in federal and provincial elections. In 1948, this right was extended to municipal elections (Mayer, 1959). Another discriminatory law which required the fingerprints of East Indians on legal documents, was also revoked (Mayer, 1959). It is instructive to note that these measures correspond to the end of direct British colonialism in India.

While domiciled Indians were granted franchise, the entry of new immigrants from India was still restricted. In 1952, a quota of 150 was established from India, subsequently raised to 300 in 1957 (Bolaria and Li, 1988:173). These changes were brought about for political reasons. In 1955, the minister of citizenship and immigration stated: 'We agreed upon this quota as a gesture for the improvement of Commonwealth relations' (cited in Hawkins, 1972:101). The admission for non-whites continued to be discriminatory. The large demand for labour during the post-War period was met through the aggressive recruitment of white Europeans (Law Union of Ontario, 1981). Immigrants from India continued to be relatively small in numbers, only exceeding 1,000 in 1964 and over 2,000 in 1965 and 1966. Thus, the total population of Indian background in Canada remained small. However, this began to change due in particular to the immigration regulations enacted in 1967.

INDIAN IMMIGRATION: SINCE 1967

The increasing demand for professional–skilled workforce led to basic changes in immigration policy in 1967. To achieve this, education and skills became the primary criteria in new regulations for admission to Canada and racial quotas were eliminated. For instance, in the 1967 regulations, points were allocated to potential immigrants based on such factors as age, education, occupational demand, skill, knowledge of the language, adaptability, and the like. For example, 12 points were assigned to education, 15 to vocational preparation, 8 to experience, 10 to occupation, 10 to arranged employment, 10 to age (two units subtracted per year if under the age 21 or over the age of 44), 15 points if immigrants were fluent in English or French, 10 points for personal suitability, 10 points for level of control (location where immigrants want to live and number of years they are willing to stay there). Ten points were given to those independent applicants who had some relatives in Canada willing to support them financially. Out of the total possible score of 100, a minimum 70 points were required to qualify in the 'independent immigrant' category. This system benefited non-white immigrants who had traditionally been barred from immigrating to Canada. While in the year before the introduction of the point system, 76 per cent of the immigrants were Europeans, this proportion declined to 39 per cent by 1973 (Hawkins, 1988). Even incentives in the form of tax exemptions in some professions were not always sufficient to attract immigrants from white countries. The 'European immigration had declined to the point that Canada was forced to admit non-European immigrants in order to meet the demand for labour' (Law Union of Ontario: 1981:40).

Canada was the world's second-largest recipient of people from Third-World countries, including India. There was a noticeable change in the characteristics of immigrants from the Indian subcontinent. After the new regulations came into effect, a high proportion of immigrants from India destined for the Canadian labour force were in the professional, managerial, financial, and entrepreneurial groups. However, in subsequent years the proportion of professional–skilled immigrants consistently declined. For instance, the percentage of professionals among immigrants from India has fallen from 42.6 per cent in 1968–72 to 21.5 per cent in 1973–74, 10.4 per cent in 1978–82, and 1.5 per cent in 1983–84. There was also a shift toward the 'sponsored relative' category from the 'independent immigrant' category in the early 1980s.

Aside from those East Indians who have come to Canada as landed immigrants, others enter the labour market as non-immigrant transient workers. These workers enter the country under the Non-Immigrant Work Authorization Programme, to work in specific jobs for a specified time period. For instance, in 1982, 5,245 workers from India entered Canada on employment visas. India ranked third, accounting for four per cent of the total workers receiving such authorizations (Wong, 1984:89). The labour market profiles of the workers on temporary work visas are substantially different from other workers (Wong, 1984; Trumper and Wong, 1997). Similarly, the labour market profiles of racial minority workers are substantially different from that of the white workers.

The immigration regulations of 1978 continued to favour immigrants with skills. Although there are no blatant racist provisions in the law, the discriminatory treatment of immigrants from non-white countries is evident in the distribution of immigration offices in various regions. Through various administrative procedures and inadequate staffing, immigration from non-white countries is indirectly discouraged. The discretionary powers given to individual immigration officers makes it possible for prejudiced officials to make discriminatory judgements (Law Union of Ontario, 1981:46).

In spite of a substantial increase in immigration from the Indian subcontinent in the 1960s and 1970s, in comparison to earlier periods, these immigrants still constitute one of the smallest groups in Canada. However, as would be expected, the demographic and socio-economic characteristics of Indo-Canadian communities have also changed in recent years. This is primarily due to the changes in immigration requirements and the development of conjugal families and Canadian-born population. This community is now more heterogeneous in regard to income levels, educational achievements, labour force participation, and occupational differentiation. In the case of the Sikh community, the Sikhs are predominantly a young population and a majority of whom are still foreign-born, recent immigrants.

Overall, the proportion of the non-white population in Canada has increased over the years. This change in the Canadian population has also contributed to diversity in the labour force. Foreign-born workers from Asian countries have been an important component of the professional, scientific, and skilled workforce since the late 1960s. The Sikh population, like other minorities, is now represented in all sectors of Canadian society (Singh, 1994; Minhas, 1994; Chadney, 1985; Redway, 1984; Basran, Gill, and Maclean, 1995). Even with all the changes and recent increase in immigrants from non-traditional sources, the overall proportion of non-whites in Canada is relatively small.

Immigration levels, characteristics of immigrants, place of origin, and settlement patterns continue to be important subjects of debate in this country. In particular, there is concern about the increase in family sponsored immigrants. Recent policy initiatives tend to favour young, highly educated, professional, language-proficient (English or French), independent immigrants whose occupational skills correspond to the labour force needs in Canada (Simmons and Keohane, 1992). The Canadian state continues to face contradictory pressures with regard to immigration. The necessity to procure cheap labour from non-traditional sources and in capital accumulation comes into conflict with the conception of some Canadians of a Canada as a white-man's country (Satzewich, 1995). One strategy to resolve this contradiction has been to import non-white workers under the Employment Authorization Programme to work in certain sectors for a specified period of time and then 'send [them] home' at the expiry of their work contracts.

From the perspective of racial minorities, racism and racial inequality and discrimination in the labour market and in political and social institutions has been a crucial element of the Canadian mosaic. Resistance to racial inequality formed an important dimension of the social and political activities of 'pioneer immigrants' from India.

POLITICAL CONSCIOUSNESS AND RESISTANCE

An examination of the history of immigration from India indicates that the Canadian immigration policy has been to control and limit the volume of immigrants from India. This ranged from total exclusion based upon explicitly racist policies to measures such as continuous journey requirements and annual immigration quotas. Those who did make it to Canada found themselves in a hostile environment facing institutional racism and discrimination in the social, economic, and political spheres. In their daily lives they often faced personal ridicule and social segregation because of their 'appearance' and national origin. These experiences, while a constant reminder of their common low status, also contributed to community, nationality, and political consciousness among the Indian immigrants (Puri, 1993).

The early form of community activities centered around religious institutions and organizations, predominantly the Khalsa Diwan Society and the Sikh Gurdwara. The Gurdwara became a center of religious, social and political activities. The newcomers, regardless of their religious background, received assistance in the form of *langars* (free community meals), social support, and help in finding jobs. These community activities in response to hostilities and discrimination strengthened kinship and nationality bonds among the Indian immigrants (Puri, 1993). Puri cites the words of Nihal Singh (1909): 'When others are kicking you, you cannot but feel affiliating with others of your kin and country and pulling together' (Puri, 1993:45).

Puri argues that political consciousness emerged due to three factors: experience of hostility and discrimination; development of national/ethnic identity; and British colonialism in India (Puri, 1993:43). These three factors are interrelated. However, it was the recognition of the linkage between the discriminatory treatment and everyday experience in North America and colonialism in India that 'became an important part of the consciousness' of Indian immigrants (Puri, 1997:162). Consequently, many of the Indian immigrants came to the conclusion that they would never be treated as equals in Canada and the US so long as India was a colonial country and they were colonized people. Thus their role and participation in the anti-colonial struggle is an important aspect of the history of Indian immigrants in Canada.

Appeals for equal treatment based upon consideration of being British and commonwealth subjects and loyalty to the Empire met with failure. It became evident to many that only *ghadar*; a violent revolutionary change could transform the situation of inequality and discrimination. Political work by nationalists and nationalist organizations even changed the orientation of organizations such as Khalsa Diwan Society whose primary initial concern was to fight the 'corrupting influence of foreign environment ... and to maintain the purity of the Sikh religious norms' (Puri, 1993:44). For instance, at its meeting of 23 October 1909, the executive committee of the Sikh Gurdwara of Vancouver not only condemned the British pillage of India, but also resolved not to wear any medals and other British insignia signifying British rule and supremacy (Puri, 1993:53). The cooperative and independent activities of organizations such as Khalsa Diwan Society, Hindustan Association, Hindi Association and United India League contributed to the politicization of the community in the US and in Canada.

The emergence of the Ghadar movement in 1913 and the important political role it played in the mobilization of the Indian immigrant communities for anti-colonial activities has received considerable attention (Puri, 1993). Led by a small group of revolutionary nationalists, most prominent among them Har Dayal and Sohan Singh Bhakna, provided leadership and direction to the movement. The principal objective of the movement was to liberate India from British colonialism through armed struggle. This strategy was based upon the premise that the racial oppression and exploitation of the Indian immigrants was linked to colonial oppression and British rule in India. The secular orientation of the organization without any formal affiliation with any religious organization allowed it to focus on the solidarity of all groups: Hindus, Muslims, Sikhs (Josh, 1977; Puri, 1993). There was widespread support for the Ghadar movement. Membership came predominantly from Punjabi immigrants, mostly Sikhs (Dhillon, 1981; Puri, 1993; Singh and Singh, 1966; Singh, 1977). The newspaper of the party, *ghadar* published in various Indian languages became the principal organ of the party's political writings and served to politicize the community.

The political activities of the Ghadar Party did not go unnoticed by the colonial government, and it started to receive considerable attention and surveillance from secret service agents and agencies. Concerned about the revolutionary potential of the work of the party and its leaders, the colonial government in India put pressure on the US government to curtail their political activities. The arrest of Har Dayal on 24 March 1914 and other actions taken by the state led to the decline of the Ghadar movement. While recognizing that the party continued its activities under the name Hindustan Ghadar Party up to 1947, commenting on the period 1913 to 1918, Puri (1993:8) states: 'The distinct movement, launched with the formation of the Hindi Association of the Pacific Coast in May and its main organ Ghadar from 1 November 1913, collapsed following a series of conspiracy trials in India and the 'Hindu German Conspiracy' trial in USA'. When the Party was revived in 1919, the change in the international political situation, the different social and political context and the concerns of Indian immigrants, the anti-colonial struggle and strategy under Mahatma Gandhi in India, all led to a change in the political strategy and programme of the Ghadar Party (Puri, 1993). The Ghadarites never received the expected support from the leading political parties in India for their movement and political tactics and strategy to achieve Independence. This and other factors such as British total control of the Indian state and its law enforcement agencies, loyalty of the feudal lords (rajas and maharajas), contradictory and conflicting class and political interests, and lack of class consciousness among the masses in India at the time, made it easier for the colonial government to control and eliminate any direct threat to its rule from the Ghadarites and the Ghadar movement (Josh, 1977).

While the precise impact of the Ghadar movement on pre-Independence politics in India and India's Independence struggle is difficult to determine, this movement clearly had a profound influence on the Indian immigration in the US and Canada. Its political analysis, programme, and strategy were widely disseminated through its weekly newspaper. This greatly enhanced the political consciousness and political awareness in the Indian community. Most importantly, they became aware of the linkage between their material existence and the social inequality they faced in Canada and US, and colonialism in India, the irreconcilability of Indian and British interests, and the anti-imperialist struggles in other countries (Puri, 1993:206–12). The secular orientation of the movement helped to undermine divisions of religion and caste. The liberation of India through armed struggle and call to arms was a frequent theme of political propaganda (see Box 5.2). Brave young men were asked to sacrifice their lives in this struggle to liberate mother India. The response to this call was overwhelming. According to Dhillon (1981:171), 'over 10,000 prosperous Sikhs from Canada and

America had responded to the call and sacrificed their properties worth crores of rupees', The high involvement of the Sikhs is not surprising given that among the large number of Punjabi immigrants who joined the Ghadar movement most were Sikh unskilled workers, farmers, and farm labourers (Puri, 1993:3).

BOX 5.2

CALL TO BRAVE YOUNG INDIAN MEN TO TAKE UP ARMS FOR GHADAR IN INDIA

WANTED	Fearless brave soldiers to start Ghadar (Armed revolution – mutiny) in India
WAGES	Death
REWARD	Martyrdom and Freedom
BATTLEGROUND	Hindustan (India)
BHARAT MATA	(Mother India) calls her children for her protection (security/rescue) and to achieve independence)

The Hindustan Ghadar (Urdu), vol. 1, no. 18, August 11, 1914
Source: Harish Puri, *Ghadar Movement* (Amritsar, India. Guru Nanak Dev University Press, 1993), (Urdu text p. 216; English translation and commentary, p. 213).

It is apparent from this brief review of the political activities of 'pioneer' immigrants that they did not passively accept institutional racism and social inequality. An important aspect of their political consciousness was the linkage between their material existence and everyday lived-experience, and their experience as a colonized peoples. The Ghadar movement played a crucial role in the politicization of the Indian community.

SUMMARY

This chapter provides historical and contemporary dimensions of Canadian immigration policy and migration patterns from India to Canada. An examination of the history of immigration indicates that Canadian immigration policy has been to control and limit the volume, the demographic characteristics, and legal–political status of immigrants. Various measures used to achieve these objectives ranged from total exclusion based upon racialized hierarchy of preferred immigrants and assimilability of new immigrants to the continuous journey stipulation and annual immigrant nationality quotas. Under the more recent universal entry regulations, the entry of immigrants is tempered by labour force needs and other demographic, economic and political considerations.

Institutional racism has been most explicit in the immigration legislation and regulations, legal and political rights, conjugal rights and labour market inequalities. The consequences of these measures are manifested in demographic and socio-economic characteristics of Indian immigrants. The early immigrants, for instance, were predominantly single, male, manual workers, largely employed in lumber mills, and railroad and road construction. Because of changes in immigration regulations and requirements, and achievement of legal–political rights the Indian community is now more heterogeneous in regard to income levels, educational achievements and occupational differentiation. The majority of this community are still foreign-born and recently arrived immigrants.

Resistance to racism and racial inequality has been an important dimension of social and political activities of immigrants from India. The pioneer immigrants, in particular, found themselves in a hostile environment and experienced social, economic, and political institutional and individual discrimination. They did not passively accept their situation. The linkage between their material existence and everyday lived-experience and their colonial oppression as colonized peoples formed an important dimension of their political consciousness. They were not only active in Canada in their resistance to inequality but made financial and other sacrifices for India's liberation and freedom for their people.

The explicitly racist immigration policy and overt institutional racism is now replaced by more subtle forms of racism. Our discussion in the next two chapters indicates that racial minorities continue to face socio–economic inequality.

NOTES

1. The first Sikh arrived in Canada in 1904, named Bhai Bakhsish Singh of village Sur Singh Wala (Dhillon, 1981:185).

2. In 1908, Professor Teja Singh, who was studying law in the US, came to visit Vancouver. He was part of the group which, along with Raja Singh and Dr Sunder Singh, went to Ottawa to make a case to the Canadian government on behalf of the Sikh community to allow entry of wives and children of domiciled Indian immigrants. Their efforts were unsuccessful.

3. At the time of our field-work in 1985, Sikhs in Golden, B.C., brought it to our attention that Sikhs had worked in the Columbia River Logging Company during the 1890s and had built a gurdwara around 1900 (a room of 20' by 40' in size). We interviewed Norman King from Golden, B.C., to obtain some information regarding the gurdwara and the Sikh community at that time. In 1900, at the age of six, he visited the gurdwara in Golden. King's parents had close relations with the Sikhs. According to Norman King, there were about 40 Sikh men working in the mill around 1910. King, who was a good friend of the mill managers at that time, visited Sikh homes, the gurdwara and the mill quite frequently. Norman King talked affectionately about these pioneer Sikhs in Golden and described the Sikhs as hard working and diligent individuals. According to him, all but one of these Sikhs was turbaned, and Hardit Singh was their leader. Three of these Sikh men brought their wives to Golden in the 1920s.

The Columbia River Logging Company building burnt down around 1927. All the Sikhs then relocated to Vancouver and Vancouver Island. They left the King family the temple carpet. We consulted the local library in Golden as well as the land title office to determine the ownership of the land on which the gurdwara was built, but we have not been able to establish the exact date of the arrival of the Sikhs in Golden or the year when they built the gurdwara. We speculate that the gurdwara in Golden was built c. 1900 on the property of the Columbia River Logging Company. Some other lumber companies at that time also assisted in building gurdwaras for the Sikhs. According to one report, the Sikh gurdwara in Golden was built on Lot 1, Plan 5874 a dot of land formerly owned by the Columbia River Logging Company and now owned by the Crown (*Golden Gazett*, 11 June, 1980:16).

Sikh gurdwaras and religion played an important role in the everyday lives of early immigrants. They were attended by Sikhs, Hindus, Muslims, and other East Indians. Gurdwaras were places of religious worship as well as important cultural, social, political, and economic centres. In Vancouver, after the Khalsa Diwan Society was established in 1907, Sikhs built a gurdwara at 1866 2nd Avenue West in 1908. Gurdwaras were subsequently built in Abbotsford, Victoria and elsewhere in B.C. and they were all under the management of the Khalsa Diwan Society. According to James G. Chadney, typical leaders of the Khalsa Diwan Society possessed the following characteristics:

He is a Jat male in his mid-forties, who can speak both Punjabi and English fluently, who has adapted western style of dress and appearance, yet can trace his ancestry (if not his birth) to the Doabha region of the Punjab, who has been in Canada for at least two decades, who is a professional or holds an executive position, who has proven himself by performing multiple services for the community [Chadney, 1984:131]

4. Daljit Singh was the great uncle of the Maharaja of Kapurthala and Sir Bijoy Chand Mahtab, the Maharaja of Burdwan), lackeys of the British government.

REFERENCES

Basran, G.S., C. Gill, and B. Maclean (1995): *Farm Workers and Their Children* (Vancouver: Collective Press).

Bolaria, B.S. and Peter S. Li (1988): *Racial Oppression in Canada* (2nd edn) (Toronto, Ontario: Garamond Press).

British Columbia Magazine (1919): 'The Position of Hindus in Canada', vol. 8. Vancouver, B.C.

Chadney, James G. (1984): *The Sikhs of Vancouver* (New York: AMS Press).

—— (1985): 'India's Sikhs in Vancouver: Immigration, Occupation and Ethnic Adaptation', *Population Review* 29, 1–2: 59–66.

Dhillon, Mahinder Singh (1981): *A History Book of the Sikhs in Canada and California* (Vancouver: Shromani Akali Dal Association of Canada).

Golden Gazette (1980): 'Sikhs Want Land Back for New Temple', 11 June, p. 16. Golden B.C.

Grace, Elizabeth Ross (1913): 'East Indian Immigration', *British Columbia Monthly*, vol. 3, no.3, Vancouver, B.C.

Hawkins, Freda (1972): *Canada and Immigration: Public Policy and Public Concern,* (Montreal: McGill - Queen's University Press).

—— (1988): *Canada and Immigration: Public Policy and Public Concern,* 2nd ed. (Kingston: McGill - Queen's University Press).

Helweg, A.H. and U.M. Helweg (1990): *An Immigrant Success Story: East Indians in America* (Philadelphia: University of Pennsylvania Press).

Holland, Robert (1943): 'Indian Immigration into Canada: The Question of Franchise', *Asian Review* 39:167–72.

India Canada Committee (1916): India's Appeal to Canada or an Account of Hindu to the Dominion (Toronto: India Canada Committee).

Jagpal, Sarjeet Singh (1994): *Becoming Canadians: Pioneer Sikhs In Their Own Words* (Madeira Park, B.C.: Harbour Publishing).

Johnston, Hugh (1989): *The Voyage of the Komagata Maru: The Sikh Challenge to Canada's Colour Bar* (Vancouver: University of British Columbia Press).

—— (1992): 'Voyage of the Komagata-Maru: The Sikh Challenge of Canadians Colour Bar', *American Review of Canadian Studies*, vol. 22, no. 1, Spring.

Josh, Sohan Singh (1977): *Hindu Gadar Party: A Short History* (New Delhi: People's Publishing House).

Kurian, George and R.P. Srivastava (1983): *Overseas Indians: A Study in Adaptation* (New Delhi: Vikas Publishing House).

Law Union of Ontario (1981): *The Immigrant's Handbook* (Montreal: Black Rose Books).

Mckay, Principal (1914): 'Problems of Immigration, VII, Komagata Maru', *Westminster Hall Magazine and Farthest West Review*, vol. 5, no. 6 (July) Vancouver, B.C.

Mayer, Adrian C. (1959): 'A Report on the East Indian Community in Vancouver'. Working Paper, Institute of Social and Economic Research, University of British Columbia.

Minhas, M.S. (1994): *The Sikh Canadians* (Edmonton: Reidmore Books Inc.).

Muthana, I.M. (1975): *People of India in North America* (Bangalore, India: Lotus Printers).

O'Connell, T. et al. (1988): *Sikh History and Religion in the Twentieth Century* (Toronto: University of Toronto Center for South Asian Studies).

Puri, Harish K. (1981): 'Ghadar Movement: An Experiment in New Patterns of Socialization', *Journal of Regional History* 1:1(1980):120–41.

Puri, Harish K. (1993): *Ghadar Movement: Ideology, Organization and Strategy.* Amritsar, India: Guru Nanak Dev University (2nd ed.).

—— (1997): 'The Ghadar Movement: A New Consciousness', pp. 157–79, *in* Indu Banga (ed.), *Five Punjabi Centuries: Polity, Economy, Society and Culture c 1500–1990* (Delhi: Manohar).

Redway, Brian (1984): Spotlight on Indo-Canadian National Association of Canadians of Origin in India (NACOI), B.C. Chapter, Vancouver.

Satzewich, Vic (1995): 'Capital Accumulation and State Formation: The Contradictions of International Migration', pp. 318–35, *in* B. Singh Bolaria (ed.), *Social Issues and Contradictions in Canadian Society*, 2nd edn (Toronto: Harcourt Brace). (2nd ed.).

Simmons, A. and K. Keohane (1992): 'Canadian Immigration Policy: State Strategies and the Quest for Legitimacy'. *Canadian Review of Sociology and Anthropology*, vol. 29, no. 4, (Nov).

Singh, Kesar (1989): *Canadian Sikhs (Part-one) and Komagata Maru Massacre* (Surrey, B.C.).

Singh, Khushwant (1977): *A History of the Sikhs, vol. II* (Delhi: Oxford University Press).

Singh, Khushwant and Satinder Singh (1966): *Ghadar 1915: India's First Armed Revolution* (New Delhi: R and K Publishing House).

Singh, Nihal Sant (1909): 'The Triumph of Indians in Canada', *Modern Review* (Aug.):99–108.

Smith, Mannan W. (1944): 'Sikh Settlers in Canada', *Asia and the Americas*, 44:359–364.

Trumper, L. and Lloyd Wong (1997): 'Racialization and Genderization: The Canadian State, Immigrants and Temporary Workers', pp. 153–91, *in* B. Singh Bolaria and Rosemary von Elling Bolaria (eds), *International Labour Migrations* (New Delhi: Oxford University Press).

Ward, W. Peter (1978): *White Canada Forever: Popular Attitudes and Public Policy Towards Orientals in British Columbia* (Montreal: McGill–Queen's University Press).

Wong, Lloyd (1984): 'Canada's Guest Workers: Some Comparisons of Temparary Wokers in Europe and North America', *International Migration Review*, 18:85–97.

Colonialism and Indian Labour
Work and Life in the Colonies

❧

INTRODUCTION

The early years of influx of Indian labour to Canada and the conditions that both structured their emigration from India and their work and life in Canada, needs to be discussed in the context of the increasing demand for workers within the British empire. The urgent need for an alternate source of cheap, easily controllable and exploitable workforce arose with the abolition of slavery. The Indian colony became the primary source of such labour to meet the needs of British capital in various parts of the empire. The British colonial authorities developed wide-ranging policies, including legal contractual obligations of Indian workers overseas, conditions of employment, duration of the indentured period, and their legal–political status in various colonies. Their entry and legal–political rights varied considerably between the white dominions such as Canada and non-white colonies. An understanding of the historical context and the structural conditions of labour transfer and its use during the colonial period are essential to fully understand Indian migrations.

It is in this broad framework that the early period of Indian immigration to Canada is analysed. The first part of this chapter examines the structural necessity for the importation of Indian labour within the empire and the conditions for emigration of such labour from India. The labour force participation, work experience, and life of immigrants are then discussed with particular focus on migrants to Canada. Our discussion is based both on primary and secondary sources. A major part of the findings is based on our own research into the history of early Indian migrants to Canada (British Columbia Study).[1] The qualitative data reported here is entirely from this study (Bolaria and Basran, 1986). While details of this study are reported in note 1, a brief comment here, we hope would help readers to fully appreciate the content of responses. The interviews were conducted in English, Punjabi and sometimes in both languages, and were taped. Taping helped us to report the responses in verbatim, that is, 'in the words of the respondents' without editing, and in translation from Punjabi to English every attempt was made to present a 'literal translation' and capture the intention and context of the responses. All transcription and translation was done by one person, other than the authors, who was fluent in both languages and was familiar with the use of both languages in Indian and Canadian cultural and social contexts. The authors, who are also fluent in both languages, made every attempt to ensure that consistency was maintained in the translation and transcription of the interviews.

COLONIALISM AND INDIAN LABOUR[2]

While Indian workers have been migrating abroad in small numbers, primarily as artisans, tradesmen, and merchants; large-scale, organized, and systemic export of Indians began with the abolition of slavery in 1833–4. The need for such labour arose out of the demands of British capitalists for a cheap and ample supply of workers and an easily controllable workforce (Gangulee, 1947; Tinker, 1974; Saha, 1970; Sandhu, 1969; Kondapi, 1951; Gillion, 1956).

After the abolition of slavery, it became necessary for various colonial plantations to look for a supply of labour elsewhere (Tinker, 1976). An attempt was made to use other labour sources, such as 'freed' slaves and Chinese labour, but in many instances the newly freed slaves virtually refused to work on plantations; and the experiment with white European labour also met with failure (Kondapi, 1951; Saha, 1970). The cost of introducing Chinese labour was high, and there were legal and other difficulties (Saha, 1970). As the plantation economy could not survive without a secure labour supply, planters now looked to the Indian colony as a source of assured cheap labour.

Labour migration to plantation economies in particular took the form of indentured labour because of its many advantages for employers (Sandhu, 1969). The indenture system 'bound' the worker to a particular employer and/or plantation under a contract, usually written and 'voluntarily' agreed to, which bargained away the freedom of the employee for a specified period of time (Sandhu, 1969). At the end of the indenture period the worker could have the status of 'free labour', or be reindentured, or return to India. Of course, the employer would want to renew the contract if the worker was still productive, or to 'dispose' him of if he was not (Cumpston, 1956; Gillion, 1956; Sandhu, 1969). In this regard, the indenture system was preferable to slavery for employers, because they could rotate the healthy and productive labour force, either by hiring new indentured workers or through renewing old contracts, and discard unproductive workers.

The labourers recruited under the indenture system were known as 'coolies', and worked under conditions not dissimilar to those of slavery. Indian workers inherited all the features of plantation slavery (Tinker, 1974; Sandhu, 1969). Even if the work was intolerable, they had no freedom to withdraw from the contract. The worker could not change his employer or place of employment. Breach of contract was placed in the category of criminal liability. The system clearly had many of the characteristics of slave labour (Gangulee, 1947; Kondapi, 1951).

The general attitude of the British colonial governments was that Indians were accepted as a labouring or subordinate class and not as competitors with European interests. As Sir Thomas Hyslop, a South African planter, said: 'We want Indians as indentured labourers but not as free men' (Kondapi, 1951:7) The conditions for the recruitment of indentured labourers were created by colonial policies and practices.

By the mid–nineteenth century, virtually the whole of India had come under the political and economic control of the British empire. Henceforth, the interests of India were subordinated to the interests of the empire and 'India was to be an economically vassal state' (Sandhu, 1969:32). Particularly after the industrial revolution, the political economy of the UK required the, 'conversion of India from an exporter of manufactured goods to that of a supplier of raw materials to the British industrial complex and a market for the consumption of the products of those machines' (Sandhu, 1969:32). Through various restrictive tariffs and legislative means, industrial and commercial enterprises in India were made subservient to British enterprises (Sandhu, 1969:33).

British policies in India brought about the decline of the domestic handicraft industry, throwing many craftsmen out of work (Sandhu, 1969). British rule also had a profound effect on the agrarian structure. Agriculture was transformed from a subsistence to a commercial enterprise, and land became a source of investment and income for the money-lenders and landlords. Subsistence farmers were obliged to borrow money to pay heavy taxes; as their debt burden increased a large number became tenant farmers, while many others were simply thrown off the land (Kondapi, 1951; Sandhu, 1969).

Destruction of their traditional sources of livelihood and famines in some parts of India created conditions for labour recruitment and exploitation (Cumpston, 1956, 1968; Saha, 1970:73; Tinker, 1974). Recruitment was done through deception and false promises of prospects in the colonies (Kondapi, 1951:5; Saha, 1970). The mode of recruitment differed in detail but not in substance. It was not an escape to opportunity. Many found themselves exiled into bondage and servitude and many only found death and disease in 'a lifeless system, in which human values always mattered less than the drive for production, for exploitation' (Tinker, 1974:177).

The recruitment of male individuals and not families was the norm under the indenture system (Kondapi, 1951; Tinker, 1974). The conditions of transportation were appalling (Gangulee, 1947), and mortality was high during transportation and at the workplace (Tinker, 1974). To be sure, the forms of legal bondage varied, but the basic conditions of existence were the same. Living conditions were degrading and segregated in what was referred to in some countries as the 'Nigger Yard' (Tinker, 1974:177). The exploitation and degradation of their labour were reflected in low wages, cruel punishments, and high rates of suicide. Many workers were obliged to wear convict uniforms, and many Indian women were driven into prostitution (Tinker, 1974, 1976).

The bonded Indian labourer was sent overseas to serve the interests of the colonial masters who despised him. The statutory colour bar was in operation in many colonies, providing a series of political, economic, and social restrictions to maintain the supremacy of the ruling classes (Gangulee, 1947). Economic exploitation 'lies mainly at the root of racial problems and brings into play the colour bar in social and political relations. The colour bar is, in truth, an economic weapon' (Gangulee, 1947).

The establishment of British rule in many areas also required the service of English-speaking clerks, small businessmen, and white-collar workers to perform services that were needed for the empire to work (Sandhu, 1969; Tinker, 1976). The British brought the Indians as subordinate administrators, clerks, and other junior staff to work in railway stations and post offices as caretakers, policemen, and the like. Due to lack of opportunities in India, the English-educated Indians, like their less educated brethren, were following the path of labourer compatriots (Sandhu, 1969). Indians in these positions served as buffers between the colonial masters and the indigenous population in various parts of the empire, and performed a dual role. As buffers, the Indians had contact with the natives; though they were in positions of subordinate administration, they were seen to be in positions of authority. People did not see the colonial masters who were really controlling their destiny. They were also despised by the natives and were seen as the pariahs who performed the most menial tasks, which the natives would not undertake (Tinker, 1976).

It is obvious that through deliberate colonial policies and practices conditions were created in India to assure a steady and continuous source of labour to meet labour force needs after the abolition of slavery. The labour procurement systems and the conditions of their employment varied depending upon the production requirements and administrative needs of various regions and territories. Some commonalities are, however, evident, including recruitment of male individuals and not families, legal–political subordination of Indians in colonies, the colour bar and segregation, and exploitation.

Colonialism and the concomitant racial ideology which facilitated and rationalized domination and exploitation of people and resources in India, also justified their differential treatment and exploitation in other parts of the empire. Of particular significance in the present context are the policies and practices that governed the migration and settlement of Indians in white dominions. There has been a great deal of similarity regarding Indian immigration to these dominions, characterized by two main features: (1) to strictly regulate the volume of Indian immigration, and (2) to deny full citizenship rights to domiciled Indians in various dominions (Gangulee, 1947). This, however, violated the official proclaimed principles of the empire, which, to quote Chamberlain, 'makes no distinction in favour of, or against any race or colour' (Huttenback, 1976:278). The way out of this contradiction was found in regulations that appeared not to be directed specifically against the Indians, such as language dictation tests in English or other European languages, and health-screening tests (Gangulee, 1947). Another way out of this dilemma used by the imperial government was to give autonomy to various dominions in matters concerning the composition of their populations. The 1911 Imperial Conference agreed to the resolution: 'His Majesty's Government fully accepts the principle that each of the Dominions must be allowed to decide for itself which elements it desires to accept in its populations' (Tinker, 1976:28). This principle was reaffirmed at the 1918 Imperial Conference (Gangulee, 1947:73). Dominion governments exercised this prerogative to take steps to restrict the entry of Indians into their respective countries. The dominions also used this autonomy to define the legal and political status of domiciled Indians and impose restrictions and constraints in other areas, such as labour force participation and conjugal family life.

In sum, colonial policies and practices forced many Indians to migrate to sell their labour power overseas. However, they soon found that emigration from their country did not substantially change their colonial status. They remained in a disadvantaged position and were subjected to political and legal control, economic exploitation and racism, discrimination and social subordination. Their experiences in Canada were not dissimilar to their treatment in other parts of the empire, in particular in white dominions. Migration to Canada did not change their colonial status. Even in their passage to Canada they faced many obstacles and discriminatory treatment on the ships.[3] When in Canada many of them found that it was not an escape to opportunity.[4] The following sections discuss the work and life of early migrant workers from India. In particular, the focus is on the structural conditions under which Indian workers were incorporated into the labour market and the policies and practices that kept them as a low-cost, subordinate, and a highly exploited segment of the workforce.

SIKH WORKERS: REPRODUCTION OF LOW-COST LABOUR

Capitalism and employers seek every means to reduce labour costs and to increase the output of workers so that they reap even larger surplus (profits). To preserve the rate of profit against labour shortages and higher labour costs, the strategies used include: increasing the intensity of labour exploitation (increase their productivity) and having recourse to sources of low-cost labour (Portes, 1978a, 1978b; Dixon et al., 1982; Buroway, 1976; Braverman, 1974, 1975). The search for low-cost labour takes two primary forms: (1) locating enterprises to areas of cheap labour, and (2) importing such labour to replace or supplement the local labour force. In the present context, our focus is on the immigrant and migrant workers and the use of this labour to check labour costs.

Immigrant labour is advantageous in many respects. In the case of imported labour, labour renewal costs are borne in other countries; immigration laws facilitate the externalization of these costs. Immigration laws, for instance, are often designed to separate workers from their families, they come alone and remit small amounts to their families to support and reproduce labour. The circulation of workers across the borders helps to reduce the cost of renewal of labour at the point of production (Burawoy, 1976), and emigration is considered by some as 'capital export' similar to the export of other factors of production (Berger and Mohr, 1975). In short, the countries of immigration transfer a substantial cost of labour to countries of emigration.

The usefulness and importance of immigrant labour goes beyond mere quantitative increase in the supply of labour; it is to increase the supply of particular labour: cheap, docile, submissive, socially subordinated, often confined to undesirable, arduous, and dirty work (Portes, 1977, 1978a, 1978b; Dixon et al., 1982; Castles and Kosack, 1972, 1973; Cockcroft, 1982). Subordination, docility, and cheapness of immigrants is not inherent in the personality of the immigrants, but is achieved through deliberate legal–political manipulation and immigration laws.

There are other specific strategies used to highly-exploit this segment of the workforce. These include: racial labour policies in workload assignments, promotion and training, colour line and segregation into different work areas and work shifts, unfree labour and single male/female workers (Bolaria and Li, 1988; Bolaria and Bolaria, 1997a, 1997b; Das Gupta, 1996; Trumper and Wong, 1997; Sassen-Koob, 1978, 1980).

These preliminary observations provide the framework for the discussion of employment patterns and work experience of the early Sikh workers and the structural constraints and labour processes that made them an easily exploitable workforce. These workers came to Canada with many of the features that typically make foreign born labour especially useful and desirable to the employers.

Single Male Labour

From the vantage point of the receiving countries, immigrants are ready-made workers, with the cost of labour reproduction borne by their countries of origin. Immigration laws, accordingly, are designed to recruit the required labour at the lowest cost possible. In this sense, immigrant laws and regulations are in fact labour laws used to regulate foreign-born labour by controlling their conditions of entry. The restrictions on immigrants from some countries and on preventing racial/ethnic minority workers bringing their families may be seen as a measure to reduce the cost of labour reproduction. As Table 6.1 indicates, the Indian workers, almost all of them Sikhs, were primarily males. Only a few adult females were admitted to Canada. For instance, prior to 1920, 5,252 males, but only 23 females came from India. This pattern of entry of Indian immigrants continued even after 1919 when immigrants from India were allowed to bring in their wives and children. Even after this change, few could afford to take advantage of the situation because of lack of financial resources and the fear of racial discrimination. The social cost of maintenance of workers without families is quite low. The recipients of this labour force save on a whole range of social costs: housing, schooling, and so forth. These workers commonly lived in logging camps or cookhouses with other males, and were denied a conjugal family life (Smillie, 1923; Srivastava, 1974). Separation from their families produced a marginal existence for many without emotional and social support from immediate family members. Also, given such living arrangements there was no physical separation between the workplace and the personal lives of these workers. This situation potentially extends control

TABLE 6.1

IMMIGRATION TO CANADA BY SOUTH ASIAN ETHNIC ORIGIN, ADULTS, 1904–66

Years	Adult male	Adult female	Total adult
1904–9	5,167	16	5,183
1910–19	85	7	92
1920–9	89	144	233
1930–9	26	90	116
1940–9	142	69	211
1950–9	1,214	525	1,739
1960–6	728	336	1,064
1904–66	7,451	1,187	8,638

Sources: Canada Division of Immigration, Immigration Statistics 1896–1961, Immigrants Admitted to Canada by Ethnic Origin, *Annual Reports*, Sessional Papers, Fiscal years, 1904–5 to 1907–8, calendar years 1908–66. (Compiled from Helen Ralston, *The Lived Experience of South Asian Immigrant Women in Atlantic Canada: The Interconnections of Race, Class, Gender* (Lewiston, New York: The Edwin Mellen Press, 1966). App. A, pp. 122–3.)

and surveillance by employers over workers' lives even after the working hours.

There were other consequences for the workers and the community. Exclusion of females was also intended to ensure that Sikh workers did not become permanent settlers with families (Doman, 1984), and were largely viewed sojourners (Trumper and Wong, 1997). This policy did have the intended effect. Under the circumstances of their reception the workers saw themselves as sojourners. Speaking of early migrant workers, a Sikh respondent described their orientation as follows:

... thinking that they [workers] would make money in Canada, spend four or five years and whatever debt we have to pay we can return and buy some land and put in the well, do the farming when we go back.

Another respondent stated:

The white people had turnover rate quite a bit but our people ... wanted to work steady four or five years, did not want to lose any time.

This has also meant a considerable delay in the development of a native-born Indo-Canadian community. As temporary transient workers (sojourners), with families to support in the 'home country', they faced additional pressure to accept any available job and at any wage level in order to enable them to meet these normative obligations and expectations. In short, importation of foreign-born workers as temporary transient workers, in particular without families, is advantageous in many respects for the labour importing countries. The racialized segment of this workforce is subject to additional constraints which makes it even more vulnerable.

COLONIAL STATUS, RACISM, AND LEGAL–POLITICAL RIGHTS

Racist ideology, which justified imperial expansion and colonization, also provided rationalization for economic exploitation of racial-minority workers (Brown and Cook, 1974). The notion of racial inferiority and non-assimilability of colonial immigrants justified both their restricted entry and differential treatment of those already in Canada. The state and its representatives propagated this notion through immigration laws and denial of legal–political rights to non-white immigrants. For instance, Indian immigrants like other Asians were denied the right to vote. As a consequence, they could not enter certain occupations such as law and pharmacy, because eligibility to those fields was limited to those on the voters' list

(Krauter and Davis, 1978; Bolaria and Li, 1988; Trumper and Wong, 1997). This formal legal subordination of workers not only restricted their labour market opportunities, but also reaffirmed their unsuitability as citizens and permanent settlers. This was in reality legalization of racial oppression, differential treatment, and subordination of Indian workers (Bolaria and Li, 1988). Denial of legal–political rights made Indian workers more vulnerable to threats and repression by the employer than workers who had these rights.

The role of the state is significant in this context. By making their position legally weak, the state creates the conditions for employers to potentially make use of political threats, including threats of deportation, to discipline the workers and obtain docility and compliance. These workers can be easily deported if they 'cause trouble' or are no longer needed. Their tenuous legal–political status and its associated powerlessness has special significance for the employers to impose discipline on alien defenseless workers.

Immigrants from India were conscious of the link between their colonial status and legal–political rights in Canada. As one of the respondents stated:

When I came our country was still under British rule. ... We did not have our own government, no support from our own country, so we did not have the rights ...

This theme was evident in responses by other respondents:

They did not accept us as citizens of this country while our India was under British rule, we were mere workers; since we got our own government, we got these rights.

[They] used to call [us] Hindus. When we got the freedom they started calling us East Indian but not before that ...

They [employers, white people] used to say that you are slave [colonized people]. They used to hate [us] because they would say we are slave.

Other respondents were cognizant of the change in their status in Canada after India's formal Independence. One respondent remarked in stark terms:

... with freedom the conditions became better, it made a difference, before that [they] would not think that we are also human beings ...

Furthermore, these foreign-born workers could be forced to work in undesirable and low-wage sectors. These conditions would not be socially acceptable in other sectors of the society and the indigenous workers would not put up with these working conditions. Ascribing inferior characteristics justifies the presence of these workers in low-wage sectors and masks the deliberate policies and practices that confine them to these sectors and extend employers' control.

RACIAL LABOUR POLICY

In addition to denial of normal conjugal family life (single male labour) and denial of legal–political rights, workers of Indian origin also faced other structural constraints and obstacles in the labour market and at their place of work. An understanding of the characteristics of the labour market inequalities, enforced racial segregation in the labour market and at the place of work, and the maintenance of social differentiation is essential to an understanding of the structure and process of labour exploitation. Labour market segmentation and stratification and allocation of workers in different sectors creates differential opportunity structures, with different working conditions and differential rewards within each sector (Gordon, Edwards, and Reich, 1982; Bonacich, 1972; Piore, 1975; Szymanski, 1976; Phillips, 1989). Allocation of workers in different sectors and within the same sector is often based upon social ascriptive factors such as race and gender. Non-market sanctions may be required to procure and retain workers in the lower strata of the labour market characterized by low-paying, arduous, and dead-end jobs (Bolaria and Bolaria, 1997a). Foreign-born workers with tenuous legal-political status and unfree labour help to supplement and sustain the workforce in the lower stratum.

The early Sikh immigrants filled jobs in the segmented and lower strata of the labour market. They were employed predominantly in lumber mills and farms, working under very undesirable conditions and extreme exploitation. Racism, discrimination, both at the workplace and off-work, made them particularly vulnerable. The organization of the workforce and work on racial and ethnic lines further created conditions in which Sikh and other racial minority labour could be utilized at the lowest possible cost. Various dimensions of these processes are of particular significance and are discussed below.

Racially Segregated Labour and Living Conditions

The early Sikh workers mostly lived at their place of work, such as logging camps and bunkhouses. As they were not allowed to migrate with their families, these 'unattached' males lived with other males, at or near their place of employment. This was also necessitated by racial discrimination in housing (Smillie, 1923). These bunkhouses were segregated by race or nationality groups. As one of the respondents in our study stated:

... and the company built the bunkhouses for the people to live there and there used to be [a] cookhouse in there where people would eat their meals. Usually the white[s] had the houses in the city but they would also live in the bunkhouse. These bunkhouses were separate for all different kinds of people: the white people had their own bunkhouse and the Chinese had their separate cookhouse, Japanese had different, and we Hindustani [Indian] had a separate bunkhouse, at that time families were not many and so we would live in the bunkhouse.

Another respondent said:

They [mill owners] had bunkhouses for Chinese, Japanese, Germans and East Indians. For all kinds of nationalities.

These bunkhouses were shabby places, poorly constructed. 'We used to put newspapers on the walls ... The wall had the single layer of planks', noted one respondent.

The living conditions were not very different for those who were farm workers.

People who came first: they used to work in the fields and used to sleep in the cow barns. They used to throw or spread their cloth on the hay or grass and they used to sleep there.

It was hard to get work at that time; living was in the barns; used to spread hay on the ground in the barn and used to sleep on it ...

The strategy to separate and segregate the workforce on racial and ethnic bases is not uncommon in some sectors. One of the authors experienced this in the early 1960s when he had a summer job as a farm worker in California.[5] The labour was segregated in different camps usually referred to as 'Mexican camp', 'black camp', white camp', and 'student camp'. Almost all of the workers in the 'student camp' were from the Third World on student visas who had to obtain permission from the Immigration and Naturalization Service to work during the summer months. Living and working conditions for student workers were only marginally better than those experienced by early immigrants. The foreman responsible for hiring was aware of the students' vulnerability, given that they had only a short summer period to earn money and limited alternative employment opportunities. A large number of students lived in somewhat crowded bunkhouse(s), with inadequate toilet and shower facilities. Often student workers had to wash in the nearby river. Workers were exposed to toxic sprays at work and sometimes while they had lunch breaks in the fields, because spraying was done from planes. To be employed one was required to eat in the 'cookhouse' owned by the foreman for which he deducted a substantial amount from individual wages. Indeed, this amount was levied by the foreman regardless of whether or not an individual ate 'meals' there. In addition, an Immigration and Naturalization Service (INS) representative sometimes made 'surprise' visits in the field to verify if student(s) had legal permission (work permits) to work. This also served as a reminder to the students of their temporary status with restricted legal access to work in the US.

Workers in one camp had virtually no contact with their counterparts in other camps, and in the field at the place of work. This was thus a workforce segmented on lines of race, ethnicity along racial, ethnic, and nationality, analogous to the situation of early Punjabi/Hindustani migrants in Canada. Workers in different contexts and different periods of time faced similar working and living conditions.

Racial Preference in Employment and Blocked Alternative Opportunities

Labour market opportunities for Sikh workers were constrained due to racial discrimination. This meant that they only got the job if white workers were not available or were jobs they would not accept because of the nature of work and terms employment. This also meant that the Sikh workers were vulnerable to exploitation by employers at places where they had a job, because the employers were aware that these workers did not have very many alternative employment opportunities.

One respondent describes the labour market practices at the time in the following words:

... The difficulty was finding work, like if the white would go to apply for work then it seemed that he would not have any problem, if there would be a job, because he would get it if there was one. But our people and all the Asiatics would feel that they give us the jobs which the white men would not like to do. Specifically, there were white people's companies which were in great or large numbers, Japanese or Hindustani companies were very few ... so white people had the first preference, and we would get job the last. If the white people would not do that job then they [white mill owners] would give us the job, ... so this was the one factor, the other was the wages, and the third dissatisfaction was advancement at work, ... become millwright or any kind of technical machinist.

Blocked labour market opportunities and racial preference in hiring by some white mill owners also created objective conditions for exploitation by some Hindustani (Indian) mill owners. As one respondent stated:

... It was not only the white owners who would get more work from us with less wages but our Hindustani mill owners would do the same thing. They would take as much advantage of us as the white mill owners.

According to another respondent:

... at that time our people who were owners of mills used to get the time mixed up. Like if somebody had worked 50 hours they used to write 40 hours.

Another respondent said that the bookkeeper (a relative of the mill owner) in one of the companies 'cheated' workers by falsifying their work hours and thereby their wages.

... We had [number deleted] companies or mills which were owned by our own people, they would not treat our people right ... Our people used to show less hours worked. Especially in [name deleted] company, the bookkeeper used to cheat like that ... He [the bookkeeper, name deleted] told about cheating when he got in a fight with the mill owner or something, his name was [deleted].

The general situation of exploitation is reflected in statements like: 'work for our own people [Indian] was harder', 'used to pay less', and 'used to mix up the hours'.

Limited and blocked employment opportunities created conditions for exploitation of early immigrants irrespective of place of employment, employers often taking advantage of the workers' vulnerability.

Differential Wages: Racism and Price of Labour

Differential labour market opportunities for white and non-white workers and vulnerability of non-white workers forced them to accept lower wages than their white counterparts. In other words, a split labour market operated where the price of labour for racial minority workers was less than that for white workers. Hindustani [Indian] and other Asian workers were paid substantially lower wages for doing the same work. This was a common practice at the time, and of course helped to keep the wage bill low for the employers. The following representative statements from the B.C. Study describe the situation well:

Paid less because one thing the colour, and second from a foreign country. And they [employers] were thinking that if they would give the same wage as to the white people then they would mind about it ... They used to hate [Indian workers] because they would say we are all slaves.

We did the work for less money because we had to and we needed the work. They [employers] used to discriminate [against] us on these things. That game was going on, 15 cents less. We [Indians] would accept whatever they [employers] would pay us.

They used to discriminate against our people at that time.

The minimum wage legislation was understood to have in fact legitimized the differential wage rate. As one of the respondents described it,

Yes, there was difference in wages ... and the rate of pay it was higher for the white workers and the Asians, Chinese and others including Hindustanis [Indians] it was lower than the white workers. But the first Minimum Wage Act, I do not remember the exact date of it, I think it came in 1935 or 1936, it was made by the government, in that Act they put minimum wage 35 cents an hour but along with it they wrote that the companies could pay 25 cents to the 25 per cent of people. Usually that was the interpretation, that the Asiatics are 25 per cent here, so the government would say pay 35 cents to the white workers and 25 cents to the Asiatics. So, that was the difference.

Even in some instances where Sikh workers were paid at the same hourly rate as white workers, the foreman and/or the mill owner managed to 'take back' part of the wages paid to them. One method often used was to charge the workers a 'fee' for cashing a cheque. The official wage cheque would be issued for the correct amount that the workers were entitled to, yet when the cheque was endorsed by the workers they would receive cash payments with considerable deductions for 'cashing fees'. Sikh workers were also 'cheated' on the number of hours they worked—'owners used to get the time mixed up'—and did not receive any different wage rate for overtime work, and in addition most of them worked six days a week. They worked 'for less money' because they 'had no other alternatives' was a common characterization of the situation of vulnerability for early Sikh workers. Because of the absence of any collective organization of workers at the time, they were at the whim of the employers:

Whenever they [owners/management] wanted they would kick you out, like sometimes at 3:30 p.m. they would bring the slip and give it to you and tell you not to come tomorrow.

Increase in any wage rate was also clawed back through rent for bunkhouse accommodation. As noted earlier, Sikh workers were single males who lived in bunkhouses at the workplace. While the accommodation was crowded and poor, it was usually 'free'. However, in some cases where the wage rate increased, the owner started levying rent for such accommodations. As one respondent stated:

We did not have to pay the rent. As soon as the pay increased more than 40 cents an hour then they [mill owners] started getting the rent from us. Whatever more wages we used to get actually it used to go to rent, and we would receive the same 40 cents an hour.

It is evident that the employers used various methods to keep the wage bill low. This low-cost labour was primarily foreign-born, the Sikhs and other racial minority workers. The differential wage rate, it would appear, was legally sanctioned by the state. Some of the practices of unequal treatment continued in the lumber industry even in the 1950s; for instance, unpaid labour performed during 'training' shifts and overtime work (Bains and Johnston, 1995:62). Workers of Indian background often had to give gifts to their bosses to keep their jobs; jobs which entailed hard and arduous work under poor working conditions, and when at times the worker did not even have the use of the wash room for an entire shift (Bains and Johnston, 1995:62,79). Differential work assignments and workloads and segregation of workers in different work areas within the same company/mill on the basis of race and nationality are discussed below.

Racialized Work and Segregated Work Areas

Sikh workers also faced discrimination and exploitation in other respects at their place of work. They were assigned physically demanding and exhausting work to be done under difficult and undesirable working conditions. In lumber mills, they usually worked outside in uncovered open yards (referred to as 'green chain' by the respondents), in rain and cold. It would appear that workers were segregated on the basis of race in different work areas. Race was also an important consideration in the division of labour and social differentiation at the workplace. Several respondents in the B.C. study described this differential treatment in lumber mills in the following terms:

They [employers] used to give us quite hard and heavy work and the whites used to get good and light work.

Another respondent stated:

In those days they [employers] were not giving good work to our people. [We] used to work outside to load the lumber: the work was heavy and hard. It improved when we got the Independence. Before, our people always got work outside.

Another respondent noted:

[Our] people used to work outside in the yards ... in the winter. In the rain they used to wear plastic clothes and plastic caps. [They] used to feel hot. ... It was very hard.

Yet another respondent commenting on the nature of work, workplace, and the division of labour stated:

No, they [mill owners] would not put them on better jobs or work. The hard work was outside on the chains, there was no roof, it was open. When there was rain they used to work outside lifting the lumber and carry it around in the water, the work was very heavy and hard. The conditions were very bad and hard. ... Our people would not get the work inside the mill, they worked outside in the lumber yard.

It is evident that in the lumber mills, the employers exploited the vulnerability of Sikh workers not only in terms of differential wage rates but also in assigning to them the hard and heavy work to be performed under difficult conditions. There was obviously racial segregation of workers into different work areas: white workers had better jobs inside, whereas Sikh and minority workers were relegated to poor jobs in the lumber yards, which white workers would not accept and with working conditions that would not be socially acceptable.

The characteristics of workers appear to conflate with the characteristics of the jobs. Yard work was largely done by 'our people'. The assignment to them of low paid and inferior work reinforced and sustained their inferior status and perpetuated the notion that Indian workers were only capable of and suitable for certain work. This self-fulfilling prophecy was also evident in other aspects of social differentiation and social stratification of labour at the workplace.

Racialized Occupational and Social Hierarchy

The labour force was also stratified along racial lines with respect to technical/skilled jobs and positions of authority and power. Sikh and other racial minority workers rarely occupied positions of manager and foreman, and rarely held jobs as technicians, electricians, and millwrights. These jobs were 'reserved' for white workers. As one respondent stated:

The ones who were technicians they were all white people. Engineers were white workers in the mills, electricians were white people, and millwrights were white men, and all technical jobs or work were for the white men or the white men were in these jobs, the jobs which were not technical or ... dangerous ones, in those jobs were Japanese, Chinese and our Hindustanis.

The racialized occupational hierarchy and social subordination of racial minority labour were commonly practiced in mills owned by whites. Because of the segregated workforce, even if Sikhs were appointed as foremen, they were foremen of Indian workers only. At the time in a few 'our mills', 'Hindustani mills', as respondents referred to mills owned by Indian entrepreneurs, 'our people' usually held jobs as foremen and managers.

... In our mills [Hindustani mills] our people would be the foremen too, but they [our people] were not the top ones. They [Hindustani mills] used to hire the white men for the higher positions where they would think our men could not do that work. But, usually [in] our mills, the Hindustani mills, they had our people foremen and the manager ... they were our Punjabi Sikhs.

It is important to note that in 'Hindustani mills' the workforce was predominantly and perhaps even exclusively, composed of workers of Indian origin. These workers would not be opposed to a foreman of Indian background. White workers, on the other hand, were often unwilling to accept an Indian as a supervisor/foreman. One of the respondents described a case in point:

... one man ... [name deleted], he knew quite bit grading and knew the language too, there [in the mill] they had the opening from grading to foreman, so he applied for that job, they [mill owners] offered him that job. But at the same time the white workers went to the company and said, we would not take [accept] him, we will not be here, we would go [quit], so he was fired from that work ... so he had to quit that work ...

Thus, there was racially stratified social hierarchy where white workers would not accept positions where they were subordinate to a non-white foreman. White workers also would not accept jobs in Sikh-owned mills and farms, obliging the owners to rely upon racial minority workers. As one respondent reported, 'Chinese were working on our farm. At the time these people [white] did not like to work for us'.

Race was also the criterion in the selection of workers for further occupational and skill training. Sikh and other minority workers were denied such opportunities which would make them eligible to become graders and the like. Even those who already had professional education and training faced discrimination in the labour market. Many could not get jobs congruent with their education and training. As one respondent noted:

It was even harder for educated people to get jobs. Some educated people were working with us in mills. There was one man named [name deleted] who was an engineer, he was a pilot too. He could not get any job ...

Other evidence indicates that professional Hindustanis [Indians] faced discrimination and often were compelled to work on the green chain (Jagpal, 1994:90).

Race also played a part in evaluation of one's ability, capability, and capacity to undertake certain work and assume certain responsibilities. One respondent stated:

You had to be satisfied with the job because you could not do anything about it ... One time I was working in [name deleted]. There was some kind of opening which paid more money. I said to the superintendent that I want to take that job, he said that you would not be able to do that, he said you cannot do it ... they would not give our people the work where the pay was more.

In the above case, the job for which the respondent wanted to be considered paid 25 cents more an hour than the job he held at the time. Jobs with better pay and working conditions were often denied to Sikh workers. Because of blocked opportunities for occupational mobility at the place of work, and limited alternative opportunities in the labour market, these workers often worked at the same jobs throughout their working lives or at a similar low-paying job at another mill.

The racially stratified occupational and social hierarchy thus kept the Sikh workers confined to only certain jobs in the mills and kept them in socially subordinated positions vis-à-vis the white workers and bosses. These policies and practices also reinforced and perpetuated the colonial and racist views concerning the intellectual (ability and capacity) and social superiority of whites over non-white colonial subjects.

Undesirable Immigrants, Preferred Workers

The greater exploitation of foreign-born workers in various countries is repeatedly documented (see Bolaria and Bolaria, 1997b). This exploitation is not inherent in their personality, their cultural background, their social and cultural practices, and lower aspirations, but is conditioned through the structural vulnerability of these workers. The legal, political, and social subordination of workers creates objective conditions which make them a vulnerable and easily exploitable workforce. In Canada, while state policies and practices often characterized immigrants from India as 'undesirable' and 'non-preferred', and they faced racism and discrimination, they were at the same time preferred workers because they were relatively cheap, stable, and docile workers. As one of the respondents stated:

... Our people used to get less pay and would work very honestly and always had the fear too. Our people would not say anything no matter where they were being put for the work or job, but white people used to be very pushy and used to argue. So these qualities [less pay, honesty, accept any job] made them likeable but otherwise they did not like our people ...

Employers preferred Sikh workers because of their availability and readiness to do any kind of work at any time. As one respondent recalled:

They [mill owners] would prefer these people [Sikh workers]. Sikh immigrants would do any kind of work ... and our people [Sikh workers] would never ask how much money they would get for the job. They would accept whatever was given. The employer would get as much work as he could with the least wages. This is how our people used to work. They never said no if the employer would ask them to work in the middle of the night. They would go and do any type of work at any time.

Along with Indian labour, Chinese workers were also exploited. As the following responses demonstrate, Chinese and Indian workers were preferred because of 'less pay and more work'.

Our people and the Chinese used to get less pay and work more, they kept on working.

Yes, less wage to the Chinese too. That is why there were more Chinese and our people who worked for them. When the unions came to power they had to pay the fixed wage for the same work to everybody.

Chinese and Hindustanis were 'preferred' by the mills: 'less pay and more work'.

Yes, that is true. That is why there were so many of our people and the Chinese working over there [in mills]. They got less pay and did more work. That 'willingness' to accept the work without inquiring about the wage rate and not questioning the actual payment—'our people would not say anything no matter what they were paid for the work or job'—are mentioned frequently as characteristics that 'made them likeable' as workers, even when 'they [employers] did not like our people. ...'

Respondents point out the contradiction between racism and the need for labour. While some employers harboured racist beliefs and attitudes toward Sikhs, they preferred them as workers because of their availability, docility, stability, and low wages. For these reasons they were 'much sought after' as workers (Srivastava, 1974). At the same time they were often accused of working for low wages and scabbing, and were frequently assaulted by white workers (Reid, 1941).

Racism and racial discrimination meant low wages for racial minorities, on the one hand, and a split between white and non-white workers, on the other. One of the respondents in our B.C. study describes this situation:

... that white people, the ones who worked with them, used to hit them. It was because our people used to work for lower wages. But the white people would get mad and say why you have agreed to get less money [wages]. On the other hand the owner of the mill wanted them to work and offer them the job. So, our people always used to think, what we will do by sitting around without work, and used to accept any kind of work for less wage.

At that time there were no unions and things like that. So that was the case. Those white people used to say that you should get full wage, why are you willing to work for half or less wage. These white people used to get mad ... Because when the white man was working for full wage, then our countrymen used to agree to work for less money. The mill owner wanted that.

While the availability of cheaper racial minority labour was profitable for the mill owner, it threatened the wages of white workers and split the workers along racial lines. The unions began to transform this situation. The union organizers were quite aware of that without the cooperation and involvement of Sikh workers they could not effectively organize at the workplace and would not have successful and effective unions. The Sikh workers also clearly recognized the potential benefits of labour unions to protect their own and the collective interests of all workers. After unionization at the workplace the racially stratified occupational and social hierarchy began to weaken. As a respondent stated:

Unions did useful things for all kinds of people or nationality, Chinese, East Indians and Japanese too, any nationality they belonged to, the unions did very good work. The unions had them pass the law that whether someone is Japanese, Chinese, East Indian or any nationality he belongs to he should get the same wage for the same work as the white people. So that is why with the help of the unions we would get the grading work, machinery work ... so, unions helped everybody.

Another respondent stated:

No, before the unions they [mill owners] would not give any good work to our people. After the unions they used to give better work to our people, and the other reason we got our own government [Independence] in India. With the freedom the conditions became better, it made a big difference'.

The unions also provided job security for the workers and support in case of grievance.

First the foreman was all in all then the unions came in power, so when the unions came if you had any trouble to go to the union and they had to back you up ...

Respondents attributed the improvement in working conditions primarily to unionization in the lumber mills. Unions also mediated antagonisms and hostilities between white and non-white workers.

Our discussion of the early Sikh migrants to Canada indicates that the Sikh workers were a racially stratified and extremely exploited segment of the labour force. Racist immigration policies and practices, the structural constraints under which they entered Canada, and racial labour policies and practices which limited their opportunities, created conditions for extreme exploitation of these workers. Economic necessity, social and cultural isolation, and denial of legal-political rights contributed to their vulnerability. These juridical weaknesses and their precarious status in Canada made them docile, submissive, and easily exploitable. Racial labour policy was manifested in segregated living accommodation with poor living conditions, racial preference in hiring and blocked opportunities, differential wages, racially stratified work and segregated work areas, and racially stratified occupational and social hierarchy.

Sikh workers were in many respects a sub-proletarian, marginalized, and subordinate segment of the working class. Leggett (1968:14) described the marginal working class as, ' ... a sub-community of workers who belong to a subordinate ethnic or racial group which is unusually proletarianized and highly segregated'. Oppenheimer (1974:10) defines sub-proletarian labour as 'unskilled, physically exhausting and uncomfortable (as in a hot kitchen, stoop labour) working utilizing a minimum of machinery ... unionization tends not to exist, hence there is a low level of job, wage and safety protection ...' To be subordinated means to be 'disadvantaged with regard to the labour market or labour process in comparison with another group of workers' (Berrera, 1979:39). The working condition of the 'sub-proletarians' are markedly different from those of even many unskilled manual workers, and the work is regarded as the leas desirable and 'dirtiest' (Oppenheimer, 1974).

While these pioneer workers from India were seen as undesirable immigrants, they were preferred workers. Because of the structural conditions of their existence in Canada, they were mostly a docile, submissive, reliable and low-wage workforce. These workers faced no less racism and discrimination in their daily lives beyond the workplace.

Everyday Lived Experiences of Sikhs

Sikh workers also faced racism, discrimination and social subordination in their daily lives beyond the workplace. They were called 'ragheads'; in trains people would not sit beside them, and they could not go to a movie in their native attire. They even faced physical abuse (Smillie, 1923; Norris, 1971; Scanlon, 1977; Raj, 1980) and could not own property in some sections of Vancouver (Norris, 1971). Because of discrimination in housing, many of them lived in miserable conditions (Smillie, 1923:229). Proposals were even made to relocate them in British Honduras (Ward, 1978). In short, they faced what (Essed, 1991) refers to as 'everyday racism', daily insults, and humiliations. Sikh workers had to endure and cope with discrimination in housing, restaurants, hotels, and bars. The general social environment in some communities was quite inhospitable and even downright hostile, and personal abuse and insults were a common occurrence. Respondents in our B.C. study almost uniformly referred to the discriminatory policies and practices of various business and service establishments.

Discrimination in housing, both purchase and rental, was a common and persistent problem for Sikh workers. They were prevented from buying homes and property in certain areas by both formal and informal means. Formal means often involved the use of city and municipal regulations and informal means often involved the use of public meetings and petitions by neighbourhood residents. As one respondent stated:

There were some areas where they had restrictions for us people ... they [whites] were concerned about the value of their land [property]. They used to put the petition [start a petition] if some East Indians bought the house there [neighbourhood, area] ... They used to prevent us from buying houses through petitions.

Another respondent commented that, 'White people used to hold meetings when they would see that the East Indian family bought the house in their neighbourhood'. One of the respondents indicated that the city council objected to construction of his house because he was 'building a house on a high spot where he could look down on other houses'. The city officials would resort to any regulations to maintain restrictive neighbourhoods. It is these formal and informal discriminatory policies and practices that in the long run produce ethnic and racial ghettoes.

Sikhs often were unable to avail of overnight accommodation in hotels owned by whites. One respondent stated:

... At first they would not give them room in the hotel. In [name of the place deleted] they could get into the hotel [could not stay] ... For staying there was one Chinese restaurant and they had one room there, if that room was available then you could sleep there, but if it is occupied [taken] then you go to the bus depot and pass your night there ...

The alternative to 'passing the night' at the bus depot where one could find space to stay was some distance away. The same respondent continued:

And there was [name deleted] mill which was four miles away from [name deleted], so you walk there and can stay there overnight, there was our cook in that mill ...

The reference in this instance is to an Indian bunkhouse in the mill where workers would hire 'one of their own' to cook for the bunkhouse crew. In essence, Sikh workers had only a few options for overnight stay.

Many restaurants and bars also followed discriminatory practices. They would not get service in restaurants. One respondent described an 'incident':

... One time one incident happened to us, my dad used to sell the wood in Victoria. We went from here, we had to take the truck from the mill for the wood ... one of my cousins was there, he had his hair and beard, they [his father and cousin] felt we should eat our meal here, there was [name deleted] cookery and we went inside and sat there. I was young at that time. We sat for a long time, they were serving to the white people and they did not give anything to us ... they would not serve us, they would not look at us. We got up and came out of that place and bought fruit from the corner store and went in our truck.

In bars Sikhs were restricted to certain areas on the premises and were asked to sit in segregated facilities with other racial minorities, such as aboriginal people. As one respondent stated:

... there they had a small beer room in that bar, they used to say to Hindustanis, if you want to have beer, then you go there and sit, they did not let them [Hindustanis] sit with public.

Another respondent described the discriminatory practices of a particular hotel in a Vancouver Island community:

... there was commercial hotel, which is still there, it is on the other side of the railway track. There, if our people with turban and hair would go and wanted to have beer, then these people had the separate place where they put four–five chairs around the table, they could only go to that separate place and sit there. They were not allowed to sit anywhere else.

The same respondent stated that another hotel altogether excluded Sikh workers from its premises.

The other hotel ... I do not remember the name. There was no permission for the people who had hair and beard. So in that hotel they could not even go.

So, in some bars and hotels Sikhs were not even permitted to enter while in others they were restricted to the use of only segregated areas on the premises. Yet, in other places, even if they went in they were denied service by the waiters.

Then in the beer parlours where the people would go with their turbans, they would not serve us. Then we hired a lawyer, there were few others with me, one was [name deleted], his father was my friend, we told him that we want to do this [challenge the discriminatory practices]. So, we went to the beer parlour, the bar tender [waiter] did not serve us. We came out and went to the lawyer and told him the story. He [the lawyer] said, is that right? We said, you can come with us, so we went there [back] and sat at a table. They [the waiter] put the glass in front of him [the lawyer] and we were not served. Then he [the lawyer] called the bartender ... and told him that I am lawyer [and said] why did you not serve these guys? He [waiter] said, I am not allowed. He [the lawyer] asked him where is it written? He [the lawyer] said you put the sign outside, and they would not come inside. Then he [waiter] talked to his boss,

then the boss came and talked to the lawyer who was with us. He said that
these people [Sikh workers] make too much noise.

The respondent continued:

Yes, boss said that ... He [the lawyer] said, if you do not want to serve them
then you put the sign outside that we are not going to serve East Indians. They
[bar owner] would not do that, I [respondent] mean they could not put the
sign like that ... This happened in front of me [respondent] so this kind of
discrimination they used to do with us.

Racism and discrimination were practiced in various forms: total exclusion;
allowed in some establishments but asked to use segregated area or a
separate table on the premises; and allowed in but ignored and denied
service. Sikh workers, as the above response indicates, did not altogether
passively accept the discriminatory practices of hotels and bars.

In cinema (houses), there were also segregated areas for the minorities at
the time, and they were not allowed to use swimming pools in some areas
and one respondent even mentioned that 'in those days they would ask our
people to go to the bottom level' on the Vancouver Island ferry.

Sikh workers also faced racism and discrimination in other areas. For
instance, Sikhs who decided to shave their beards and cut their hair were
refused service by white barbers, and could obtain these services only in
barber shops owned and operated by Chinese and Japanese.

... They [whites] were not cutting our hair. ... There was one Japanese and one
Chinese and our people used to go to these places for haircut ... but white
people would not cut our hair. So, in [name of community deleted] there was
quite a bit of discrimination.

According to a respondent even a very well-off Indian did not get service
from a white barber. He, a millionaire [name deleted] 'went to a barber in
[name deleted], but the barber said no.' Another respondent also made the
following comments on this issue:

... They [whites] would not cut our people's hair. There was one Chinese and
one Japanese who would cut our hair'.

On the other hand, those Sikh workers who kept their beard, hair and
turban often faced ridicule and insults. They were suspected by some whites
of having lice in their hair and sometimes, ' ... they [whites] would stop the
car when they would see the person with beard and hair, and they [whites]
would act like [mimic] goat, so this way they used to insult our people ...'

They faced insults because of their religion and 'appearance' and mode of dress. Some had expected that by cutting their hair, ceasing to wear a turban, and shaving off their beard they would escape racism and discrimination. However, at the time, both in official immigration statistics and by the general public, all people of Indian origin were considered and referred to as Hindus. No distinction was made on a religious or any other basis. Sikhs resented being addressed as Hindus. As one respondent commented, 'They [whites] were calling Hindu to everyone whether he is clean shaven or keeping the turban. We used to feel hurt when they would call us Hindus'. Bunkhouses with Indian workers were also called 'Hindu bunkhouses'.

While there was some level of racism and racial discrimination every where, people in one community on Vancouver Island were at the time particularly hostile to people of Indian origin. This was attributed to a significant presence of white people of British origin, who had been in India as civil servants or in the army before their retirement in this community. They maintained their colonial attitudes toward the Indians and treated them as 'colonial subjects' and despised them. As one respondent stated:

Actually, most of the officers were the pensioners who came from India. They were majority in [name deleted]. We were their slaves and how could they stand us here.

The link between their colonial background and racial discrimination and differential treatment was almost uniformly recognized by our respondents. In their everyday lived experience, and insults and humiliations, they were constantly reminded of their colonial background. During our interviews words such as *ghulami* and *ghulam* [English translation 'slavery' or 'enslaved' or 'colonized'] and *azadi* and *azad* [English translation 'free' or 'freedom'] were used frequently by the respondents to characterize their status and background. This shared *ghulam(i)* status became a source of unity, cooperation and mutual assistance among Indian workers regardless of their socio-economic and religious background, and united them in the cause of *azadi* for India from colonial rule. In Canada, shared external hostility and racism united the community to fight against the racist policies and practices of the Canadian state, institutions, and employers, and individual prejudice and racism. For instance, Indian workers sent financial aid for the fight against colonialism in India and raised funds to assist passengers on the *Komagata Maru* and to support the Ghadar party.

The Sikh gurdwara became the nucleus of and played a critical and pivotal role in virtually all the political, social, economic, educational, and philanthropic activities. Indians of all backgrounds and different religious affiliations participated in religious observance and other functions. At the time, communal antagonism and religious conflict in the Indian community was virtually non-existent, as is evident in the reference to 'our people' and 'our Hindustani' in responses during interviews. As noted earlier, they were all as Hindustanis united in the common cause of India's Independence and against racism and discrimination. The contradictions within the Sikh community based on regional origins in India and differences in 'correctness' of religious observance were minimal.[6] Gurdwara congregations became a source of job information, *langar* (free communal meal), and even for some transients and recently arrived migrant workers and students a place to stay free of any cost. The early migrants, in providing these services, were following the best traditions and teachings of the Sikh religion and its practices.

The discussion presented above indicates that the early Sikh migrant workers were the object of 'everyday racism' enduring racism, discrimination, racial insults, and humiliations. They faced discrimination in housing, were often denied overnight accommodation in hotels, refused service in restaurants and bars, had to sit in restricted areas in some establishments, refused service by white barbers, and were insulted and ridiculed for their adherence to their religious faith, religious observance, and practices. Their common shared experience of racism and discrimination united them as Hindustanis in support of India's freedom movement and in opposition to racism and discrimination. At the time, the Sikh gurdwara became the nucleus of the social, religious, political, and community activities of Hindustanis.

SUMMARY

After the abolition of slavery, the Indian colony became the primary source of labour to meet the needs of British capital and colonial expansion. British colonial authorities created conditions in India to assure a continuous supply of labour and developed a wide range of policies for the transfer and use of this labour in various parts of the empire. The labour procurement and recruitment systems, and the conditions and duration of their employment, varied considerably depending upon the nature of the economy, labour force needs, and production requirements. There were certain commonalities, however, including recruitment of single-male labour, denial of legal–political rights, and subordination of Indian workers, racial labour policies, and exploitation. The early Sikh workers in Canada were the most disadvantaged group in the labour market. They were not allowed to bring their wives and children with them and were denied legal–political rights. Racism and racial discrimination limited their labour market opportunities, and racial labour policies at the place of work relegated them to low-paying and subordinate jobs in segregated work areas. They also lived in segregated bunkhouses with poor living conditions. The structural conditions and constraints under which they entered and lived in Canada made them an easily exploitable work force.

These workers faced no less racism and discrimination in their daily lives beyond the workplace. They had to endure and cope with discrimination in housing, restaurants, hotels and bars, and were denied other services. Sikh workers were insulted and ridiculed for their appearance and mode of dress. The common shared experiences of Hindustani workers united them in their support for India's freedom and against racist immigration policy and racism and racial discrimination. At the time, the Sikh gurdwara was the centre of many social, political, religious, and community activities of Hindustanis of every background and faith.

While considered as 'undesirable' immigrants, for employers they were preferred workers because they were docile, submissive, reliable, and constituted low-wage workforce. In short, they were a highly-exploited racial segment of the labour force and in many respects they were a sub-proletarianized, marginalized, and subordinated segment of the working class.

NOTES

1. The authors conducted extensive interviews with respondents to collect information on the individual and collective work experience and life of Indian workers in Canada. In addition, the interviews yielded information about labour policies and practices involving other racial and ethnic groups.

For our initial contact with respondents knowledgeable about the early years we relied on our contacts within the Sikh gurdwaras. These respondents then became the source of further contacts. Given the objectives of our study, we consider this method of selection of respondents to be the most appropriate. Within the limits of our resources and time frame, we conducted interviews with 33 Sikh respondents.

All the interviews except two were taped. All our respondents migrated from Punjab province. Interviews ranged from 50 minutes to two hours in duration. Twenty-two interviews were conducted in Punjabi, 10 in Punjabi and English, and one in English alone. All the interviews were conducted by the authors.

Our respondents had varied socio–economic backgrounds. Before migration to Canada, nine were in agriculture-related work, 16 were students, one a labourer, one a bank manager, one a marketing inspector, three were house-wives, and two came as dependant children. There were 30 males and three females in our sample. All the males came alone as immigrants, while all the females came with their families. Most were young at the time of migration (24 under 20 years of age). Among the adults, 19 were single and 13 were married.

Open-ended questions and taping of interviews yielded rich qualitative data from our study. Earlier analysis of this data was also reported in B. Singh Bolaria and G.S. Basran (1985): 'Sikhs in Canada: History of Sikhs in British Colum-bia: A Research Report', Saskatoon (Saskatchewan: Department of Sociology) and B. Singh Bolaria and G.S. Basran (1986), 'Racial Labour Policy and Exploitation: The Case of Sikh Immigrant Workers', paper presented at the annual conference of the National Association of Ethnic Studies, Fresno, California, 26 Feb.-1 March.

2. Extensive material in this section is used from Chapter 7 in B. Singh Bolaria and Peter S. Li (1988): *Racial Oppression in Canada* (2nd edn) (Toronto: Garamond Press).

3. In our British Columbia Study we also asked the respondents about their travel to Canada and the condition of their passage. Most of our respondents as well as other immigrants travelled by merchant ships from Calcutta (India) to Hong Kong and then by a passenger ship to Vancouver (Canada). Those who could not afford to travel on a passenger ship often took a cheaper freighter. Travellers also had to undergo a medical examination in Hong Kong before they were allowed to travel to Canada.

The primary accommodation (room and board) for many travellers in Hong Kong was the Sikh gurudwara. Respondents spoke highly of the facilities, services, and other assistance which they received from the gurdwara. In accor-dance with the Sikh tradition travellers received food and accommodation free of any charge, barring for voluntary donations.

Respondents also spoke of the undesirable ('terrible') conditions on mer-chant ships. They often had to sleep on the deck and did not have enough space to sleep comfortably, sit, and relax. For their travels, Indian passengers often brought their own cots to sleep on and food supplies to enable them to cook their own meals on the ship.

Conditions on passenger ships were better for travellers in regard to food and other facilities. Most of our respondents traveled by economy class (third class), white passengers largely travelling in the first class or business class cabins. Passengers on some ships were segregated into racial and nationality groups including segregated dining facilities (rooms). Racial discrimination and racial attitudes were common experiences of Indian travellers: 'Some whites used to ignore the Sikhs and treated them as inferior and undesirable'.

Indians living in Canada had to have a return document issued by the Immigration Department before leaving Canada for India for admittance to Canada or were re-admitted on the basis of a medical examination. These early immigrants did not have passports or other travel documents.

4. In our British Columbia Study, data were also collected about reasons for migration (why did they leave Punjab, India?). Many factors contributed to emigration from India during colonialism. For most of them the potential of better economic opportunities in Canada was the primary reason. Respondents in our study, were largely from rural backgrounds, mostly Jat Sikhs (agriculturalists), considered themselves as being middle class ('not poor but not rich either'), with small landholdings providing a 'comfortable' living. Other reasons mentioned for leaving India included: 'Conditions in villages were bad; we did not have easy access to water, there was no electricity. People were living from hand to mouth'; 'Corruption and favouritism in India'; 'religious prejudice against Sikhs'; 'British government in India was not interested in giving Indians education so they could maintain rule in India'.

At the time of emigration, our respondents mostly had low educational achievement (grade school or high school education), with only one respondent with two years university education. The primary source of information about Canada was other family members, followed by information from the mass media.

5. B. Singh Bolaria worked in California picking peaches during the summer months on two separate occasions in the 1960s.

6. One major conflict within the community emerged due to anti-community activities. One of these conflicts involved Bella Singh and his group and their collaboration with Hopkinson, an agent of the state to spy on the community. Bella Singh was also implicated and charged with shooting two Sikhs in the gurdwara around 1913. He was acquitted of these charges and resumed his anti-community activities and spent time in prison. In 1932–3 Bella Singh was killed in India. Mewa Singh in 1914 killed Hopkinson for his activities and was convicted and hanged.

References

Bains, T.S. and H. Johnston (1995): *The Four Quarters of the Night: The Life Journey of an Immigrant Sikh* (Montreal: McGill-Queen's University Press).

Berger, John and Jean Mohr (1975): *A Seventh Man: Migrant Workers in Europe* (New York: The Viking Press).

Berrera, Mario (1979): *Race and Class in the Southwest: A Theory of Racial Inequality* (Notre Dame: University of Notre Dame Press).

Bolaria, B. Singh and G.S. Basran (1986): Racial Labour Policy and Exploitation: The Case of Sikh Immigrant Workers, paper presented at the Annual Conference of the National Association for Ethnic Studies, Fresno, California, 26 Feb.–1 March.

Bolaria, B. Singh and Rosemary von Elling Bolaria (1997a): 'Immigrants, Migrants, and Labour Market Opportunities': *in* B. Singh Bolaria and Rosemary von Elling Bolaria (eds), *International Labour Migrations*: 192–209 (New Delhi: Oxford University Press).

—— (1997b): *International Labour Migrations* (New Delhi: Oxford University Press).

Bolaria, B.S. and Peter S. Li (1988): *Racial Oppression in Canada* (2d edn) (Toronto, Ontario: Garamond Press).

Bonacich, Edna (1972): 'A Theory of Ethnic Antagonism: The Split Labour Market', *American Sociological Review*, 37:547–59.

British Columbia Magazine (1912): 'The Position of Hindus in Canada', vol. 8, Vancouver, B.C.

Braverman, H. (1974): *Labour and Monopoly Capital* (New York: Monthly Review Press).

—— (1975): 'Work and Unemployment', *Monthly Review*, June:18–31.

Brown, R.C. and Ramsay Cook (1974): *Canada 1896–1921: A Nation Transformed* (Toronto: McClelland and Stewart).

Burawoy, M. (1976): 'The Functions and Reproductions of Migrant Labour: Comparative Material from Southern Africa and the United States', *American Journal of Sociology*, 81 (March): 1050–1087.

Castles, Stephen and Godula Kosack (1972): 'The Function of Labour Immigration in Western European Capitalism', *New Left Review*, 73: 3–21.

Castles, Stephen and Godula Kosack (1973): *Immigrant Workers and Class Structure in Western Europe* (Oxford: Oxford University Press).

Cockroft, James D. (1982): 'Mexican Migration, Crises and the Internationalization of Labour Struggles', *in* M. Dixon and S. Jonas (eds), *The New Nomads: From Immigrant Labour to Transnational working Class* (San Francisco: Synthesis Publications).

Cumpston, L.M. (1956): 'A Survey of Indian Immigration to British Tropical Colonies to 1910', *Population Studies*, 10: 158–65.

—— (1968): *Indians Overseas in British Territories, 1836–1854* (London: Dawsons of Pall Mall).

Das Gupta, Tania (1996): *Racism and Paid Work* (Toronto: Garamond Press).

Dixon, M., Susan Jonas, and Ed McCaughan (1982): 'Reindustrialization and the Transnational Labour Force in the United States Today', *in* Marlene Dixon and Susan Jonas (eds), *The New Nomads* (San Francisco: Synthesis Publications), 1010–15.

Doman, M.S. (1984): 'A Note on Asian Women in British Columbia 1900–1935', *in* B.K. Latham and R.J. Pazdro (eds), *Not Just For Money: Selected Essays on the History of Women's Work in British Columbia* (Victoria, B.C.: Camosun College), 99–104.

Essed, P. (1991): *Understanding Everyday Racism: An Interdisciplinary Theory* (Newbury Park: Sage).

Ferguson, Ted (1975): *A White Man's Country* (Toronto: Doubleday Canada).

Gangulee, N. (1947): *Indians in the Empire Overseas* (London: The New India Publishing House).

Gillion, K.L. (1956): 'The Sources of Indian Emigration to Fiji', *Population Studies*, 10: 139–57.

Gordon, David M., Richard C. Edwards, and Michael Reich. (1982): *Segmented Work, Divided Workers* (Cambridge: Cambridge University Press).

Huttenback, R.A. (1976): *Racism and Empire* (Ithaca: Cornell University Press).

Jagpal, Sarjeet Singh (1994): *Becoming Canadians: Pioneer Sikhs in Their Own Words* (Madeira Park, B.C.: Harbour Publishing).

Kondapi, C. (1951): *Indians Overseas 1938–1949* (London: Oxford University Press).

Krauter, Joseph F. and Morris Davis (1978): *Minority Canadians: Ethnic Groups* (Toronto: Methuen).

Leggett, J. (1968): *Class, Race and Labour: Working Class Consciousness in Detroit* (New York: Oxford University Press).

Norris, John (1971): 'People of India and the Moslems', *in Strangers Entertained: A History of the Ethnic Groups of British Columbia* (Vancouver: Evergreen Press).

Oppenheimer, M. (1974): The Sub-Proletariat: Dark Skins and Dirty Work. *Insurgent Sociologist*, 4: 7–20.

Phillips, P. (1989): 'Through Different Lenses: The Political Economy of Labour', *in* W. Clement and G. Williams (eds), *The New Canadian Political Economy* (Montreal and Kingston: McGill-Queen's University Press), 77–98.

Piore, Michael J. (1975): 'Notes for a Theory of Labour Market Stratification', *in* Richard L. Edwards et al. (eds), *Labour Market Segmentation* (Lexington, Mass.: Heath), 125–50.

Portes, Alejandro (1977): 'Labour Functions of Illegal Aliens', *Society*, 14: 31–7.

—— (1978a): 'Toward a Structural Analysis of Illegal (Undocumented) Immigration', *International Migration Review*, 12: 469–84.

Portes, Alejandro (1978b): 'Migration and Underdevelopment', *Politics and Society*, 8;1:1–48.

Raj, Samuel (1980): 'Some Aspects of East Indian Struggle in Canada, 1905–1947', *in* K.V. Ujimoto and G. Hirabayashi (eds), *Visible Minorities and Multiculturalism: Asians in Canada* (Toronto: Butterworths).

Reid, Robie L. (1941): 'The Inside Story of the Kamaguta Maru', *British Columbia Historical Quarterly*, 5: 1–23.

Saha, P. (1970): *Emigration of Indian Labour (1834–1900)* (Delhi: People's Publishing House).

Sandhu, Kernial Singh (1969): *Indians in Malaya* (London: Cambridge University Press).

Sassen-Koob, Saskia (1978): 'The International Circulation of Resources and Development: The Case of Migrant Labour', *Development and Change*, 9(Fall): 509–45.

—— (1980): 'Immigrant and Minority Workers in the Organization of the Labour Process', *The Journal of Ethnic Studies*, 8: 1–34.

Scanlon, Joseph T. (1977): *Ethnicity and the Media: An Analysis of the Media Reporting in the United Kingdom, Canada and Ireland* (London: H.M.S.O., UNESCO).

Smillie, Emmaline (1923): 'A Historical Survey of Indian Migration Within the Empire', *The Canadian Historical Review*, 4: 217–57.

Srivastava, Ram P. (1974): 'Family Organization and Change Among the Overseas Indian Immigrant Families of British Columbia, Canada', *in* George Kurian (ed.), *The Family in India—A Regional View* (The Hague, Netherlands: Mouton Publishing), pp. 369–91.

Szymanski, Albert (1976): 'Racism and Sexism as Functional Substitutes in the Labour Market', *Sociological Quarterly*, 17: 65–73.

Tinker, Hugh (1974): *A New System of Slavery* (Oxford: Oxford University Press).

—— (1976): *Separate and Unequal* (Vancouver: University of British Columbia Press).

Trumper, Richard and Lloyd L. Wong (1997): 'Racialization and Genderization: The Canadian State, Immigrants and Temporary Workers', *in* B. Singh Bolaria and Rosemary von Elling Bolaria (eds), *International Labour Migrations* (New Delhi: Oxford University Press), pp. 153–91.

Ward, W. Peter (1978): *White Canada Forever: Popular Attitudes and Public Policy Towards Orientals in British Columbia* (Montreal: McGill-Queen's University Press).

Post-War Immigrants
Opportunities and Constraints

⸙

INTRODUCTION

In the post-war decades, especially since the 1960s, the changes in the Canadian immigration policies have had a profound impact on the place of origin, the characteristics, and background of immigrants. The sources of immigrants have changed in recent years. Growing numbers of immigrants are from Asia, the Middle East, and Africa rather than the traditional sources such as the UK and Europe, and the US. The changes in entry criteria have also meant that recent immigrants are better educated, a relatively large number with university education and university degrees, professional–skilled workers often from urban middle- and upper-class backgrounds. These changes have led to an increasing diversity and hetero-geneity in the Canadian population. The changing racial, ethnic, cultural, religious, and linguistic composition of the Canadian population has also refuelled debate among academics, politicians, and others on subjects such as immigration levels, labour market opportunities, socio–economic status of racial minority immigrants, their economic contributions, and their impact on the social and cultural fabric of Canada.

As in the case of other immigrants, a noticeable change took place in the characteristics and background of immigrants from the Indian subconti-nent after the changes in the immigration policy. The removal of specific regulations restricting and limiting the entry of Indians to Canada, exten-sion of franchise, and formal legal equality facilitated immigration from India for professional–skilled workers and those with high educational achievement. A high proportion of immigrants, particularly during the sixties and early seventies, were professional–skilled workers (Bolaria and Li,

1988:161–84). These changes have led to a more diverse and heterogeneous Indo-Canadian community and their labour market profile is quite different from that of the early immigrants from India.

While visible minority immigrants now have relatively better opportunities in Canada, they still face numerous constraints and disadvantages in the labour market and racism and discrimination in their daily lives. Given historical and contemporary constraints and disadvantages, the incidence of low income among members of visible minorities and their families remain above the Canadian average.

In this chapter we first provide an overview of the socio-economic profile of visible minorities in Canada and then go on to discuss the socio-economic profile of Sikhs with particular focus on their labour force participation. Subsequent sections of the chapter cover topics related to Sikh politics, media and the Sikhs, and the social profile of Sikhs in Canada. Our discussion indicates that racism and discrimination continue to structure the experiences of Sikhs and other visible minorities in the labour market and in their daily lives.

Post-War Immigrants

The post-war period is marked by a gradual change in immigration policies of many countries, including Canada (See Bolaria and Bolaria, 1997). This change is characterized by formal elimination of racist policies and a shift toward professional–skilled workers. By the late 1960s it became evident that Canada could not meet its labour force needs in professional, skilled, managerial, and technical jobs without importation of foreign workers. Consequently, Canada along with other advanced countries, entered into the 'international market of brains'. The immigration regulations enacted in 1962 and the subsequent point system deracialized immigration controls and personal qualities and professional educational qualifications, particularly those corresponding to the labour force requirements, became the primary criteria of admissibility for an independent class of immigrants. In particular, these changes opened up immigration from non-traditional sources. As noted by the Law Union of Ontario, '... European immigration to Canada had declined to the point that Canada was forced to admit non-European immigrants in order to meet he demand for labour' (1981:40). Non-availability of professional and skilled workers from traditional sources (white countries) forced Canada to recruit these workers from non-traditional (non-white countries) ones (Hawkins, 1974). Canada benefited from this 'brain drain' without bearing the cost of producing this labour force (Bolaria, 1987). Canada was the world's second largest recipient of professional-skilled labour in the years after the war (Hawkins, 1972), and a significant proportion came from Third-World countries. These developments changed the complexion of immigrants and the characteristics of post-war immigrants.

IMMIGRANTS INCREASINGLY FROM NON-TRADITIONAL SOURCES

The data presented in Table 7.1 demonstrate the trend in immigrant sources from 1950 to 1991. It is evident that there was a consistent decline in the proportion of immigrants from Europe and a consistent increase from Asia and Africa. For instance, in 1950–5, 88 per cent of immigrant arrivals were from Europe, and only 3.2 per cent of the immigrants arrived from Asia and Africa. The contribution from Asia and Africa increased to 9.4 per cent and the contribution from Europe decreased to 73.5 per cent during the 1962–7 period. The major shift in source areas became more evident in the 1968–73 period. European contributions to immigrant arrivals declined to less than 50 per cent in 1968–73, and Asian and African arrivals jumped to slightly over 20 per cent during the same period. These trends continued during the seventies and by the 1980s Asian and African arrivals outstripped the arrivals from Europe. In the 1980–5 period, 46.4 per cent of immigrants came from Asia and Africa, and just over 30 per cent from Europe. By the 1986–91 period the European contribution further declined to about 24 per cent and Asian and African increased to just over 54 per cent. The arrivals from the US during this period were only 4.3 per cent.

In short, the proportion of European-born immigrants has declined steadily in recent years. On the other hand, there is a steady increase in immigrants from Asia and other non-white countries. To put it differently, nearly 42 per cent of the immigrants who lived in Canada in 1991 were from the UK, Italy, the US, Poland, Germany, and the Netherlands. However, of arrivals to Canada between 1981 to 1991, slightly over 33 per cent came from Hong Kong, the People's Republic of China, India, Vietnam, the Philippines, and Lebanon (Badets and Chui, 1994:14, Table 1.1). These developments have not only contributed to the ethnic and racial diversity of

TABLE 7.1
DISTRIBUTION OF IMMIGRANTS BY SOURCE AREA, 1950–91

(Per Cent)

Area	1950–5	1956–61	1962–7	1968–73	1974–9	1980–5	1986–91
Europe	88.0	84.8	73.5	49.9	36.3	30.2	24.2
Asia	2.8	2.7	7.2	16.8	28.6	42.7	48.2
Africa	0.4	1.0	2.2	3.3	4.9	3.7	6.0
United States	6.3	7.7	10.4	15.2	11.1	7.8	4.3
Americas and others	2.5	3.8	6.7	14.8	19.1	15.6	17.3
Total	100.0	100.0	100.0	100.0	100.0	100.0	100.0

Source: Includes North, Central and South America. Figures recalculated from: Vic Satzewich, 'Capital Accumulation and State Formation: The Contradictions of International Migration' Table 3.3, p. 60)

the Canadian population but also to its linguistic diversity (Badets and Chui, 1994).

RECENT IMMIGRANTS BETTER EDUCATED

Because of the importance of personal characteristics and professional–educational qualifications of potential immigrants, after the sixties, recent immigrants tend to be better educated than those who arrived prior to 1961. For instance, 6.1 per cent of women and 11.5 per cent of men who arrived before 1961 had university degrees. The corresponding figures for the period 1981–91 were: 14.6 per cent women and 20.2 per cent men had university degrees (Ghalam, 1995:128). The proportion of immigrants with less than grade nine education has also declined over the years. While a little over 30 per cent women and 26 per cent men who immigrated prior to 1961 had less than grade nine education, these figures declined to 16.2 per cent and 11.1 per cent, for women and men, respectively, who arrived during the period 1981–91 (Ghalam, 1995:128). From these figures it is also evident that immigrant men tend to have a higher level of formal education than their female counterparts.

There was considerable variation in the level of education among immigrants from different regions. Immigrants from Asia, Africa, and the

US tend to have the highest educational levels and those from southern Europe and central America the lowest (Badets and Chui, 1994:45). The proportion of immigrants from the former regions who had university degrees ranged from 22 per cent to 28 per cent and for those from southern Europe and central America the proportion with university degrees were 4 per cent and 8 per cent (Badets and Chui, 1994:45, Table 4.2).

Overall, immigrants also tend to be better educated than their Canadian-born counterparts. This is primarily due to the higher educational levels of recent immigrants (Badets and Chui, 1994; Ghalam, 1995). As noted above, the proportion of recent immigrants (1981–91) with university degrees is much higher than earlier immigrants (before 1961). These differences in educational achievement are more pronounced for those 25 years of age and older. For instance, 25 per cent of men in this age group who came during the period 1981–91 held a university degree as compared to 19 per cent of all immigrant men. The corresponding figures for women were 17 per cent of recent immigrants as compared to 12 per cent of all immigrant women (Badets and Chui, 1994:40–1).

LABOUR FORCE PROFILE OF IMMIGRANTS

Successive waves of immigrants have been an important source to meet the specific labour force needs in Canada. Educational achievement, age, sex, and country of origin of immigrants have significant influence on the labour force participation of immigrants. Overall, in 1991 the labour force participation rate of immigrants (65.2 per cent) was lower than that for the Canadian-born (68.7 per cent). The differences in labour force participation were greater for women than for men. Younger immigrants were less likely but older immigrants were more likely than the Canadian-born to form part of the labour force (Badets and Chui, 1994:47–8).

The labour force activity also varied by length of time in Canada and place of origin of immigrants. The labour force participation rate was higher for those who immigrated in the 1960s than the recent immigrants. Among the immigrants, labour force participation rates were higher for those with university degrees than those with less than grade nine schooling. However, immigrants with university degrees had lower and those with less than grade nine schooling had higher labour force participation than their Canadian-born counterparts with the same education (Badets and Chui, 1994).

The occupational profile of immigrants differed from the Canadian-born population. In 1991, immigrant men were more likely than Canadian-born men to be employed in professional, managerial, service, product fabricating, and processing occupations. The occupational profile of immigrants varied by place of origin, particularly for those who arrived during the 1981–91 period. In 1991, nearly one-third of immigrant men from the US were in professional jobs. Other recent immigrant men who had relatively high representation in professional jobs were from UK, northern and western Europe, and Africa. Recent immigrant men (those who arrived between 1981 and 1991) from regions such as central America, eastern Asia, and South-East Asia were more likely to be employed in service occupations. Also, men from southern Europe had a high concentration in the construction occupations, and those from South East Asia, South America and the Caribbean were more likely to be in product fabricating occupations.

As with immigrant men, recent immigrant women from the US, UK, northern and western Europe were more likely to be in professional occupations. Recent immigrant women were proportionately more concentrated in service, processing, and product-fabricating occupations than their Canadian-born counterparts, but their proportion in professional and clerical occupations was lower than that of the Canadian-born. Overall, immigrant women, like the Canadian-born women, were concentrated in clerical and professional jobs (Badets and Chui, 1994:55–8). Immigrant men and women are more likely to have low incomes (Statistics Canada Low-Income Cutoffs) than the Canadian-born. In 1990, nearly 21 per cent of all immigrant women and about 18 per cent of immigrant men lived with low incomes compared with 16.3 per cent Canadian-born women and 13.2 per cent Canadian-born men (Ghalam, 1995:131, Table 9.14).

In summary, the post-war changes in immigration policy have had a profound impact on the sources of immigration and their characteristics. Recent immigrants tend to come from non-traditional sources and are better educated than the early immigrants and the Canadian-born population. The labour-market profiles of immigrants differ from the Canadian-born and the occupational profiles and labour force participation of immigrants vary by their place of origin and educational achievement. These changes in immigration patterns have also increased the racial and ethnic diversity of the Canadian population.

VISIBLE MINORITIES:
NON-WHITE IN COLOUR OR NON-CAUCASIAN IN RACE

Visible minorities refers to 'persons other than aboriginal peoples, who are non-Caucasian in race or non-white in colour'. As the previous discussion on post-war immigrants indicates, the proportion of immigration from non-traditional sources has substantially increased in recent years. This has also meant increasing racial and ethnic diversity in Canada, in particular the increase in visible minorities, also often referred to as racial minorities or people of colour. Given the demographic and labour force presence of visible minorities in Canada, the discussion in this section covers selected socio–economic characteristics of this group. This presentation provides a broader framework for subsequent discussion of the labour force and socio–economic profile of Sikhs.

The data presented previously indicate that educational achievement and place of origin of immigrants have an important influence on their labour market opportunities in Canada. Table 7.2 provides data on the educational attainment of persons of visible minority and other persons aged 15 and over, for 1991. It is evident that visible minority men and women are more likely than their counterparts to have university degrees. A little over 21 per cent of visible minority men and 15 per cent of the women had university

TABLE 7.2

EDUCATIONAL ATTAINMENT OF PERSONS IN A VISIBLE MINORITY
AND OTHER PERSONS AGED 15 AND OVER, 1991

	Visible Minorities		Other Persons	
Educational attainment	Women	Men	Women	Men
Less than Grade 9	14.6	9.2	14.2	14.0
Grades 9–13	35.2	34.3	41.2	37.6
Some post-secondary	17.3	17.9	13.9	13.1
Post-secondary certificate/diploma	17.9	17.2	21.2	23.3
University degree	15.0	21.4	9.4	12.0
Total	100.0	100.0	99.9	100.0
Total Population (000s)	956.0	925.3	9,926.5	9,496.9

Source: Statistics Canada (1995): *Women in Canada: A Statistical Report* (Ottawa: Minister of Industry). (Table 10.7), p. 142.

degrees as compared to 12 per cent of other men and a little over 9 per cent of other women. While a lower proportion of visible minority women had university degrees as compared to their male counterparts, they nevertheless were more likely than non-visible minority men to be university graduates. As compared to other persons, visible minorities are more likely to have some post-secondary education but less likely to have a post-secondary certificate or diploma. Visible minorities tend to have degrees in science-related fields, commerce/management/business administration, and the health professions more frequently than other persons. For instance, a little over 20 per cent visible minority women and nearly 48 per cent men had degrees in science-related fields as compared to 11 per cent of other female and 30 per cent of male graduates (Chard, 1995:143, Table 10.8). Visible minorities were less likely than other university graduates to have degrees in fields such as education and counseling.

In spite of the educational attainment of visible minorities, they were slightly less likely than other Canadians to be employed. In 1991, 60 per cent of visible minority women and 70.5 per cent of men aged 15 to 64 were employed (percentage employed in the week prior to the 1991 Census), as compared to 63 per cent of other women and 77 per cent of men in the same age group (Chard, 1995:143, Table 10.9). These data also show that visible minority women and men in the age groups, 15–24 and 25–44 were less likely than other Canadian women and men in the same age categories to be employed. The gap in employment levels was much wider in the younger group (15–24 years) than in the group 25–44 years of age. Visible minority women experienced greater disadvantage in the job market than visible minority men.

Visible minority men and women were less likely than other persons to be self-employed (Chard, 1995:137). Visible minorities were more likely than other persons to experience unemployment. In 1991, about 13 per cent visible minority men and 13.4 per cent women aged 15 to 64 were unemployed, compared to 10 per cent of other men and 9.9 per cent of women in the same age group (Chard, 1995:145, Table 10.12).

The labour force profiles of visible minorities differ from their non-visible minority counterparts. Visible minority persons are less likely than other persons to hold professional and managerial jobs. In 1991, among those with university degrees, 3.4 per cent visible minority women as compared to 8.2 per cent of other women worked in professional jobs. The corresponding figures for visible minority and other men are 38.3 per cent and 45.1 per cent, respectively. Among the university graduates, 8.4 per cent visible minority women and 14.9 per cent men as compared to 11.8 per cent of other women and 21.1 per cent of other men were in managerial positions (Chard, 1995:144, Table 10.11). A little over 18 per cent visible minority women with university degrees worked in clerical jobs, compared to about 10 per cent of their non-visible minority counterparts. The figures for visible minority men and other men are 6.9 per cent and 3.7 per cent, respectively. Visible minorities were also more likely than their non-visible minority counterparts to work in sales, service, and manual occupations (Chard, 1995:144).

Because of differential occupational and professional opportunities, the average employment (full-time, full-year employed) earnings of visible minorities were lower than that of others. In 1990, the average earnings of visible minority women aged 15–64 were $24,712 as compared to $26,160 for other women. The corresponding figures for visible minority and other men were $34,597 and $39,345, respectively (Chard, 1995:145). These differences amount to nearly $1,500 for women and slightly over $4,600 for men. Average employment earnings of visible minority men and women were lower than their counterparts in all age categories. The total average earnings of persons in a visible minority were lower than non-visible minority persons. Visible minorities are also more likely than others to have low incomes. In 1990, approximately 28 per cent of visible minority women and a little over 26 per cent of visible minority men had incomes below Statistics Canada Low Income Cut-Offs. The corresponding figures for non-visible minority women and men were 16.3 per cent and 12.9 per cent, respectively (Chard, 1995:146). Members of the visible minority population are more likely than the general population to live on low incomes. For instance, in 1995, about 36 per cent of the members of the visible minorities, compared to 20 per cent of the general population lived on low incomes. A high proportion of visible minority children live in low-income families. Approximately 45 per cent of visible minority children under six years of age lived in low-income families, compared to 26 per cent of all children. The incidence of low income was also higher among visible minority seniors than the national average, 32 per cent and 19 per cent, respectively (Statistics Canada, 1998).

The above discussion indicates that visible minority men and women tend to have higher educational achievement, compared to other Canadians, yet the labour force profile of visible minorities differs significantly from other Canadians in regard to their employment status and type of jobs. They are less likely than other Canadians to be in professional, managerial positions. Because of labour market inequalities, differential employment earnings and incomes, the incidence of low income among members of visible minorities remain above the Canadian average.

It should be noted also that the socio–economic status of the visible minority population varies from group to group. These differences are largely a reflection of differences in the historical immigration patterns of each group and conditions and constraints under which each entered Canada. There is also considerable heterogeneity within each visible minority group. In the following section we present a labour force and socio–economic profile of Sikhs.

SOCIO-ECONOMIC AND LABOUR FORCE PROFILE OF SIKHS

The early immigrants from India arrived under many restrictions and constraints and had a limited range of opportunities in the labour market. They were ghettoized in a few sectors and jobs, discriminatory hiring practices of employers and racial labour policies at the workplace often created conditions of extreme exploitation of these immigrants. The changes in the immigration policy and regulation in the sixties have had a significant impact on the characteristics of immigrants, their reception in this country, and their labour force opportunities. Although pre-immigration factors, such as class background, educational achievement, and professional–skills training, have opened up diverse employment avenues, sectorial concentration and inequality continue to persist. These inequalities are the result of a number of factors including racial immigration controls, historical immigration patterns, the legacy of racism, and contemporary employment practices. The denial of conjugal family life has limited the growth of the Canadian-born population in several racial minority communities in Canada. For instance, 1981 data on immigrant status show that 97 per cent of the Indo-Pakistani males and 96.4 per cent of the females in the labour force were born outside Canada. While a little over 87 per cent of the British males and 86.3 per cent of females in the labour force in 1981 were born in Canada (Abella, 1984:83, Table 1). With the exception of the Japanese community, members of all other racial minorities are still predominantly foreign-born.

The data on immigration status and period of immigration of Sikhs and other Indo-Canadians in the labour force in 1981 indicate that they were still predominantly a foreign-born population. As Table 7.3 shows, only about 5 per cent of the Sikhs and under 4 per cent of other Indo-Canadians in the labour force were born in Canada. These data also show that a large majority of them arrived in Canada during the period 1967–77. Those in the employed labour force were largely male workers (Table 7.4).

TABLE 7.3

INDO-CANADIANS (SIKHS AND OTHERS) IN THE EMPLOYED
LABOUR FORCE BY IMMIGRANT STATUS AND PERIOD OF IMMIGRATION,
CANADA, 1981*

(percentage)

Immigrant status and period of immigration	Sikhs	Others
Born in Canada	4.7	3.7
Born outside Canada		
Arrived before 1946	0.4	0.1
Arrived between 1946 and 1966	9.2	10.0
Arrived between 1967 and 1967	69.7	75.2
Arrived between 1978 and 1981	16.0	11.0
Total number	27,120	69,020

* Employed labour force, 15 years of age and over, 'East Indian' ethnic origin
Source: Statistics Canada. Unpublished data from the 1981 Census.

TABLE 7.4

INDO-CANADIANS (SIKHS AND OTHERS) IN THE EMPLOYED LABOUR
FORCE BY GENDER, CANADA, 1981*

(percentage)

Gender	Sikhs	Others
Male	63.7	61.2
Female	36.3	38.8
Total Number	27,120	69,020

* Employed labour force, 15 years of age and over, 'East Indian' ethnic origin
Source: Statistics Canada. Unpublished data from the 1981 Census.

The data on educational achievement are presented in Table 7.5. Nearly 40 per cent of the Sikhs in the workforce had less than secondary school

TABLE 7.5

INDO-CANADIANS (SIKHS AND OTHERS) IN THE EMPLOYED LABOUR
FORCE BY EDUCATIONAL ATTAINMENT, CANADA, 1981*

(percentage)

Educational attainment	Sikhs	Others
Less than secondary school graduate	39.7	18.4
Secondary school graduate or trades	14.7	10.3
Other non-university	14.8	23.6
Some university (no degree)	13.1	15.0
University degree (Bachelor degree or higher)	17.7	32.7
Total Number	27,121	69,020

* Employed labour force, 15 years of age and over, 'East Indian' ethnic origin
Source: Statistics Canada. Unpublished data from the 1981 Census.

TABLE 7.6

INDO-CANADIANS (SIKHS AND OTHERS) IN THE EMPLOYED LABOUR
FORCE BY OCCUPATIONAL STATUS, CANADA, 1981*

(percentage)

Occupational status	Sikhs	Others
Managerial, administrative and related	3.2	10.9
Professional[1]	8.8	23.2
Clerical and related	8.8	24.0
Sales and service	18.5	16.5
Farming, horticulture, animal husbandry	4.5	0.5
Processing, machining, construction, transportation[2]	46.1	20.4
Other	10.1	4.5
Total Number	27,121	69,020

* Employed labour force, 15 years of age and over, 'East Indian' ethnic origin.
[1] Occupations in natural sciences, engineering, social sciences, teaching, medicine, artistic, literary.
[2] Processing; machinery and product fabricating, assembling, and repairing; construction trades; transportation equipment operating.
Source: Statistics Canada. Unpublished data from the 1981 Census.

education. On the other hand, about 18 per cent were university graduates, and 13 per cent had some university education. Among the other Indo-Canadians, nearly 33 per cent were university graduates and 15 per cent had some university education.

The occupational distribution of Sikhs shows (Table 7.6) that a very small proportion of them were in managerial, administrative, and professional occupations. Sikhs were mostly (46.1 per cent) in the processing, machinery, construction, and transport operation occupations. Another 18.5 per cent were employed in sales and service jobs. A comparatively higher proportion of other Indo-Canadians were in professional, managerial, and administrative positions. Nearly 11 per cent were in managerial/administrative jobs, and 23.2 per cent in professional occupations, and another 24 per cent in clerical jobs.

TABLE 7.7

INDO-CANADIANS (SIKHS AND OTHERS) IN THE EMPLOYED LABOUR FORCE BY EMPLOYMENT EARNINGS, CANADA, 1981*

(percentage)

Employment earnings	Sikhs	Others
Less than $8,000	35.5	27.7
$8,000–$15,999	25.9	31.9
$16,000–$23,999	23.5	21.5
$24,000–$31,999	10.5	10.4
$32,000–$39,999	2.9	4.4
$40,000 and over	1.7	4.1
Total Number	27,121	69,020

*Employed labour force, 15 years of age and over, 'East Indian' ethnic origin.
Source: Statistics Canada. Unpublished data from the 1981 Census.

The data on employment earnings are reported in Table 7.7. Figures show that a little over 35 per cent Sikhs and nearly 28 per cent other Indo-Canadians had incomes below $8,000. Another 25.9 per cent Sikhs and 31.9 per cent of the others had incomes of $8,000 to $15,000. A very small proportion of the Indo-Canadians, both Sikhs and others, had employment earnings in the highest income categories. Under 2 per cent Sikhs and slightly over 4 per cent of others had employment incomes over $40,000. Nearly 3 per cent Sikhs and 4.4 per cent other Indo-Canadians earned

$32,000 to $39,900. While nearly double the proportion (8.9 per cent) of other Indo-Canadians as compared to Sikhs (4.6 per cent) had incomes in the top two categories, there was virtually no difference between the two groups in the lower income categories. A little over 61 per cent Sikhs and nearly 60 per cent of the others had incomes under $16,000.

It is evident that primarily because of historical racial immigration controls and patterns, a very small proportion of Indo-Canadians, Sikhs and others, in the workforce in 1981 were born in Canada. Most of them arrived in Canada after the changes in immigration regulations during the sixties. While relatively better educated, a small number of the Sikhs were in managerial–administrative jobs, and a significant proportion of them worked in processing, trades, transportation, and construction. On the other hand, a relatively higher proportion of other Indo-Canadians were in managerial, administration, and professional occupations. These differences between the Sikhs and other Indo-Canadians in employment patterns may be due to the differences in the educational attainment of the two groups. These differences in employment profiles were also manifest in the earnings of the two groups in the top income categories. However, in both groups, a very high proportion had low incomes. About 60 per cent of workers in both groups had incomes under $16,000. These data suggest that notwithstanding relatively better educational attainment, a small proportion of them were in high status jobs and most of them had relatively low employment earnings.

While still relatively small numerically, by the 1991 Census there was a substantial increase in the Sikh population in Canada and in the Canadian labour force as compared to the data reported above for 1981. It should be noted, however, that the Sikhs remain a predominantly foreign-born population. Nearly two-thirds of the Sikh population in 1991 were immigrants. The data on educational attainment, labour force characteristics, and income are reported in the following pages. Comparative data are presented on two Indo-Canadian ethnic groups and all Canadians. The data on educational attainment (Table 7.8) indicate that about one in five Sikhs had less than grade 9 education as compared to 10.5 per cent Hindus, and nearly 14 per cent of all Canadians. These data also show that a significant proportion of Canadians had grade 9 to 13 education. For Sikhs the figure in this category was 38.9 per cent as compared to 36 per cent for Hindus, and 39 per cent for all Canadians. On the other hand, nearly 14 per cent Sikhs were university graduates as compared to 22 per cent Hindus, and

TABLE 7.8

EDUCATIONAL ATTAINMENT OF INDO-CANADIANS AND
ALL CANADIANS, 1991

(percentage)

Educational attainment	Indo-Canadians		All Canadians
	Sikhs	Hindus	
Less than grade 9	20.5	10.5	13.9
Grades 9 to 13	38.9	36.0	39.0
Trade school	16.6	20.3	26.2
Some university	10.2	11.2	9.4
Completed university	13.8	22.0	11.4
Total Number	108,167	115,000	21,258,347

Source: Compiled from the 1991 Census of Canada, Public Use Microdata File on Individuals, based on a 33.3 per cent probability sample of the population. The figures in this table have been weighted to population size.

TABLE 7.9

OCCUPATIONAL DISTRIBUTION OF INDO-CANADIANS AND
ALL CANADIANS IN THE EMPLOYED LABOUR FORCE, 1991*

(percentage)

Occupation	Indo-Canadians		All Canadians
	Sikhs	Hindus	
Managerial, administrative and related	5.0	8.2	9.5
Professional and technical	8.4	19.0	18.5
Clerical and related	10.5	19.0	16.9
Sales and service	26.4	23.7	26.0
Supervisors and related	3.0	3.1	5.4
Crafts, trades and other manual	46.6	27.0	23.7
Total Number	85,500	89,433	15,451,852

* Employed labour force, 15 years of age and over.
Source: Compiled from the 1991 Census of Canada, Public Use Microdata File on Individuals, based on a 33.3 per cent probability sample of the population. The figures in this table have been weighted to population size.

11.4 per cent of all Canadians. Also, a slightly higher proportion of Indo-Canadians than all Canadians have had some university education.

The data on occupational distribution (Table 7.9) show that Sikhs are less likely than others to be in managerial, administrative, professional, and technical occupations. Only 13.4 per cent of the Sikhs were in these occupations, compared to 27.2 per cent Hindus, and 28 per cent of all Canadians. Sikhs are also more likely than other groups to be in sales and service occupations. The differences between the Sikhs and other groups are particularly large with respect to crafts, trades, and manual occupations. Nearly 47 per cent of Sikhs were in these occupations, compared to 27 per cent Hindus, and almost 24 per cent of all Canadians.

Sikhs are more likely than the other two groups to be in agriculture, manufacturing, and construction, and in transportation and communication, but are less likely to be in the service sectors (Table 7.10). Over 10 per cent Sikhs were in agriculture, compared to less than 2 per cent Hindus, and 6 per cent of all Canadians. A higher percentage of Indo-Canadians, both Sikhs (31.9) and Hindus (27.8) than all Canadians (20.8) were in manufacturing and construction. A little over 33 per cent Sikhs were in the service sectors. A much higher percentage of Hindus (46.3) and all Canadians (48.5) worked in the service sectors. As in the case of occupational

TABLE 7.10

INDUSTRY CLASSIFICATION OF INDO-CANADIANS AND ALL CANADIANS
IN THE EMPLOYED LABOUR FORCE, 1991*

| | | | *(percentage)* |
| | Indo-Canadians | | All |
Industry	Sikhs	Hindus	Canadians
Agriculture and other primary industry	10.5	1.6	6.1
Manufacturing and construction	31.9	27.8	20.8
Transportation and communication	8.5	5.8	7.3
Trade (wholesale and retail)	15.9	18.5	17.3
Services	33.2	46.3	48.5
Total Number	85,500	89,433	15,451,852

* Employed labour force, 15 years of age and over.
Source: Compiled from the 1991 Census of Canada, Public Use Microdata File on Individuals, based on a 33.3 per cent probability sample of the population. The figures in this table have been weighted to population size.

distribution, the sectorial employment profile of Sikhs varies considerably from the other two groups.

TABLE 7.11

TOTAL INCOME OF INDO-CANADIANS AND ALL CANADIANS, 1991

(percentage)

Total income	Indo-Canadians		All Canadians
	Sikhs	*Hindus*	
Less than $10,000	41.0	41.9	33.9
$10,000–$19,999	25.3	19.8	22.3
$20,000–$29,999	14.5	17.2	16.6
$30,000–$39,999	9.6	9.3	11.7
$40,000 and over	9.6	11.8	15.5
Total Number	108,167	115,000	21,258,347

Source: Compiled from the 1991 Census of Canada, Public Use Microdata File on Individuals, based on a 33.3 per cent probability sample of the population. The figures in this table have been weighted to population size.

The data on income are reported in Table 7.11. Indo-Canadians are more likely than other Canadians to have lower incomes. Forty-one per cent Sikhs and about 42 per cent Hindus had incomes under $10,000, compared to about 34 per cent of all Canadians. A little over two-thirds of the Sikhs, and about 62 per cent of the Hindus had incomes below $20,000. The corresponding figure for all Canadians was a little over 56 per cent. Sikhs were less likely than the other two groups to have incomes in the top category; under 10 per cent Sikhs, close to 12 per cent Hindus, and 15.5 per cent of all Canadians had incomes of $40,000 and over. Indo-Canadians, both Sikhs and Hindus, are less likely than other Canadians to be in the top two income categories. A little over 19 per cent Sikhs, 21 per cent Hindus, and 27 per cent of all Canadians had incomes of $30,000 and over.

In general, these data suggest that notwithstanding better educational attainment (measured by university education), Indo-Canadians are less likely to be in managerial, administrative, and professional jobs, and more likely to have low-incomes, compared to all Canadians. These data also show variation in educational attainment, occupational and sectorial distribution, and income levels among the Indo-Canadians. In terms of occupational distributions and industry, Sikhs were concentrated in crafts, trades, and other manual jobs. Hindus, on the other hand, were concentrated in the service sectors.

MEDIA AND THE MINORITIES: PROBLEMETIZING THE SIKH COMMUNITY

The socio–economic status and public image of a community are a function of a number of factors including immigration policy, country of origin, their racial and ethnic background, and their employment opportunities and patterns. No less important is the role of the media in shaping public opinion and the perception of a community. This is particularly significant in the case of racial minority communities because of their often spatial and social isolation from the 'mainstream'. In the absence of personal contact and knowledge about the group, the general public perception and images may be based primarily upon what they see and read in the media. The media's construction and presentation of the issues and problems of a community are of particular significance in the case of minorities. Given the increased presence of racial minorities, the media's 'treatment' of these communities has come under critical scrutiny. The principal points of critique of the mainstream media include the relative absence of racial minorities in the media (invisibility of visible minorities), racialization of immigration policy, racialization of crime, stereotypical portrayal, miscasting and misrepresentation of minorities, and minorities as 'social problems' (Fleras and Elliott, 1992, 1999; Fleras and Kunz, 2001; Henry and Tator, 2002; Henry et al., 2001; Henry et al., 1995).

We do not intend to present here a detailed discussion of numerous aspects of media–minority relations, but confine our discussion to the coverage by the print media of specific gurdwara elections in British Columbia. We also do not attribute any deliberate malicious intent, motives, or conspiracy on the part of the reporters–columnists of these newspapers against the Sikh community in their reporting on the elections. Even when the media 'treats' and 'maligns' everyone and every community 'equally' in their quest to compete for circulation, the effect on the minorities of any negative coverage is greater because of their specific vulnerabilities.

From the headlines, use of language, and the media's construction of the issues, a particular image of the Sikh community emerges. This image is not particularly flattering. It characterizes the community as conflict and violence ridden, with a tendency to settle disagreements and disputes through violence; one with no aptitude for reasoning and democracy, as a 'troubled' community requiring inordinate use of public resources including the police and courts to maintain harmony and peace within it and to reduce its threat to the general public. The coverage is intense, repetitive, sensational, without substance, and devoid of analysis to inform and promote understanding of the issues.

The headlines and sub-headlines of the articles covering the Ross Street Gurdwara election included: 'Sikh Temple Dispute Ends in 2 Arrests: Trouble escalates at Vancouver's Ross Street site when fundamentalists attempt to push aside tables and chairs' (*Vancouver Sun*, Monday, 27 July 1998:B1); 'Police Hope For Calm as Sikh Temple Reopens: They are investigating why a rifle and box of shells were found inside a closet' (*Vancouver Sun*, Saturday, 8 Aug. 1998:B4); 'Locked Out: Police Stopped a Vote at the Ross Street Temple Yesterday After Scuffle Broke Out. Several People Received Minor Injuries' (*Province*, Monday, 30 Aug. 1999, Front page headlines); 'Cops Interfered: Sikh Leader: Ross Street President claims victory after vote cut short amid scuffles' (*Province*, Monday, 30 Aug. 1999: A3). The national newspapers characterized the situation with similar headlines, for example, 'Fearing Violence, Police Shut Doors of a Temple Divided' (*Globe and Mail*, Tuesday, 4 Aug. 1998:B1); 'Police Halt Vote After Violence Erupts at Sikh Temple' (*National Post*, Monday, 30 Aug. 1999:A4).

The election was a daily 'play by play' contest, who is on top between moderates and fundamentalists, and who has won the latest skirmish between these two contending factions. Framing the main issue as a conflict between the moderates and radicals simplified the reporting, for example, 'Sikh Election Hopeful Gets Death Threat. The target is Jarnail Singh Bhandal, a moderate presidential candidate ...' (*Vancouver Sun*, Saturday, 21 Nov. 1998:A3); 'Moderates Sweep Elections at Ross Street Temple' (*Vancouver Sun*, Monday, 7 Dec. 1998); 'Moderates at Sikh Temple Face Challenge Over Voting' (*Vancouver Sun*, Monday, 5 April 1999:B3).

Continuation of skirmishes and squabbles between the moderates and the fundamentalists in courts were the subject of other headlines, for example, 'Sikh Temple to Close Indefinitely'. Religious leaders say they are receiving legal counsel about taking the matter to court' (*Vancouver Sun*, Wednesday, 5 Aug. 1998:B1); 'Moderates Ask Court to Reopen Sikh Temple' (*Vancouver Sun*, 6 Aug. 1998:B1); 'Judge Gives Temple Control to Moderates": The winning side is overjoyed by the court's decision while fundamentalists say the religious dispute is far from over. The temple was closed by police after threats of violence were made' (*Vancouver Sun*, 7 Aug. 1998:B1).

Similar patterns of newspaper coverage of elections in the other principal Sikh gurdwaras are evident from the headlines. This is a picture of violence and police involvement, and a battle between the moderates and the fundamentalists. Headlines of the Abbotsford Gurdwara election included: '"Fight Shuts Temple": Abbotsford police arrest four after man stabbed in belly with dagger. Charges Expected Today in Sikh Temple Stabbing' (*Province*, Monday, 24 August 1998:A1, A3); 'Sikh Temple Closed After Stabbing, Arrests' (*Vancouver Sun*, Monday, 24 Aug. 1998:A1); '"Alleged Sikh Fundamentalist Charged in Stabbing at Temple": The 37–year-old suspect was released in his own recognizance. The wounded man was reported in stable condition in hospital'. (*Vancouver Sun*, Tuesday, 25 Aug. 1998:A3); '"Police to Monitor Site of Sikh Vote": Abbotsford officers will be on hand Sunday to keep the peace in an election that some link to a murder'. (*Vancouver Sun*, Saturday, 21 Nov. 1998:B6); 'Sikh Vote Under Police Watch in Wake of Moderate's Murder' (*Globe and Mail*, Monday, 23 Nov. 1998:A5).

The Abbotsford Gurdwara election was also characterized as a skirmish between the moderates and the fundamentalists over the principal issue of 'tables and chairs'. For example, headlines in the Vancouver Sun read: '"Sikh Vote Overseer Appointed": Abbotsford lawyer sees the election as a means to heal wounds in the community (Friday, 18 Sep. 1998:B3); 'Sikh Temple Election Battle Heating Up in Abbotsford' (Wednesday, 4 Nov. 1998:B3). The other provincial newspaper, *Province*, headlined: '"Sikh Election Uneasy": This is no protest says fundamentalist leader as group demonstrates. That would come later if we're not being heard' (Sunday, 11 Oct. 1998:A3).

Other headlines included: 'Moderate Sikhs Want Chair Removers Charged' (*Vancouver Sun*, Friday, 26 June 1998:B6); 'Sikh Opponents Hold Own Rallies in Abbotsford: Extremism condemned at rally' (*Vancouver Sun*, Monday, 20 July 1998:B1, B3)'. '"Temple Victorious Moderates Plan to Take Control": While the moderate slate won Sunday's election at Abbotsford Sikh Temple, fundamentalists have occupied the building since June when they removed tables and chairs from the dining hall' (*Vancouver Sun*, Wednesday, 25 Nov. 1998:B3); '"Tables and Chairs Returned to Abbotsford Sikh Temple": Temple leaders hope to avoid any clashes' (*Vancouver Sun*, Thursday, 3 Dec. 1998:B1, B4).

The principal themes of conflict and violence appear in headlines about the Surrey Gurdwara as well, 'RCMP Shut, Scour Temple. Four Suspects, One a Fugitive, Face Charges in Bloody Sikh Riot' (*Province*, Monday, 13 Jan. 1997:1); '"Timetable of Violence at Temple in Surrey": As moderates tried to carry in furniture, swords flashed and people fell bleeding' (*Vancouver Sun*, Monday, 13 Jan. 1997:B3); '"Three Charged in Riot at Temple Ordered Held": 4th Suspect Surrenders to Police' (*Vancouver Sun*, Tuesday, 14 Jan. 1997:A1, A4); '"Police Occupying Sikh Temple Seek End to Standoff": Four men appear in court today to face charges stemming from Saturday's bloody riot in Surrey. Members Fear for Their Lives' (*Vancouver Sun*, Wednesday, 15 Jan. 1997:A1).

The incidence of 'bloody Sikh riots', 'Saturday's bloody riot in Surrey', 'Members fear for their lives', and 'violent clash' appear again in a somewhat different form in reports covering court proceedings. The Sikh temple 'Melee Case' was extensively reported as illustrated in the following headlines: 'Temple Violence Recalled in Court' (*Vancouver Sun*, Wednesday, 14 Oct. 1998); '"Temple Trial Hears Swords Drawn as Furniture Broken": Witness says he can identify all 10 of those charged in connection with violent incident in 1996' (*Vancouver Sun*, Wednesday, 14 Oct. 1998:B3); 'Tape of Temple Fight Shown at Trial. Officer Identifies One of the Accused as Masked Man Carrying Metal Paddle' (*Vancouver Sun*, Tuesday, 22 January 1999:B1, B3); '"Election Losers Caused Temple Melee, Court Told": Accused Denies Stabbing Moderate' (*Vancouver Sun*, 22 January 1999:B1, B3); '"Judge Weight Verdict in Sikh Temple Melee Case": Four Sikh fundamentalists face a variety of charges, including attempted murder and assault, in connection with a bloody fight at the Guru Nanak temple in Surrey just over two years ago. Verdict Due to be Given Feb. 12' (*Vancouver Sun*, Friday, 29 January 1999:B1, B3); '"Temple Fracas Suspects Cleared": While one man was convicted of possessing a weapon, three others were cleared of charges as judge cited witness inconsistencies' (*Vancouver Sun*, Saturday, 13 Feb. 1999:B5).

Even the most benign news of an election win by the moderates are blemished with messages of 'divided' and 'troubled': 'Moderates Win in Peaceful Vote at Divided B.C. Sikh Temple' (*Globe and Mail*, Tuesday, 26 Oct. 1999:A5); 'Sikhs Return Moderate to Head Troubled Temple—Elections Were Fractious' (*National Post*, Tuesday, 26 Oct. 1999:A8).

Headlines covering other stories of Sikhs conjured up images of violence, arson, fear and law violation, for example: 'Controversial Khalsa School Director's Vehicle Torched' (*Vancouver Sun*, Thursday, 15 Oct. 1998:B7);

"'Edmonton Sikhs Fear B.C. Style Violence": Members of the community say there are fewer tensions than in Vancouver but that could change quickly' (*Vancouver Sun*, Saturday, 17 July 1999:B4); and "'Sikh Temple Open Despite Not Having City Permit": The Surrey temple used by fundamentalists continued holding events in spite of citations. Sikh Temple Lacks Several Permits' (*Vancouver Sun*, Thursday, 9 July 1998:B1, B4).

The images of Sikhs as conflict-ridden remained in newspaper headlines when the top high priest of Sikhism from the Golden Temple in Amritsar, Punjab, India, issued a religious edict against the use of chairs and tables for community meals (*langar*) in the temples. Whether to use chairs and tables or to sit on the floor for *langar* was identified with the two 'warring' factions in gurdwara politics, the moderates and the fundamentalists, respectively. The issue of religious edict to remove chairs and tables and excommunication of those who refused to do so remained in the headlines for some time. For instance, the *Globe and Mail* carried the story(ies) under headlines: "'B.C. Sikh Leaders Ousted Over Temple Dispute": High priest excommunicates men after refusal to remove tables and chairs: President [Sikh temple] vows to ignore decision' (Monday, 27 July 1998:A3); "'Ruling Hits Canadian Sikhs": Traditionalists win bitter dispute' (Tuesday, 28 April 1998:A1); "'Sikh Leaders in Western Canada Fight Religious Edict": 1997 Surrey temple brawl sparks order for removal of tables and chairs in power struggle between moderates and traditionalists' (Tuesday, 19 May 1998:A3); and "'Moderate Sikhs Defy Order to Sit on the Floor": Several elders risk excommunication to use chairs and tables in the temple's dining rooms' (Saturday, 30 May 1998:A2).

The *Vancouver Sun* also covered this event. For example: 'Sikh Groups Demanding Resignation of High Priest. Majority Wants to Keep Chairs, Tables, Vote Shows' (Wednesday, 27 May 1998:B1,B3); "'Punjab Leaders Come to Defence of Canadians": Leaders in Punjab have called for the resignation of a Sikh high priest over his excommunication decision' (Tuesday, 4 August 1998:B4); "'Sikh Excommunication in Dispute": Two of Sikhism's five high priests in India disagree with the way six B.C. leaders had their religion stripped from them. The priests refuse to participate in subsequent excommunication meetings' (Friday, 21 August 1998:B1,B3); 'Sikh High Priest Demands Answers from Moderates' (Friday, 6 November 1998:B6); "'Indian High Priest Urged To Resign": A moderate elected despite his excommunication says officials in India are guilty of fuming division' (Monday, 7 Dec. 1998:B4).

The *Vancouver Sun* continued to focus on conflict, fear and volatility in the Sikh community in their headlines on the visit of the 'controversial High Priest' to the United States, and the 'moderates' fear' that this would 'stir up divisions' in the 'already volatile Sikh community'. "'Sikhism's Controversial High Priest to Visit U.S.:'": Moderate Sikhs fear that Ranjit Singh may attempt to visit Canada and he may use his first-ever foreign visit to further stir up divisions in British Columbia's already volatile Sikh community' (Monday, 4 Jan. 1999:A3); "'U.S. Officials Will Monitor Visit by Controversial Sikh": Officials say high priest Ranjit Singh's conviction for the murder of a religious rival is insufficient grounds to bar him' (Tuesday, 5 Jan. 1999:A3). The paper also carried headlines of the meeting between the high priest 'who ordered [Canadian] Sikhs to eat on the floor' and Canadian High Commission officials (*Vancouver Sun*, Saturday, 23 Jan. 1999:A4).

The negative depiction of the Sikh community continued after the unfortunate and tragic murder of Tara Singh Hayer. The theme of conflict between the moderates and radicals remained the primary context of headlines and sub-headlines in newspapers. For example: "'Moderate Sikh Publisher Shot Dead in His Garage'": An assassination attempt against Tara Singh Hayer a decade ago left him in a wheelchair. Publisher Lauded for Fight for Liberty' (*Vancouver Sun*, Thursday, 19 Nov. 1998:A1,A2); 'Moderate Backlash Likely After Sikh Murder' (*Vancouver Sun*, Saturday, November 21, 1998:A1); 'Publisher Fought Against Sikh Radicals' (*StarPhoenix* (Saskatoon), Saturday, 21 Nov. 1998:A14).

Other headlines alluded to a 'hit list' of moderate Sikhs and a 'link' between Hayer's assassination in Surrey and one in England. The *Vancouver Sun* headlines read: "'Police Examining Sikh Hit List in Wake of Hayer Assassination'": Seven names, including those of moderate Sikhs excommunicated by an Indian priest, and a reporter, are said to be on the list' (Friday, 20 Nov. 1998:A1); "'Link Suspected in Two Sikh Killings'": The murder of Surrey Sikh editor was similar to the still unsolved killing in 1995 of a fellow Sikh editor in England' (Saturday, 28 Nov. 1998:A1). *The Province* headline, on the other hand, two days after the *Vancouver Sun* read: "'No Evidence of Hit List: Police'": Potential for violence but no formal roll of names, RCMP says' (Sunday, 22 Nov. 1998:A22). However, *The Province* added its own intrigue and mystery in headlines on the same page: "'Is His Killer on the Tapes?'" Sikh editor's home-surveillance videos scanned by cops for clues to his murder'.

The newspaper editorials, forums, and headlines continued to project

Tara Singh Hayer as an independent voice of moderation: 'Martyr to Moderation. Hayer: An example of Fearless Journalism': 'Death Threats Taken in Stride'; 'The Fearless and Fatalistic Voice' (*Vancouver Sun*, 20 Nov. 1998:a1,A20); and 'B.C. Civil Liberties Group Honours Assassinated Newspaper Publisher' (*Vancouver Sun*, Thursday, 11 March 1999:B1,B3).

There appear to be common themes in all the headlines and stories about Sikhs, be it about the Sikh gurdwaras, or the high priest's edict or Hayer's assassination. In almost every instance the conflict and contradictions are reduced to a battle between the fundamentalists and the moderates, and the issue of religious convictions and traditions reduced to 'tables and chairs' and 'floor' relating to the community *langar* (meals). The political conflict in Punjab, India, regarding Khalistan (independent Sikh homeland) and the links to Sikhs in Canada figured prominently in a few articles. The central thrust and implications of these articles were that the politics of the home country is being played out in Canada and that the Sikhs have inappropriately brought their troubles and problems with them to this country, that these links are inappropriate, and that these political and religious conflicts pose a threat to peace and security in Canada. The content remained basically the same in all articles over time, but under different headlines.

The distinction between fundamentalists and moderates, though never clearly enunciated and defined, by inference is made on the basis of their commitment to establish Khalistan, political means to achieve their goal, and adherence to Sikh traditions. For instance, fundamentalists are defined by their commitment to the creation of Khalistan even by violent means and their strict adherence to Sikh traditions, including eating *langar* while seated on the floor. The moderates, on the other hand, are those who are less likely to support Khalistan and use violence in their political cause, and are more likely to support 'reforms' such as eating *langar* on tables and chairs. Moderates are also seen to be 'modern', 'adjusted', to the 'Canadian ways' and 'progressive', and most of them arrived in Canada before the 1970s. Fundamentalists mostly arrived in Canada after the 1970s, and are often seen as 'traditionalists' in their 'dress' and 'appearance' and 'not adjusted' to 'Canadian ways'.

The recent newspaper articles are not unique. The headlines of articles in *The Province* on Sikhs in 1985 (cited in Henry et al., 1995:326) included: 'Guns Alarm Cops' (27 March 1985); 'Close Watch on City Sikhs' (20 Oct.1985); 'Sikh Militancy Grows' (7 Nov. 1985). The Sikhs have been in the headlines off and on ever since the downing of the Air India flight over the North Atlantic in 1985. More recent headlines, with photographs of two suspected Sikhs on the front page of the *Globe* and *Mail* (28 Oct. 2000) read: '"Air India Suspects Charged": RCMP arrests two after 15–year probe of jetliner bombing that killed 329'. A third suspect who was extradited from England has also been charged. The trial of these suspects in a specially renovated courthouse in Vancouver for security reasons is likely to keep the Sikhs in the news for some time in the future.

While we have pointed to some selected events and their coverage in the newspapers, particularly in B.C., other headlines also project a negative image of the community. For instance, '"Gangland Slayings Confound B.C. Police": Violence among young Indo-Canadians tied to turf wars over lucrative drug trade' (*Globe and Mail*, Friday, 4 Jan. 2002:A5); '"One Dead, Four Hurt in Wedding Shooting": Richmond RCMP Suspect Gangland Slaying' (*Vancouver Sun*, Monday, 24 Dec. 2001:A1). These headlines portray the image of a community involved in the 'drug trade' and 'gang turf wars'.

The incidents of domestic abuse and homicides in the Indo-Canadian community are often presented in the context of the cultural, religious and ethnic background of the accused and the victims. This often turns to an 'attack' and 'blame' on the system of 'arranged marriage', loss of 'honour', and 'face', and 'shame' embedded in Indian culture. These incidents are not seen as the aberrant acts of individuals and individual responsibility as is the case with the mainstream community but rather as the product of the minority community's culture and customs, and present a stereotypical, monolithic, static, and deterministic image of culture and behaviour. The often unintended consequence and negative outcome of such an analysis goes far beyond the few visible incidents occurring within the minority community. Indeed, the entire community is maligned and stereotyped for the acts of a few individuals. In a way this also keeps the focus on the place of origin (where they are from) of minorities, who are often seen as 'outsiders' rather than 'real Canadians' (Fleras and Kunz, 2001).

The news media employ double standards in covering minorities and 'often hold entire communities accountable for the actions of individuals; by contrast, mainstream actions are regarded as the actions of individuals who have fallen outside the orbit of normalcy', and 'individual minority women and men tend to be portrayed as representatives of their race when they fail, yet are often deemed to be an exception when they succeed' (Fleras and Kunz, 2001:84). The success of a few in politics, academia, business, the arts, and other fields may not have a positive impact on social status and image of the whole community because they are seen as an 'exception to the rule'. Those who are successful are even 'held up' as an example of the 'openness' of Canadian society, where there is equality of opportunity for all regardless of individuals' background, and racism, prejudice, and discrimination are things of the past.

COMMUNITY CONFLICT AND IMMIGRATION CONTROLS

Some editorials and forums even used the political and religious conflicts and other incidents within the Sikh community to argue that violence is 'distinctly non-Canadian', and places extra demands on public safety services and 'brings out the anti-immigration crowd' and even a 'push' for 'reforming sloppy [immigration] laws'. For instance, an editorial in the *Vancouver Sun* (Tuesday, 14 Jan. 1997:A12) entitled "'Limited Tolerance": Violence in the name of doctrinal purity is distinctly non-Canadian' reads in part:

One can arrive without suitcase but not, so to speak, without baggage. And, by and large, a good thing. A country like Canada needs fresh energies and new faces—not replicas.

But not old, and distant, quarrels. Not power struggles between factions violently arguing over doctrinal purity and practices. Least of all internecine bloodshed over such matters. Canada is among the most generous of nations. But nothing loses the sympathy of Canadians faster—and brings out the anti-immigrant crowd braying louder—than the kind of melee that exploded at Surrey's Guru Nanak Sikh Temple on Saturday.

The editorial continues,

Doubtless there are peaceful fundamentalists and battling moderates. The litmus test of support for an independent Sikh homeland carved out of India's Punjab region and called Khalistan is quite unreliable. Most Sikhs under both rubrics support the idea, but with wide variances of fervor, at the bottom end including funding for terrorism abroad. Apart from ethnic East Indians, few Canadians have any opinion about the Khalistan issue ....

No, the issue for the larger community, the point where intolerance becomes intolerable is simply violence. It isn't enough to shrug off the matter as a Sikh one that Sikhs can settle or unsettle as they choose. No violence is, or long will remain, internecine. The shot fired at the house of the moderate faction's leader last week was fired at all Canadians—endangering beyond symbolism, his neighbors as well as his family. The police who predictably were harshly harangued by both factions, on one side for acting at all and on the other for not acting forcefully enough, cannot be expected to serve as society's on-the-spot arbitrators.

The editorial adds:

The taxpayers cannot be expected to pay cheerfully for extra public safety services in an ostensible religious dispute over whether temple members should eat at tables or on the floor.

It concludes:

Charges have been laid. Due process will be followed. But in the end the individual Sikhs must decide. What loyalties? What values?

If they fail to answer such questions clearly, and if the history of this internationally praised and pragmatically successful country is any gauge, their children, mingling with children from many backgrounds, will answer for them.

A couple of articles on the Forum page of the *Vancouver Sun* (Saturday, 21 Nov. 1998:A23), one under the headline 'Learning Lessions From A Murder": An immigration specialist argues Tara Singh Hayer's assassination should spur Canadians to push Ottawa on reforming sloppy laws' and the other, '"Canada's Great Shame: Our Immigration Policies": We invite assassination and other crimes by opening our doors too easily to thugs and granting them rights', used Hayer's assassination, and the presence and activities of terrorist groups in Canada to argue that immigration laws be reformed and citizenship requirements tightened.

The first article considers the murder of Tara Singh Hayer 'a tragedy for all Canadians' and not just a violent act within the Punjabi community. The article states that Hayer was killed because 'he stood for moderation and fair play' and for values 'fundamental to civilized society everywhere'. The article praised Hayer for his courage and fight for justice and peace and characterized him as 'truly a Canadian hero by any standards'. In spite of Hayer's warnings of the threats of terrorist groups in this country, Canada failed to protect him or deter the activities of terrorist groups. The article used the testimony before a senate committee by the Director of the Canadian Security Intelligence Service to state 'that all of the world's major Sikh terrorist groups as well as others such as Hamas and the Tamil Tigers have been or are still active in Canada', and 'that the nature of our [Canadian] society and the related policies concerning refugees and immigrants make us particularly vulnerable to terrorist influence and activities'. This article also appealed for support for Hayer's daughter's petition for submission to parliament, 'to strengthen our laws to keep terrorists and criminals out of Canada and to remove them speedily when they are discovered'. The article concluded:

In allowing terrorists and other criminals to exploit our immigration and refugee system to establish themselves in Canada and carry on their operations from here we are helping to create disaster—even though it may be less immediately apparent than other problems. Canadians must demand now that Ottawa deals with these matters in a serious manner. We owe at least this much to the memory of Tara Singh Hayer.

The second article on the same Forum page of the *Vancouver Sun* continued the theme of strong action against terrorists and criminals, of strengthening immigration laws and citizenship requirements. The article starts with an expression of 'Outrage, total outrage' about Hayer's assassination and argues for a 'new policy of total war on terrorists and other immigrant criminals and no-goods' and to avenge his appalling murder with a 'rock-ribbed legislation that sends a powerful message to the world and to the contemptible immigrants who violate Canada's compassion and generosity'. The article chastises 'feckless politicians [who] must get a grip on their responsibilities' and immigrant lawyers who 'try to foil every attempt to clean out the thugs and scoundrels'. Further, the Canadian parliament must negate the Supreme Court 1985 judgment that extended protection of the Canadian Charter of Rights and Freedoms to foreigners when they land in Canada; and to establish a new, non-political and credible Board of 'average' Canadians to judge and examine the quality and suitability of immigrants for citizenship using standards of 'civil suits' rather than the higher standards of 'beyond a reasonable doubt'. The article argues for speedy deportation of immigrants and not to wait until they are convicted of major offenses. The author favours what he calls a 'good citizenship' test, to deport the 'unworthy and ungrateful' that would include the public threat of violence, and favours the extension of the period of what he calls 'conditional citizenship' (such as 15 years) before granting permanent citizenship. The article concludes:

My bet is that law-abiding, hard-working immigrants would be among the strongest supporters of such 'tough' action. The only threat would be to the bad ones—and to this country's spineless political class and others who wet themselves fearing a lower rating by the United Nations. This Canadian has had enough.

The headlines and the use of language in the editorial and the Forum articles sensationalize specific incidents and events within the Sikh community. Their contents are not particularly informative and lack any serious contextual analysis to inform and promote an understanding of issues confronting the community. The juxtapositioning of 'Canada among the most generous nations', 'compassion and generosity', 'distinctly non-Canadian', with 'murder', 'old and distant quarrels', 'violence', 'murder', 'internecine bloodshed', 'melee that exploded', 'endangering all Canadians', 'extra public safety services', 'terrorists and criminals', 'assassination and other crimes', 'world's major Sikh terrorist groups' helps to make the case for 'rock-ribbed legislation' 'to keep terrorists and criminals out' and even suspend due process and protection of the Charter of Rights and Freedoms to 'deport the unworthy and ungrateful'. This juxtaposition and portrayal criminalizes the entire community, reinforces stereotypes and leads to racialization of immigration policy and immigration controls.

SOCIAL IMAGE OF SIKHS AND OTHER RACIAL MINORITIES

The collective social standing of various racial and ethnic groups is a product of many factors. These include nationality and country of origin, racial categorization, racialized hierarchy of acceptability of immigrants and their location in the labour market (Bolaria and Li, 1988; Li, 1998). Racial minorities are more likely than people of European origin to be ranked low in terms of their personal and social attributes such as 'clean', 'likeable', 'hardworking', and 'competent', and to have lower social standing than Europeans (Berry, Kalin and Taylor, 1976; Filson, 1983; Li, 1979; Pineo, 1977; Foschi and Buchan, 1990). The results of a 1991 national attitudinal survey about degrees of 'comfort' with various social groups are quite revealing. The data in Table 7.12 show that white ethnic groups had relatively higher social ranking than the racial minority groups irrespective of their place of birth or immigrant status. A large proportion of respondents indicated the highest comfort levels with those of British origin and the lowest proportion of respondents with the Sikhs. For example, 83 per cent of the respondents indicated having the highest comfort levels being around immigrants of British origin and only 43 per cent said so for the Sikhs. A uniformly lower proportion of respondents indicated the 'highest comfort levels' with immigrants and Canadian-born racial minorities such as blacks, Muslims, Arabs, Indo-Pakistanis, and Sikhs as compared to groups such as British, Italian, French, and German. That racial minorities

TABLE 7.12

RANKING OF SELECTED IMMIGRANT ETHNIC GROUPS AND
CANADIAN-BORN ETHNIC GROUPS BY PERCENTAGE OF RESPONDENTS
WHO INDICATED HAVING THE HIGHEST COMFORT LEVELS BEING
AROUND INDIVIDUALS FROM EACH GROUP

Origin being evaluated	Immigrant ethnic group	Canadian-born ethnic group
British	83	86
Italian	77	83
French	74	82
Jewish	74	78
Ukrainian	73	79
German	72	79
Portuguese	70	76
Chinese	69	77
Native Canadians	–	77
West Indian Black	61	69
Muslim	49	58
Arab	52	63
Indo-Pakistani	48	59
Sikh	43	55

Source: 'Multiculturalism and Canadians: Attitude Study 1991', National Survey Report; Submitted by Angus Reid Group, Inc. to Multiculturalism and Citizenship, Canada, August 1991, p. 51.

have lower social status (ranking) than the white ethnics in Canada is revealed by such surveys. Canadians also continue to attribute differential personal and social qualities to individuals and groups with racial and national backgrounds and religious affiliations other than their own.

VICTIMIZATION AND CRIMINALIZATION OF
'LOOK-ALIKE' MINORITIES

It was noted previously that in the case of minorities, the entire community is held accountable for the actions of a few individuals. This is particularly so when the actions and activities conjure up images of conflict, violence, terrorism, and threats to public safety. These images reinforce prejudice not only against the community in question but also against other 'look-alike' minorities. For instance, the repetition of negative images and stereotypes of Sikhs reinforce prejudice against all South Asians (Khaki and Parsad, 1988).

The vulnerability of minority communities became quite evident after the attack on the World Trade Centre in September 2001 (now commonly called 9/11). Since the attackers were identified as Muslims of Arab background ('Talibans'), others who shared this faith and background became objects of surveillance, police interrogation, and of hostility and assault by ordinary citizens. Even some places of worship were attacked. The post-9/11 incidents and actions of law enforcement agencies provide a clear illustration of how a whole community is held accountable for the actions of the few.

In this case, the members of other minority communities who resembled ('look-alike') 'Talibans' were also attacked. For instance, immediately after the 9/11 attack, numerous news stories of attacks on Sikhs, including one homicide of Balbir Singh Sodhi in Arizona, were reported. According to one source, Sikhs and other Asian Americans faced 243 attacks in the three months following 11 September (*Hindustan Times*, Sunday, 7 April 2002). Sikhs were especially targeted because they had beards and turbans. One Sikh website puts the number of attacks on Sikhs alone to be 277 in a seven-month period (*Hindustan Times*, Sunday, 7 April 2002). The Sikh leaders were compelled to condemn the attack and demonstrate their 'solidarity with the American people' and disassociate themselves from the Muslims and Arabs. In a demonstration the participants carried placards that said, 'Sikhs are not Muslims', and 'Bush Educate the American People that Sikhs are not Muslims or Arabs' (www.redif.com/US/2001/Sep/17ny30.htm). Religious and community leaders were compelled to defend their faiths and demonstrate their loyalty to America.

'Sikh booted off flight for staring at passenger', read a headline (*StarPhoenix*, Saturday, 17 Nov. 2001:A14). The newspaper article began by stating: 'A Canadian Sikh won't quickly forget his planned Remembrance Day business flight to Dallas'. He and his colleague were ordered off a US Airways flight from Toronto to Dallas for staring at a passenger. The airline later apologized and conceded that he was 'wrongly denied' boarding. These incidents are manifestations of 'racial profiling' of 'look-alike' minorities and 'racialization of terrorist crimes'.

In their 'war against terrorism' the United States and its allies are considering further legislative measures to restrict and control visitors from Islamic/Muslim/Arab countries and fingerprint and photograph them upon entry. Persons of certain nationalities, names and religions, who 'fit the profile' of the 11 September attackers will face excessive scrutiny and surveillance because they are 'most likely to be associated with terrorists' and 'most likely to commit terrorist acts'. These extraordinary and extreme measures and racial profiling are justified because the 'world has changed since September 11', and are 'necessary and desirable' under the circumstances. Under the headline, 'Only Whites Defend Racial Profiling', Heather Mallick makes the point 'that those who defend racial profiling always seem to be white', and 'people are very often in favour of unpleasant things that are not going to be applied to them' (*Globe and Mail*, Saturday, 8 June 2002:F3).

Racial profiling of terrorists, creating a list of suspected terrorist groups, organizations, and individuals will create conditions and provide justification for preventive detention, criminal prosecution, and compelled testimony, among other actions, against those who are 'profiled' and are 'suspected' of 'association' with and 'support' of persons and organizations on this list (Winsor, 2001). Others have argued that the term terrorist is imprecise, ambiguous and subject to political manipulation and has been used as a synonym for 'rebellion, street battles, civil strife, insurrection, rural guerilla war, *coup d'etat* and a dozen other things', and consequently has 'become almost meaningless, covering almost any and not necessarily political acts of violence' and that 'terrorism is a term without legal significance' (Aiken, 2000; Higgins and Flory, 1997). Even the Federal courts have ruled that terrorism is 'not capable of a legal definition that would be neutral and non-discriminatory in its application' (Aiken and Brouwer, 2001:A15). The 'war against terrorism' may also be used to provide 'cover' for Western and some developing countries to enact legislation to even criminalize legal and legitimate political dissent. The state, in the name of maintaining law and order and public safety, may claim the right to use force and extra-legal means and may label opponents as 'terrorists' to justify 'state terrorism'.

As is often said, 'one person's terrorist is another person's freedom fighter'. How one is labelled depends upon political differences and which side 'we' support. This is clearly demonstrated by the immediate past history of Afghanistan. Some of the very individuals and groups now 'terrorist' were once true 'freedom fighters' supported by the US against the then Soviet Union, and when in power Pakistan was their primary ally.

In short, minority communities in the post-9/11 period find themselves not only victimized but also criminalized simply because of a common faith, nationality, and because they 'look alike'.

RACE AND COLOUR MATTER

The discussion in the previous sections of this chapter indicates that there is considerable variation in the labour market profiles of immigrants and the Canadian-born population and that the occupational profiles and labour force participation of immigrants vary by their place of origin and educational attainment. Findings also show that in spite of the higher educational achievement of visible minorities, they face disadvantage and inequality in the labour market, and low earnings. These general findings are supported by many other studies (see for example, Abella, 1984; Li, 1998, 2000, 2001; Lian and Matthews, 1998; Henry, Tator, Mattis and Rees, 2001; Henry and Ginsberg, 1985; Kunz, Milan, and Schetagne, 2000; Pendakur and Pendakur, 1996; Basavarajappa and Varma, 1985; Beaujot, Basavarajappa and Verma, 1988; Boyd, 2001; Satzewich, 2000; Seassa, 1994; Vorst et al., 1991). Race and colour matter in the life chances of individuals and social groups.

Pendakur and Pendakur (1996), using 1991 census data, concluded: 'Even when controlling for occupation, industry, education, potential experience, CMA (Census Metropolitan Area), official language knowledge, and household type, we find that visible minorities earn significantly less than native-born White workers in Canada' (Pendakur and Pendakur, 1996:19). Lian and Matthews (1998:476) conclude: 'All our evidence suggests that, while our traditional "vertical mosaic" of ethnic differences may be disappearing, it has been replaced by a strong "coloured mosaic" of racial differences in terms of income rewards and income benefits'. Based upon their evidence, they further 'conclude that there is some considerable level of racial discrimination in Canada in terms of financial rewards for educational achievement' (Lian and Matthews, 1998:476).

Foreign-born, highly educated, skilled and professional workers have been an important source to meet the labour force needs in Canada. Without these workers there would have been a substantial shortfall in this area (Bolaria, 1987, 1992, 1995; Li, 1992). While migration provides employment and career opportunities for professional workers, they also encounter numerous constraints and disadvantages in the labour market

(Battershill, 1993; Mata, 1994; Fernando and Prasad, 1986). Due recognition and evaluation of their credentials is one of the principal obstacles faced by foreign-born professionals, particularly visible minority professionals and those with credentials from developing countries (Basran and Zong, 1998; Li, 2000). This contributes to their occupational disadvantage and and hinders career advancement, leads to downward social mobility and under-utilization of human capital (Basran and Zong, 1998). These professionals often end up in less desirable locations, and in the marginal and least sought-after positions in their respective professions (Bolaria, 1995). Some professionals do not even find jobs in their areas of expertise: 'Doctors, lawyers and engineers end up delivering pizza, driving cabs or telemarketing in tough job market' (*Globe and Mail*, Monday, 24 May 1999:B3). Other authors have also made the point about devaluation of foreign professional credentials and educational attainment and degrees (Basavarajappa and Verma, 1985; Rajagopal, 1990). This lack of full and due recognition of credentials provides an explanation for low earnings of Asian immigrants and their being less likely to be in professional and managerial occupations despite their relatively high educational achievements. Kunz, Milan, and Schetagne (2000:1) note in 'Report Highlights': 'Foreign-born visible minorities experience greater discrepancies between their education levels and their occupations, compared to other groups. Less than half of foreign-born visible minorities who have a university education work in jobs with a high skill level'. The higher education yields fewer payoffs for foreign-born visible minorities. They earned, on average, only 78 cents for every dollar earned by their non-racialized counterparts (Kunz, Milan, and Schetagne, 2000).

A number of studies indicate that visible minorities face discrimination in hiring, access to and referral from employment agencies, and post-employment practices of employers in the workplace (see, for example: Henry, Tator, Mattis, and Rees, 2001; Jain, 1988; Jain and Hackett, 1989; Henry, 1989; Henry and Ginsberg, 1985; James, 1999).

Foreign-born workers, particularly racial minority workers, have become an important and perhaps sole source of labour in certain sectors of the Canadian economy. Some workers are imported for specific tasks in specific sectors where, because of low pay, arduous work, and an unsafe and unhealthy work environment, indigenous workers are unwilling to venture. Workers under the 'non-immigrant work authorization programme' facilitate recruitment under specific contractual obligations to work on certain jobs for a specified period of time (Bolaria and Li, 1988; Bolaria and Bolaria, 1994). For instance, in agriculture, domestic work, and garment work, racial minority men and women are an important source of labour (see for example: Arat-Koc, 1999; Bolaria and Bolaria, 1994; Das Gupta, 1996; Basran, Gill, and MacLean, 1995). Both the living and working conditions of farm labour are 'dangerous to their health'. Unsafe and unsanitary living conditions and exposure to dangerous chemicals (pesticides, herbicides) contribute to excessive physical health problems, injuries and premature death (Bolaria and Bolaria, 1994; Basran, Gill and MacLean, 1995).

A significant proportion of homeworkers and contract shop employees in the garment industry are immigrant racial minority women workers. In 1995, women constituted 76 per cent of garment workers; 50 per cent were immigrants and 30 per cent racial minority women (Delahanty, 1999; Yanz et al., 1999). The restructuring of the garment and knitting industry from factory to home-sewing contractual work has led to a decline in union membership from 81,000 in 1980 to 38,000 in 1992 (Delahanty, 1999; Yanz et al., 1999). This restructuring has meant further exploitation of workers in this sector. They are often characterized as an 'invisible labour force', 'invisible segments of production', and 'captive and underpaid labour force' (Lipsig-Mumme, 1987; Johnson and Johnson, 1982; Morokvasic et al., 1986; Phizacklea, 2002). Writing about British Columbia under the headlines 'The Clothes Behind Closed Doors: as union rolls shrink, exploitation of garment workers is growing', Beck (1995:13) states: 'Punjabi women were making $2 to $4 per hour knitting fake Cowichan sweaters that retail for $150'.

The exploitative working conditions of immigrant and racial minority live-in domestic workers have been well documented (see Arat-Koc, 1999). Foreign workers on non-immigrant work authorization constitute the principal segment of this workforce. Because of 'undesirable working conditions, low wages, and low value placed on domestic work, Canadian workers and landed immigrants are unwilling to accept and keep jobs as live-in domestics.

Immigrant racial minority women workers face numerous barriers and disadvantages in the workplace in almost all sectors (Chard, 1995; Ghalam, 1995; Trumper and Wong, 1997). Racial inequality and discrimination are experienced by workers in many other countries (for review see Bolaria and Bolaria, 1997; Lewis, 2001).

From the evidence reviewed here it is safe to conclude that race and colour form an important dimension of economic and social inequality in Canada.

Summary

The changes in immigration policy in the post-war decades to accommodate the labour force needs in Canada have had a profound impact on the background characteristics and place of origin of immigrants. Increasing numbers of immigrants in recent years have been from Asia, Africa, and the Middle East rather than from traditional sources. Consequently, the Canadian population is now more heterogeneous and diverse. The changes in entry requirements also meant that the recent arrivals are relatively better educated with professional qualifications and training.

Overall, immigrants tend to be better educated than their Canadian-born counterparts. However, there is considerable variation in the level of education among immigrants from different regions. Immigrants from Asia, Africa, and the US tend to have the highest educational levels. The labour market profiles of immigrants differ from the Canadian-born and the labour force participation and occupational profiles of immigrants vary by their education and place of origin.

While visible minority men and women have higher educational levels in comparison to other Canadians, they are less likely than other Canadians to be in professional or managerial positions. Labour market inequalities and differential employment earnings and incomes mean that the incidence of low income among visible minorities remains above the Canadian average. However, visible minority groups differ from each other in socio–economic status and there is considerable heterogeneity and social stratification within each group.

The changes in post-war immigration patterns also meant a more diverse and heterogeneous Indo-Canadian community and their labour force profiles are quite different from the early immigrants from India. The data from 1981 suggest that while Sikh and other arrivals had relatively better educational attainment, a small proportion of them were in professional/managerial occupations and most of them had relatively low employment earnings. More recent data (1991) also show that in spite of better educational attainment (measured by university education), Sikhs and other Indo-Canadians are less likely to be in managerial, administrative, and professional jobs and more likely to have low incomes in comparison to all Canadians.

Our discussion on media and the minorities indicates that in headlines, use of language and construction of issues, the Sikh community is often 'problematized'. The community is portrayed as conflict- and violence-ridden, lacks aptitude for democracy; is a 'troubled' community requiring inordinate use of public safety services to maintain peace within the community and reduce the threat to the general public. Some editorials and forums even used political and religious contradictions and conflicts within the Sikh community to argue for immigration reforms to keep terrorists and criminals out and even suspension of due process and protection of the Charter of Rights and Freedoms for speedy deportation of suspected individuals.

Our discussion also indicates that racial minorities are more likely than people of European origin to be ranked low in terms of personal and social attributes and have lower social standing than Europeans. The white ethnic groups have relatively higher social ranking than the racial minorities irrespective of their place of birth or immigrant status.

The low social ranking of Sikhs and other minorities is partially the product of the tendency in the media and by other individuals and groups to hold the entire community accountable for the actions of a few individuals. This is particularly so when the actions conjure up images of violence, terrorism, and threat to public safety. The post-9/11 period saw that all those who shared a common faith and background with the attackers became objects of surveillance, police interrogation, and of assault and hostility at the hands of ordinary citizens. Even the members of other minority communities who resembled the attackers, the 'look-alikes', such as the Sikhs, became the objects of numerous attacks. The 'war against terrorism' is being used against 'suspected' individuals, groups, organizations who are being singled out for excessive surveillance, immigration restrictions, finger printing, interrogation of individuals and groups belonging to particular organizations, and preventive detention of suspects, among other actions against them. The minority communities find themselves victimized and criminalized simply because of common faith, nationality and because they 'look alike'.

The visible success of a few Sikhs in politics, business, the arts, academia, and other fields masks the economic and social inequality faced by many. Success stories of the 'first Sikh' or 'first Indo-Canadian' to occupy this or that high position gloss over the fact that a large number of Sikhs are far from prosperous. Race and colour matter in the life chances of individuals and groups, and are important bases of stratification in Canada. Our discussion and findings are more consistent with the view that structural barriers and constraints, such as racism in the labour market and elsewhere, and the differential opportunity structures produce economic and social inequality rather than with individual and culturally based perspectives on inequality.

References

Abella, Rosalie (1984): 'Equality in Employment. A Commission Report' (Ottawa: Supply and Services).

Aiken, Sharryn (2000): 'Manufacturing Terrorists: Refugees, National Security and Canadian Law', *Refuge* 19:3.

Aiken, Sharryn and Andrew Brouwer (2001): 'We Could Send Back the Next Mandela', *Globe and Mail*, Thursday, 7 June:A15.

Angus Reid Group (1991): *Multiculturalism and Canadians: Attitude Survey 1991, National Survey Report.* Submitted to Multiculturalism and Citizenship, Canada.

Arat-Koc, Sedef (1999): 'Good Enough to Work But Not Good Enough to Stay: Foreign Domestic Workers and the Law', pp. 125–51, *in* Elizabeth Comack et al. (eds), *Locating Law: Race/Class/Gender Connections* (Halifax: Fernwood).

Badets, Jane and Tina W.L. Chui (1994): *Canada's Changing Immigration Population* (Ottawa: Minister of Industry, Science and Technology).

Basavarajappa, K.G. and R.P.B. Verma (1985): 'Asian Immigration in Canada: Some Findings from 1981 Census', *International Migration* 23(1):97–121.

Basran, Gurcharn S. and Li Zong (1998): 'Devaluation of Foreign Credentials as Perceived by Visible Minority Professional Immigrants'. *Canadian Ethnic Studies* 30(3):6–23.

Basran, Gurcharn S., Charan Gill, and Brian D. MacLean (1995): *Farmworkers and Their Children* (Vancouver: Collective Press).

Battershill, Charles (1993): 'Migrant Doctors in a Multicultural Society: Policies, Barriers and Equity', pp. 243–61, *in* Vic Satzewich (ed.), *Deconstructing a Nation: Immigration, Multiculturalism and Racism in 90s Canada* (Halifax: Fernwood).

Beaujot, Roderic, K.G. Basavarajappa, and Ravi Verma (1988): *Income of Immigrants in Canada: A Census Data Analysis* (Ottawa: Statistics Canada).

Beck, Dirk (1995): 'The Clothes Behind Closed Doors', *The Georgia Straight*, April (14–21):11–12.

Berry, John W., Rudolf Kalin, and Donald Taylor (1976): *Multiculturalism and Ethnic Attitudes in Canada* (Ottawa: Minister of Supply and Services Canada).

Bolaria B. Singh and Peter S. Li (1988): *Racial Oppression in Canada*, 2nd ed. (Toronto: Garamond Press)

Bolaria, B. Singh (1995): 'Foreign Professional Labour: Opportunities and Constraints', pp. 89–110, *in* Terry Wotherspoon and Paul Jungbluth (eds), *Multicultural Education in a Changing Global Economy: Canada and The Netherlands* (New York: Waxman Munster).

—— (1992): 'From Immigrant Settlers to Migrant Transients: Foreign Professionals in Canada', pp. 211–28, *in* Vic Satzewich (ed.), *Deconstructing a Nation: Immigration, Multiculturalism and Racism in 90s Canada* (Halifax and Saskatoon: Fernwood Publishing and Social Research Unit).

—— (1987): 'The "Brain Drain" to Canada: The Externalization of the Cost of Education', pp. 301–22, *in* Terry Wotherspoon (ed.), *The Political Economy of Canadian Schooling* (Toronto: Methuen).

Bolaria, B. Singh and Rosemary von Elling Bolaria (1997): *International Labour Migrations* (New Delhi: Oxford University Press).

—— (1994): 'Immigrant Status and Health Status: Women and Racial Minority Immigrant Workers', pp. 149–68, *in* B. Singh Bolaria and Rosemary Bolaria (eds), *Racial Minorities, Medicine and Health* (Halifax: Fernwood Publishing and Saskatoon: Social Research Unit).

Boyd, Monica (2001): 'Gender Inequality: Economic and Political Aspects', pp. 178–207, *in* Robert J. Brym (ed.), *New Society* (Toronto: Harcourt Canada).

Chard, Jennifer (1995): 'Women in a Visible Minority', pp. 133–46, *in* Statistics Canada, 1995, *Women in Canada: A Statistical Report* (Ottawa: Minister of Industry).

Das Gupta, Tania (1996): *Racism and Paid Work* (Toronto: Garamond Press).

Delahanty, Julie (1999): 'From Social Movements to Social Clauses: Grading Strategies for Improving Conditions for Women Garment Workers' (Ottawa: North-south Institute).

Fernando, Tissa and Kamal K. Prasad (1986): 'Multiculturalism and Employment Equity: Problems Facing Foreign Trained Professionals and Tradespeople in British Columbia' (Vancouver: Affiliation of Multicultural Societies and Service Agencies of B.C.).

Filson, Glen (1983): 'Class and Ethnic Differences in Canadians' Attitudes to Native People's Rights and Immigrants', *Canadian Review of Sociology and Anthropology* 20(4):454–82.

Fleras, Angie and Jean Leonard Elliott (1999): *Unequal Relations* (3rd edn) (Scarborough,: Prentice Hall Allyn and Bacon Canada).

Fleras, Angie and Jean Elliott (1992): *Multiculturalism in Canada* (Scarborough, Ontario: Nelson Canada, particularly Ch. 11 'Media, Minorities and Multiculturalism', pp. 233–48.

Fleras, Angie and Jean Lock Kunz (2001): *Media and Minorities* (Toronto: Thompson Educational Publishing).

Foschi, Martha and Sari Buchan (1990): 'Ethnicity, Gender and Perception of Task Competence', *Canadian Journal of Sociology* 15(1):1–18.

Ghalam, Nancy (1995): 'Immigrant Women', pp. 117–32, *in* Statistics Canada, *Women in Canada: A Statistical Report*. Ottawa: Minister of Industry.

Hawkins, Freda (1974): 'Canadian Immigration Policy and Management'. *International Migration Review* 7:141–53.

Hawkins, Freda (1972): *Canada and Immigration: Public Policy and Public Concerns* (Montreal: McGill-Queen's University Press).

Henry, Frances (1989): *Who Gets the Work in 1989?* (Ottawa: Economic Council of Canada).

Henry, Frances and Carol Tator (2002): *Racist Discourse in Canada's English Print Media* (Toronto: Canadian Race Relations Foundation).

Henry, Frances, Carol Tator, Winston Mattis and Tim Rees (2001): 'The Victimization of Racial Minorities in Canada', pp. 145–60, *in* Robert J. Bryn (ed.), *Society in Question* (Toronto: Harcourt Canada).

—— (1995): *The Colour of Democracy: Racism in Canadian Society* (Toronto: Harcourt Brace and Company), Ch. 10.

Henry, Frances and Effie Ginsberg (1985): *Who Gets the Work? A Test of Racial Discrimination in Employment* (Toronto: Social Planning Council of Metro Toronto and The Urban Alliance on Race Relations).

Higgins, R. and M. Flory (eds) (1997): *Terrorism and International Law* (London: Routledge).

Jain, Harish (1988): 'Affirmative Action/Employment Equity Programmes and Visible Minorities in Canada', *Current Readings in Race Relations* 5(1):3–7.

Jain, Harish and R. Hackett (1989): 'Measuring Effectiveness of Employment Equity Programmes in Canada: A Survey', *Canadian Public Policy* 15(2):189–204.

Jakubowski, Lisa Marie (1997): *Immigration and the Legalization of Racism* (Halifax: Fernwood Publishing).

James, Carl E. (1999): *Seeing Ourselves: Exploring Ethnicity, Race and Culture.* (2nd edn) (Toronto: Thompson Educational Publishing).

Johnson, Laura and Robert E. Johnson (1982): *The Seam Allowance* (Toronto: Women's Education Press).

Khaki, A. and K. Prasad (1988): Depiction and Perception: Native Indians and Visible Minorities in the Media (Vancouver: Ad Hoc Media Committee for Better Race Relations).

Kunz, Jean Lock, Anne Milan, and Sylvain Schetagne (2000): *Unequal Access: A Canadian Profile of Racial Differences in Education, Employment and Income*

(Ottawa: Canadian Council on Social Development (CCSD); A Report Prepared for Canadian Race Relations Foundation.

Law Union of Ontario (1981): *The Immigrant's Handbook* (Montreal: Black Rose Books).

Lewis, Gail (2001): 'Black Women's Employment and the British Economy', pp. 297–318, *in* Kum-Kum Bhavnani, *Feminism and 'Race'* (Oxford: Oxford University Press).

Lian, Jason Z. and David Ralph Matthews (1998): 'Does the Vertical Mosaic Still Exist? Ethnicity and Income in Canada, 1991', *Canadian Review of Sociology and Anthropology* 35(4):462–476.

Li, Peter S. (2001): 'The Market Worth of Immigrants' Educational Credentials', *Canadian Public Policy* 26(1):23–38.

—— (2000): 'Earning Disparities Between Immigrants and Native-Born Canadians', *Canadian Review of Sociology and Anthropology* 37(3):289–311.

—— (1998): 'The Market Value and Social Value of Race', pp. 115–30, *in* Vic Satzewich (ed.) (1998), *Racism and Social Inequality in Canada* (Toronto: Thompson Educational Publishing, Inc.).

—— (1992): 'The Economics of Brain Drain. Recruitment of Skilled Labour to Canada, 1954–86', pp. 145–62, *in* Vic Satzewich (ed.), *Deconstructing A Nation: Immigration, Multiculturalism and Racism in 90s Canada* (Halifax, Nova Scotia: Fernwood).

—— (1979): 'Attitudes Toward Asians in a Canadian City', *Canadian Ethnic Studies* 11(2):70–7.

Lipsig-Mumme, Carla (1987): 'Organizing Women in the Clothing Trades: Homework and the 1983 Garment Strike in Canada', *Studies in Political Economy* 22:41–71.

Mata, Fernando (1994): 'The Non-accreditation of Immigrant Professionals in Canada: Societal Impacts, Barriers and Present Policy Initiatives', paper presented at annual Sociology and Anthropology Meetings (Learned Societies), University of Calgary, June 3–18, Calgary, Alberta.

Morokvasic, Mirjana, Annie Phizacklea, and Hedwig Rudolph (1986): 'Small Firms and Minority Groups: Contradictory Trends in the French, German and British Clothing Industry', *International Sociology* 1(4):397–420.

Pendakur, Krishna, and Ravi Pendakur (1996): 'Earning Differentials Among Ethnic Groups in Canada' (Ottawa: Strategic Research and Analysis, Department of Canadian Heritage).

Phizacklea, Annie (2002): 'Women, Migration and the State', pp. 319–30, *in* Kum-Kum Bhavnani, *Feminism and 'Race'* (Oxford: Oxford University Press).

Pineo, Peter (1977): 'The Social Standings of Racial and Ethnic Groupings', *Canadian Review of Sociology and Anthropology* 14(2):147–57.

Rajagopal, Indhu (1990): 'The Glass Ceiling in the Vertical Mosaic: Indian Immigrants to Canada', *Canadian Ethnic Studies* 22(1):96–105.

Satzewich, Vic (2001): 'Race and Ethnic Relations', pp. 208–34, *in* Robert J. Brym (ed.), *New Society* (Toronto: Harcourt Canada).

—— (2000): 'Capital Accumulation and State Formation: The Contradictions of International Migration', pp. 51–72, *in* B. Singh Bolaria (ed.), *Social Issues and Contradictions in Canadian Society* (Toronto: Harcourt Canada).

Satzewich, Vic (ed.) (1998): *Racism and Social Inequality in Canada* (Toronto: Thompson Educational Publishing, Inc.).

Seassa, Teresa (1994): 'Language Standards, Ethnicity and Discrimination'. *Canadian Ethnic Studies* 26(3):105–21.

Simmons, Alan (1998): 'Racism and Immigration Policy', pp. 87–114, *in* Vic Satzewich (ed.), *Racism and Social Inequality in Canada* (Toronto: Thompson Educational Publishing, Inc., 1998.

Statistics Canada (1998): *The Daily*, (February 17).

—— (1998): *The Daily*, May 12.

—— (1997): *The Daily* (November 4).

—— (1995): *Women in Canada: A Statistical Report* (Ottawa Minister of Industry.

Trumper, Ricardo and Lloyd L. Wong (1997): 'Racialization and Genderization: The Canadian State, Immigrants and Temporary Workers', pp. 153–91, *in* B. Singh Bolaria and Rosemary von Elling Bolaria (eds), *International Labour Migrations* (New Delhi: Oxford University Press).

Vorst et al. (eds) (1991): *Race, Class, Gender: Bonds and Barriers* (2nd rev. edn) (Toronto: Garamond Press and Society for Socialist Studies).

Winsor, Hugh (2001): 'The Danger of Listing Terrorists', *Globe and Mail*, Wednesday, 24 Oct.:A17.

Yanz, Linda, Bob Jeffott, Dena Ladd, and Joan Atlin (1999): *Policy Options to Improve Standards for Women Garment Workers in Canada and Internationally* (Ottawa: Status of Women Canada).

State Policies, Family Formation, and Inequality

❀

The point of view of the Hindu (in wanting Canada to admit wives and families) is readily understood and appreciated. But there is the point of view of the white settler in this country who wants to keep the country a white country with white standards of living and morality. ... They are not a desirable people from any standpoint for the Dominion to have. ... The white population will never be able to absorb them. They are not an assimilable people. ... We must not permit the men of that race to come in large numbers, and we must not permit their women to come in at all. Such a policy of exclusion is simply a measure of self-defence. ... We have no right to imperil the comfort and happiness of the generations that are to succeed us.

(Vancouver Sun, June 17, 1913, Editorial, p. 6)

INTRODUCTION

The legal, political, and other structural constraints under which racial minorities entered Canada have had a profound impact on the nature and development of their social and cultural institutions, yet, the nature and development of these institutions is often attributed to the cultural background, values, and practices of minority communities. For instance, it is common to conceive of family structure and composition as a consequence of individual choice and cultural patterns and practices. This orientation often fails to take into account the historical and structural determinants that have important influence on family formation. Consideration of factors other than cultural is particularly important in regard to racial minority families in Canada precisely because of racist and sexist immigration policies, and specific legal, political, and other structural constraints and limitations placed on their settlement in this country. For instance, immigrants who are only allowed to enter Canada as single male workers without wives and children, denied legal–political rights, and are made transient temporary (sojourners) rather than permanent settlers because of conditions of their entry, they are not likely to have a normal conjugal family life. In short, the nature and development of families has more to do with structural factors rather than individual preference and cultural patterns and practices. Individual choices are structured by available opportunities and cultural practices and patterns can only be maintained within a particular milieu.

This chapter examines the impact of various structural factors on the formation of the Indo-Canadian and Sikh family in both its historical and contemporary contexts. Analysis and discussion are primarily informed by two research projects, one conducted in British Columbia and the other in Saskatchewan.[1] As the following discussion indicates, the formation and structure of family and family dynamics correspond to historical changes in immigration policy as well as changes in the socio-economic characteristics of the community. The chapter concludes with a discussion of relative economic status of visible minority families in Canada and limitations of mainstream feminist theorizing and discourse which often fails to consider the interconnections of race, class, and gender.

STATE POLICIES AND EARLY FAMILY FORMATION

Focus on cultural patterns and practices tends to mask the deliberate Canadian immigration and settlement policies, which were intended to ensure that Sikh workers did not become permanent settlers with families and full citizenship rights. To achieve this goal, workers from India during the early period were primarily 'single' males without families. These workers were not allowed to bring their wives and children, were treated as transient workers and denied legal rights. Lack of normal conjugal family life also meant a considerable delay in the development of a native-born Indo-Canadian community. State policies were primarily oriented to physically separate workers' productive capacity from their place of reproduction and separating family members – husbands from wives and children from parents.(Ghosh, 1983; Chandrasekhar, 1986; Buchignani, Indra and Srivastava, 1985; Bolaria and Li, 1988). As previously discussed in Chapter 6, prior to 1920, 5,252 males, but only 23 females, came from India. This sex imbalance among the immigrants from India continued even after 1919 when workers from India could bring their wives and children. Few could afford to take advantage of the changes in immigration, because of lack of financial resources and fear of racial discrimination (Bolaria and Li, 1988). Our respondents in the British Columbia study often addressed this situation. As one of them stated, 'Families were not here at the time. We were all "single" in Canada. Some of us were married and our spouses and children were in India' (Bolaria and Basran, 1985b). Other evidence supports this observation. For example, it is estimated that at the outbreak of the second World War, the 1,100 East Indians in British Columbia were almost entirely composed of single males residing in logging camps or in apartments in Vancouver, and not more than fifteen conjugal families. Prior to the Second World War about 6,000 men migrated to Canada, as compared to only 400 Indian women and 423 children. Among the early East Indian immigrants, about 95 per cent were Sikhs (Bolaria and Li, 1988).

While specific studies of the Sikh family to 1947 are not extensive (Buchignani, Indra and Srivastava, 1985:34), it is quite likely that discrimination and social antagonism had deterred many Sikhs from bringing their families to Canada. The Royal Commission report of 1902 provided similar evidence with respect to Chinese families in Canada (Li, 1983:90).

Given various discriminatory and restrictive policies and denial of legal–political rights, many Sikh immigrants also developed sojourn orientation. For some the goal was to work hard for a few years, accumulate savings and 'retire' in India. Those with this orientation did not want to bring their families. One of the respondents in the B.C. study indicated that of the 40 Sikhs living in Duncan, British Columbia (in the 1930s),only four had their families settled with them, while the remaining Sikhs were married with their families still in India. Sikhs would work for three to four years in Canada and would subsequently visit India for a few months, eventually returning to Canada. This pattern, which did not encourage the formation of Sikh families in Canada, was followed by large numbers of Sikhs in our study in British Columbia.

Family formation may also be shaped by internal community dynamics and external opportunities and environment to court and marry 'outside' one's own community. Religious, cultural, and social norms may prohibit people from establishing exogamous bonds. Similarly, legal, racial, and social barriers and demographic factors may limit the opportunities to court and marry exogamously. For instance, in this regard, it is interesting to note that Sikh immigrants in California prior to the Second World War started marrying Mexican women. Immigration policies in the US, were similar to those in Canada at that time. However, Sikhs in Canada did not inter-marry with other groups, white or non-white. It is likely that at the time, because of racism, it was not possible for Sikh men to marry white women, and the Sikhs' class, caste and religious background did not allow them to marry Black or native women. Also there were neither Black nor native women in British Columbia in large numbers to make such relationships an option. However, Sikh immigrants in California married Mexican women until about 1946 when the Lure–Cellar Bill enabled Sikhs to become US citizens (LaBrack and Leonard, 1984:543). Between 1916 and 1949, about 300 marriages were recorded between South Asian men, mostly Sikhs, and Hispanic women, compared to only 48 with Anglo-American women, 15 with Black women, and 9 with native-American women (LaBrack, 1988:287). Sikh men may have preferred marrying Sikh women from Punjab, rather than marrying Mexican women, but this was not possible at that time (LaBrack, 1983:22). Therefore, in the absence of eligible mates, Sikh men opted for marriages (with Mexican women) that were exogamous, inter racial and inter-religious. After the changes in the US immigration policies in 1946 that allowed the immigration of families, endogamous Sikh marriage patterns were re-established and Sikh males started marrying Sikh women from Punjab (Chekki, 1988:179–180).

Early Sikh immigrants to Canada were predominantly from rural areas in Punjab province with low educational achievement. Traditionalist in outlook in terms of gender relations and gendered division of labour in the family, these families may be characterized as patriarchal in nature. Commenting on families at the time, one of the respondents from British Columbia stated:

Women were not working. They were staying home and looking after the children, cooking. So we did not ask anybody to look after our children—men did not like the idea of women working outside the home—we did not want to leave the children alone at home. So, that was the thinking of our people in those days, that the women should stay home with the children and do housework (Bolaria and Basran, 1985b).

Early Sikh immigrant women also faced contradictory pressures and demands and had to accommodate to gender inequality and patriarchy at home and to deal with racism and racial inequality in the larger society. Many of the immigrants thought that adoption of 'Western ways', and assimilation and integration would reduce racism and racial hostility toward women. Women were 'instructed' by their male relatives to discard 'Indian dress' and 'look and act like Canadians'. As one female British Columbia respondent explained, 'Our male relatives who were here would bring Western clothes at the time of our landing in Canada and asked us to wear those clothes so that we would look like Canadians'. We were instructed not to go out of the house in our East Indian dresses' (Bolaria and Basran, 1985b).

One of the significant outcomes of discriminatory immigration policies and denial of normal conjugal life has been a considerable delay in the development of a native-born racial minority population in Canada. For instance, in 1981, only 3 per cent of the Indo-Pakistani males and 3.6 per cent of the Indo-Pakistani females in the labour force were born in Canada. On the other hand, in 1981 a little over 87 per cent of males and 86 per cent females of British origin in the labour force were Canadian born (Abella, 1984:83, Table 1). Even a majority of the racial minority immigrant population currently living in Canada is foreign born.

It is evident that historical structural factors, such as immigration policies and labour procurement strategies, have been important in the formation and development of families and conjugal life in Canada. Based upon a review of literature on ethnic families, Li concludes that; 'ethnic families in North America are not necessarily a replica of families in the places of origin, nor ethnic cultures necessarily the cause of familial organization or disorganization, as the case may be' (Li, 1980:59–60).

CONTEMPORARY FAMILIES: STRUCTURAL DIVERSITY, SOCIAL RELATIONS AND CULTURAL PRACTICES

Change in Canadian immigration policies during the sixties led to a change in the socio–economic characteristics of immigrants. The change in Canadian labour force needs meant that the immigrants entering Canada after the sixties began to be better educated, professional-skilled workers from urban middle-class background with a familiarity with Western culture. Many of them migrated accompanied by their families or their families followed them soon after their arrival in Canada, and they came with the intention of settling permanently in Canada with their families.

The pre-immigration characteristics of migrants, and changes regarding family policies, have led to a diverse and heterogeneous Sikh community and has produced diversity and variation in family forms. These families show considerable diversity in structure and inner dynamics, ranging from nuclear family to modified extended familism to extended family formation with common residence (Bolaria and Basran, 1985a; Buchignani, Indra, and Srivastava, 1985). These families also show considerable variation in domestic decision-making, social arrangements, parent–child relationships, residential arrangements, and other patterns. In short, in terms of structure and inner dynamics, Sikh families are not different from the families in the general population.

In the following pages we focus on gender relations and decision–making, parent-child relations, courtship and marriage, and some of the salient concerns of Sikh families such as transmission of religion and language.

Gender Equality and Decision-Making

The shift in socio-economic characteristics of immigrants has also brought about changes in gender relations, family interaction, division of tasks, and the decision-making process. In our Saskatchewan study 70 per cent of the female respondents stated that they and their husbands jointly make important decisions in the family; only 24 per cent said their husbands make such decisions alone and 6 per cent said they made them alone (Bolaria and Basran, 1985a). The tendency toward egalitarian decision-making in these families may be a product of pre-immigration factors. It is very likely that given their high educational achievement and urban background, some of these families had adopted an egalitarian gender ethos and patterns in domestic family interaction and other relations before their arrival in Canada. Adoption of shared work practices may also have been necessitated by labour force participation of professional women in Canada.

The tendency towards greater egalitarianism in Sikh families is the result of a number of structural factors. Some of these families came from an upper or middle class background. Women from such families are more likely to participate in the Canadian labour market. Employment gives female household members economic security and resources to influence decision-making; their employment status also heightens their awareness of gender inequality. A different form of social stratification, and perhaps even less inequality in Canada, in comparison to the complex system of stratification based on class, caste, religious, ethnic, regional, and gender divisions in

India, improves conditions and opportunities for greater equality in family relations.

Participation of women in the labour market, of course, enhances their social and economic status. In our Saskatchewan study, 46 per cent of the female respondents worked outside the home, though 76 per cent earned less than $20,000 per year. Overall, those who worked outside the home were quite satisfied with their jobs and work environment. Those who were not employed outside the home reported a number of reasons: 18 per cent stayed at home to raise their children; 9 per cent did not want to work outside the home; 15 per cent could not obtain a job because of lack of recognition of their foreign qualifications; and 6 per cent mentioned racism as a factor for them not obtaining an appropriate position. Twenty-four per cent mentioned 'other reasons' and 27 per cent did not respond to this question (Bolaria and Basran, 1985a). Their evaluation of their status in Canada varied considerably. When female respondents were asked to compare the status of Sikh women in Canada to their position in India, 46 per cent said their status was better in Canada; 45 per cent felt it was the same; and 9 per cent thought that their status was lower in Canada (Bolaria and Basran, 1985a).

As one may expect, for some families the change from traditional cultural patterns and practices embedded in patriarchal–feudal family systems to more egalitarian relations between spouses, and parents and children, may not be without contradictions and conflicts. In some instances, the outcome may be conflict in the family, wife and child abuse, and separation and divorce. Increasingly, Sikh families have to deal with these emergent contradictions and conflicts between family members, as well as an often-discriminatory environment and practices of the larger society.

FAMILIES, CHILDREN, COURTSHIP, AND MARRIAGES

One response to racism and discrimination in Canadian society and the corresponding sense of powerlessness and alienation may be further isolation of Indo-Canadians from the larger society and retreat to their family and community. Family members and children in particular assume special importance in the lives of Sikh parents. Focus on children's academic achievement and their personal and social lives appear to be primary concerns. Academic achievement is seen as an important means of social and economic mobility, where minority parents often expect that their children will face racism and discrimination and therefore they have to be better than whites to get ahead (Helweg, 1986). Some parents are also concerned about transmission of cultural, social and religious values to children. In socialization and raising children mothers play a significant role, and children are more likely to approach their mothers for help and advice. In the Saskatchewan study, 43 per cent of female respondents indicated that their children approached them when they had problems, as compared to 13 per cent who approached their fathers; 19 per cent approached both; and 26 per cent of the female respondents said it depended on what they wanted to discuss (Bolaria and Basran, 1985a). When we questioned female respondents as to who is responsible for resolving most of the conflicts in reference to the children, 33 per cent of the mothers said they resolve them; 18 per cent mentioned the father; and 49 per cent said both the mother and father were involved (Bolaria and Basran, 1985a).

Parental attitudes toward children's courtship and dating behaviour vary by social class and by sex of children. Professional and educated families are likely to be more accepting of their children's courtship behaviours and choice in marriage than working class families. However, there seems to be a double standard with respect to male and female children. Male children often have more freedom in these matters than their female counterparts. This attitude partly reflects a strong patriarchal heritage that continues to shape relationships between parents and children, despite their participation in many aspects of Canadian society. Most Sikh families prefer endogamous marriages for their children. In our Saskatchewan study, in response to the question, 'How important is it to you that your children marry within the Sikh religion?', 23 per cent of the respondents said it was very important; 56 per cent mentioned that it was quite important; 10 per cent said neither important nor unimportant; and 11 per cent said it was not important (Bolaria and Basran, 1985a).

Many Sikh families appear to have accepted the fact that their children will make their own choices in marriage rather than having arranged marriages, a practice that is still widely prevalent in most parts of India. Arranged marriages, particularly between Canadian-born and -raised individuals and those born and raised in India have come under increasing scrutiny and criticism. Comments by one of the respondents in the British Columbia study, who came here as a young boy of 13 in 1942, are relevant in this context. According to him, it is relatively difficult for the marriage to be successful as children of Sikh-Canadian families are quite different from their counterparts in India. This is especially the case when a woman of Sikh-Canadian origin is married to a man from India where patriarchal values and expectations are often unacceptable to Sikh women raised in a relatively more egalitarian cultural setting.

In the British Columbia study, one middle-class female respondent commented, 'Our sons and daughters get married with their own accord, when we do not agree with them... we put pressure on them to get married to Punjabis but it is impossible, you can do it for one generation, but what about the next one?' (Bolaria and Basran, 1985b). Kurian's (1983) comparative study of Indian and Indo-Canadian youth also indicates that Indo-Canadian youth are not as supportive of arranged marriages as the youth in India, though some researchers allude to the advantages of arranged marriages (see Kalra, 1980:43–4). Research on East Indian families in England also suggests that, 'girls raised in England are not willing to be subservient like their village counterparts' (Helweg, 1986).

Kurian and Ghosh (1983) state that third generation Indo-Canadians are quite willing to accept inter-ethnic marriages. If this trend were sustained, it would probably result in a higher rate of exogamy, especially when the volume of new immigrants from India is reduced or Sikh families settle in those communities with smaller Sikh populations.

Finally, Sikh families are concerned about the relatively high divorce rates in Canadian society. It is widely held among Sikhs that exogamous marriages outside religious, racial, and class boundaries will lead to a higher divorce rate among their children. As divorce rates are quite low in Punjab, Sikh parents want their children to follow the Punjabi matrimonial system. However, many fail to realize that low divorce rates in Punjab are related to specific conditions in that province: a large rural population; low literacy among women; low rate of employment among women; strong religious and traditional values; the nature of the patriarchal and extended families which makes it difficult for Sikh women to remarry once divorced. Although many Sikhs tend to romanticize the stability of the family in Punjab, some families in Punjab experience separation and divorce, particularly when they fail to have children (Buchignani, Indra, and Srivastava, 1985:157).

Despite parental preference for endogamous marriages, Sikh families increasingly have to deal with their children's preference in mate selection and marriage. Parental attitudes toward courtship and marriage vary by social class, and the sex of their children.

CULTURAL TRANSMISSION: LANGUAGE AND RELIGION

Another concern for parents and a source of conflict between parents and children has to do with transmission of the Sikh religion and the Punjabi language. A study by Srinivas and Kaul (1987:15) in Saskatchewan found that only 17 per cent of children could speak any Indian languages and 61 per cent thought that their children had been assimilated. In our B.C. study, one respondent was concerned about the fact that his children and grandchildren do not speak Punjabi (his mother tongue) and thus cannot effectively communicate with him. Another respondent expressed disapproval that his children selected their own spouses instead of conforming to the traditional practice of an arranged marriage. He also characterized his children as more Canadian than Indian in terms of their culture, behaviour, and attitudes.

In our Saskatchewan research, 52 per cent of male respondents said their children were religious and 48 per cent said they were not religious, whereas 87 per cent of these respondents considered themselves to be religious. Consequently, there was concern that their children were not maintaining the religion in the same way as they did. When we asked them if there were any special problems which they were facing in raising children in the Canadian society, 33 per cent said none; 27 per cent mentioned either peers or conflicting cultures as having a negative influence; 10 per cent said discrimination; 10 per cent said cultural conflict and discrimination; 10 per cent mentioned peer group, cultural conflict and discrimination; and 7 per cent said cultural conflict (Bolaria and Basran, 1985a).

Loss of language and religious faith among their children appears to be a concern for many parents. One way of maintaining language and religion is for families to 'arrange' endogamous marriages for their children. With increasing courtship opportunities for Punjabi Sikhs with members of other racial, religious and linguistic groups, it is unlikely that families and communities would be able to maintain 'traditional' customs and practices in mate selection and marriage.

ECONOMIC STATUS OF VISIBLE MINORITY FAMILIES

Employment levels and labour market opportunities of visible minority men and women affect the financial security of families, the social well-being of its members, and a range of opportunities for their children. Visible minority women are more likely than others to have university education, post-secondary training, and tend to have degrees in science-related fields. However, they are less likely than other women to be employed, hold professional and managerial jobs, and are more likely to experience higher levels of unemployment (Chard, 1995:133–36). The situation of visible minority men in regard to educational levels and employment patterns is similar to visible minority women. That is, visible minority men are more likely than other men to have higher educational levels but are more likely to experience unemployment, and are less likely to hold professional jobs. Consequently, average employment earnings for visible minority women and men are less than those for their non-visible minority counterparts. Visible minority women and men are more likely than other women and men to have low incomes. For instance, in 1990, approximately 28 per cent of visible minority women and a little over 26 per cent of visible minority men had incomes below Statistics Canada Low Income Cut-offs. The corresponding figures for non-visible minority women and men were 16.3 per cent and 12.9 per cent, respectively (Chard, 1995:146).

The incidence of low income among visible minority families remains above the Canadian average. Members of the visible minority population are more likely than the general population to live on low incomes. For instance, in 1995, approximately 36 per cent of the members of the visible minorities, as compared to 20 per cent of the general population, lived on low incomes. The percentage of children under six years of age who lived in low income families was about 45 per cent in the visible minority population, compared to 26 per cent of all children. The incidence of low-income was also higher among visible minority seniors (aged 65 and over) than the national average, 32 per cent and 19 per cent, respectively (Statistics Canada, 1998).

Income levels and financial security are major factors in the overall well-being of families. Ross and Roberts (1999:5) show that 'children in low-income families are twice as likely to be living in poorly functioning families as children in high-income families'. Children in low-income families are also more likely to be living with a parent who often exhibits signs of depression and who is chronically stressed (Ross and Roberts, 1999). Children and adolescents living in these circumstances are more likely than others to exhibit behavioural and emotional problems.

The socio-economic status of the family is crucial in the family's ability to provide a healthy social environment to cope with the 'problems' of family members. It is also crucial in structuring the life chances of its members. Inadequate income, for instance, affects educational opportunities, which in turn will affect job opportunities and income levels. These inequalities are cumulative. Inequality of conditions produce differential opportunity structures, which in turn produce differential conditions.

Inadequate economic resources can also seriously hamper the family's ability to successfully sponsor relatives to immigrate to Canada under the family-class. When the state requires that sponsoring families submit legal bonds to provide support to sponsored relatives for a certain period of time, and limits access to public social programmes such as health benefits and old age benefits for newcomers, low-income families may not be able to satisfy the financial requirements imposed by the state. Other policies and practices that limit and discourage family unification/reunification include definition of the family (who is included in family and who can be sponsored), excessive screening of immigrants from certain countries, political considerations, health screening tests, 'genuine' proof of marriage in case of spousal sponsor, and 'genuine' proof of family relations to the sponsoring individuals. Notwithstanding pro-family rhetoric, these policies and practices are, in reality, anti-family and discourage family unification/reunification, and make the individuals and family legally obliged to bear the cost of settlement of family relatives in this country without assistance from the state (for an insightful discussion on this topic, see Thobani, 2001).

VISIBLE MINORITY WOMEN: RACE, CLASS, GENDER

Much feminist theory emerges from privileged women who live at the centre, whose perspectives on reality rarely include knowledge and awareness of the lives of women and men who live in the margin. As a consequence, feminist theory lacks wholeness, lacks the broad analysis that could encompass a variety of human experiences. Although feminist theorists are aware of the need to develop ideas and analysis that encompass a larger number of experiences, that serve to unify rather than to polarize, such theory is complex and slow in formation (Hooks, 1984:x).

The Canadian Employment Equity Act defines visible minorities as 'persons other than aboriginal peoples, who are non-Caucasian in race or non-white in colour'. The number of women who are non-Caucasian in race or non-white in colour has increased considerably in recent years, from 800,000 in 1986 to estimated 1.3 m in 1991. In 1991 they constituted 9 per cent of the total female population in Canada. The socio–economic and labour market profiles of these women are often different from their non-visible minority counterparts: a large proportion of them are foreign-born and most of them are recent immigrants (Chard, 1995).

Visible minority women are also often referred to as 'women of colour' or racial minority women. It is now commonly acknowledged that, overall, there is unequal distribution of social, economic, and other privileges between men and women. This gender stratification produces a differential opportunity structure and life chances for men and women. A voluminous body of literature has developed to account for gender stratification. Variant theoretical perspectives have emerged in this debate. These perspectives differ with regard to their focus and attention on gender socialization, gender discrimination, patriarchy, and capitalism. Liberal feminists and socialist feminists have received the most attention (for detailed discussion on these and other perspectives, see, e.g., Muszynski, 2000). Liberal feminists largely focus on elimination of discrimination and expansion of opportunities for women without questioning the basic organization of the society. Socialist feminists focus on patriarchy and capitalism, social subordination of women to men and women's role in the labour market. They see patriarchy and capitalism as mutually reinforcing and draw attention to the interaction of gender and class.

While feminist literature has contributed to the understanding of issues of gender inequality and gender oppression, feminist discourse and theorizing have come under increasing scrutiny and criticism. Most of the feminists assume a 'common experience' and 'common oppression' of all women based on gender alone, separately from any other experiences. While gender affects people's lives, offers privileges for some and disadvantages for others, it does not operate alone. Women of colour cannot overlook the simultaneity of the experiences of racism, sexism, and class oppression (Kline, 1989:91). There is a growing body of literature that speaks to the reality of race, class, and gender as both separate yet interconnected, and acknowledges the complexity and diversity of women's experiences and questions the universality and commonality of women's situation (e.g. Vorst, et al., 1991). The lack of inclusion of race, racism, and class in feminist theory and practice and inadequate consideration of the interconnections between race, class, and gender obsession forms the main point of the critique of mainstream feminism (e.g., Agnew, 1996; Anderson and Collin, 1995; Bannerji, 1987, 1991, 1993; Mandell, 1995; Monture, 1986, 1993; Mukherjee, 1993;

Amos and Parmar, 2001; Kline, 1989, 1991; Das Gupta, 1996; Kazi, 1986; Hooks, 1981; 1984; Thornhill, 1991; Carby, 1982; Lees, 1986; Spelman, 1982, 1988; Satzewich, 1998).

Universalization of experience of white women and omission of race excludes experiences of women of colour. Analysis and descriptions by women of colour and others point to the salience of interaction between race, gender, and class in their lives, and find it difficult to separate experience attributed to gender from race and class. As Lees states: 'In particular situations it is often very difficult to weigh the importance of different systems of stratification. Is a black woman, for example, denied a job on the basis of class, race or sex' (Lees, 1986:94). Others also point to the simultaneity of experiences of different forms of oppression in their lives. Kazi (1986:88) states: 'It is being a woman and simultaneously black that gives an added dimension to black women's oppression. In every black woman's life there are innumerable occasions when she is not only sexually but also racially discriminated against'. Carby makes the same point when she states that black women 'are subject to the simultaneous oppression of patriarchy, class and "race" ...' (Carby, 1982:213). For some feminists, race and sex are separate issues and racism is not a feminist issue. Yet for Hooks (1981), a black feminist, being born black and born female determined her destiny. Patricia Monture (1986) also argues that it is difficult to separate race and gender in actual experience, as an Indian or as an Indian woman.

The omission of race and class, argue some critics, is 'partly a consequence of the particular material circumstances in which much of contemporary feminist theory has been produced' (Kline, 1991:51). Most of the dominant theorists occupy positions of class and race privileges, are in positions to exercise choices in their lives, are not negatively affected by racism and class, and do not face contradictions in their lives experienced by many women (Ramazanoglu, 1986). Under the circumstances, it is easier for 'women who do not experience race or class oppression to focus exclusively on gender' (Hooks, 1984:14). Thornhill (1991:28) states:

The force that allows White feminist authors, for example, to make no reference to racial identity in their books about women that are in actuality about White women, is the same force that would compel any author writing exclusively about Black women to refer explicitly to their identity. That force is racism. For, in racially imperialist societies such as ours, it is the dominant group that automatically reserves for itself the luxury of dismissing racial identity.

Because of their dominant position white feminists also have the power to treat their own particular experiences as universal and wholly representative and appropriate and claim authority to speak for all women (Hooks, 1981; Bannerji, 1987; Kline, 1989). Writing on this topic Monture states that:

The notion of the commonality of all women is not agreeable to the First Nations perspective. ... My women's identity flows from my race. ... I am a Mohawk woman. ... [White women's] experience is not just as women, but also as white people. ... The women's movement, until it focuses on its own 'whiteness' is a movement of privileged women who refuse to consider their privilege (Monture, 1993:334).

The omission of race and racism is not just a manifestation of ethnocentrism but rather a reflection of 'institutionalized racism which is so totally and deeply entrenched in our [white feminist] ways of thinking and being that we cannot see clearly how we help to justify and perpetuate it (Ramazanoglu, 1986:84).

Some feminists may have also unintentionally contributed to reinforcing cultural stereotypes about Asian women by their attacks on arranged marriages and *purdah*, and the culturally structured passivity of Asian women (Amos and Parmar, 2001). The focus on cultural and gender-role socialization and cultural practices tends to mask the sex, race, and class structured distribution of power, and the role of racist and sexist immigration policies that structure the dependency of Asian women on their male relatives to immigrate and remain in the country. Racism continues to structure the experiences of women of colour in their daily lives, in their families, in their place of work. Those with 'privileges of colour' fail to recognize the significance of race and racism.

It is important to recognize that visible minority women are not a homogeneous group and the impact of various policies and practices is not uniformly felt by them. The experiences of visible minority women are far from monolithic because of their diversity of origin and background, geographical origins, culture, religion, educational background, and class. The differential opportunity structure and their location in the labour market have profound impact on the lives of women, children, and their families. For instance, in low-wage sectors, often the entire family labour is required to earn subsistence wages. Men, women, children, and even very old members of the family work in fields in order to subsist. Under these circumstances, family life suffers, children's education is affected, and the family is often exposed to an unhealthy work environment (Basran, Gill, and MacLean, 1994). Their location in the labour market (concentration in low-wage sectors) primarily accounts for their low-incomes, poverty, and social subordination rather than the gender–role socialization, docility, submissiveness attributed to their cultural background, and their biological and cultural deficiencies. Professional women often find devaluation of their 'foreign' credentials and experience, and often have to start out at the bottom of their professions.

Women of colour, whether citizens or not are often seen and treated as 'immigrants' or 'foreigners', in their daily lives, signified in questions such as, 'Where are you from?' and 'How long have you been here?' Even those who are born and raised here face similar questions (Mukherjee, 1993). The term 'immigrant' is widely used and understood to refer only to people of colour.

The social significance attached to colour and physical appearance, along with gender and immigration policies, continue to structure the experiences of women of colour in Canada. The mainstream feminist discourse and theorizing, largely based upon universalization of the experiences of white women, have failed to include the specific experiences of women of colour. The sex-, race-, and class-structured distribution of power and privileges remain permanent features of the Canadian mosaic.

SUMMARY

The presentation above indicates that historical and structural determinants have had an important influence on family formation, structure, and dynamics. Many forces have shaped Sikh families, among which were the labour procurement strategies under which Sikh workers were recruited to come to Canada, their reception in Canada, and the characteristics of the immigrants themselves. Historically, the development of Sikh families was stifled by racist and sexist immigration policies, recruitment of single-male labour, denial of normal conjugal family life, denial of legal–political rights, and limitations placed upon their permanent settlement in Canada. In the post-war decades, especially after the 1960s, the changes in immigration policies to accommodate Canadian labour force needs meant a change in the characteristics and background of immigrants. The entry criteria assured that immigrants entering Canada were better educated, professional–skilled workers, often from urban middle and upper-class backgrounds. These immigrants often arrived in Canada with their families and intended to settle permanently in Canada. These changes have led to a diverse and heterogeneous Sikh community with corresponding diversity in family forms. Their family structure and family relations differ markedly from those Sikhs who arrived earlier and were characterized by low educational achievement, predominantly rural background, and confronted by discriminatory state policies and often hostile reception in the country.

Contemporary Sikh families show considerable variation in structure, residential arrangements, and internal family dynamics, just like families in the general population. There is considerable variation in cultural practices, gender-relations, parent-children relations, and family attitudes toward courtship and marriage.

Our study also indicates that racial minority men and women face considerable inequality in the labour market and the incidence of low income among members of racial minorities and their families remains above the Canadian average. Low income and inadequate resources adversely affect the ability of the families to provide a healthy social environment, educational and other opportunities for their children, and to successfully sponsor relatives to immigrate to Canada.

We conclude with a presentation of mainstream feminist discourse and theorizing about inequality and gender oppression. Our discussion indicates that lack of inclusion of race, racism, and class in feminist theory and practice forms the central basis of the critique of mainstream feminism. Race and racism continue to structure the experiences of racial minority women in their daily lives, in their families, and in the labour market.

Notes

1. For details of the British Columbia study see endnotes to ch. 6. The Saskatchewan project, involving interviews with 30 males and 33 females, was completed in 1985 in Saskatoon, Saskatchewan. Based on a list of Sikh families provided by the Saskatoon Sikh Society, all families were contacted for interviews. Three families refused; one family was unavailable during the study period; and one female respondent declined to be interviewed. In the case of families, efforts were made to conduct independent interviews with the husband and the wife. The length of the interview varied from one-half hour to one hour. Most respondents came to Saskatoon in the 1950s and 1960s; they were primarily in professional occupations (see Bolaria and Basran, 1985a, 1985b, and 1986).

REFERENCES

Abella, R.S. (1984): *Equality in Employment: A Royal Commission Report* (Ottawa: Minister of Supply and Services).

Agnew, V. (1996): *Resisting Discrimination: Women from Asia, Africa and the Caribbean and the Women's Movement in Canada* (Toronto: University of Toronto Press).

Amos, V. and P. Parmar (2001): Challenging Imperial Feminism. In K. Bhavnani (ed.), *Feminism and 'Race'*: 17–32 (London: Oxford University Press).

Anderson, M.L. and P. Collin (1995): *Race, Class and Gender* (2nd edn) (Toronto: Wadsworth Publishing Co.).

Bannerji, H. (ed.) (1993): *Returning the Gaze: Essays on Racism, Feminism and Politics*. (Toronto: Sister Vision, Black Women and Women of Colour Press).

Bannerji, H. et al. (1991): *Unsettling Relations: The University as a Site of Feminist Struggles* (Toronto: Women's Press).

Bannerji, H. (1987): 'Introducing Racism: Notes Towards an Anti-Racist Feminism', *Resources for Feminist Research* 16(1)10–12.

Basran, G.S., C. Gill, and B.D. MacLean (1994): *Farm Workers and their Children* (Vancouver: Collective Press).

Bolaria, B. Singh and G.S. Basran (1985a): 'Profile of a Sikh Community in the Canadian Mosaic: A Research Report' (Saskatoon, Saskatchewan: Department of Sociology, University of Saskatchewan).

—— (1985b): 'Sikhs in Canada: History of Sikhs in British Columbia: A Research Report' (Saskatoon, Saskatchewan: Department of Sociology, University of Saskatchewan).

—— (1986): 'Racial Labour Policy and Exploitation: The Case of Sikh Immigrant Workers', paper Delivered at the Annual Conference of National Association for Ethnic Studies, Fresno, California, 26 Feb.–1 March.

Bolaria, B. Singh and P.S. Li (1988): *Racial Oppression in Canada* (2nd ed.) (Toronto: Garamond Press).

Buchignani, N., D. Indra, and R. Srivastava (1985): *Continuous Journey: A Social History of South Asians in Canada* (Toronto: McClelland and Stewart).

Carby, H.V. (1982): 'White Women Listen! Black Feminism and the Boundaries of Sisterhood', pp. 213–15, in *Centre for Contemporary Cultural Studies, The Empire Strikes Back: Race and Racism in 70s Britain*, 213–35 (London: Hutchinson).

Chadney, J.G. (1986): 'India's Sikhs in Vancouver: Immigration, Occupation and Ethnic Adaptation', *in* S. Chandrasekhar (ed.), *From India to Canada: A Brief History of Immigration: Problems of Discrimination, Admission and Assimilation* (LaJolla, California: A Population Review Book), pp. 59–66.

Chandrasekhar, S. (1986): *From India to Canada: A Brief History of Immigration: Problems of Discrimination, Admission and Assimilation* (LaJolla, California: A Population Review Book).

Chard, J. (1995): 'Women in a Visible Minority', *in* Statistics Canada, *Women in Canada: A Statistical Report* (3rd ed.) (Ottawa: Ministry of Industry), pp. 133–46.

Chekki, D.A. (1988): 'Recent Direction in Family Research: India and North America', *Journal of Comparative Family Studies* 19 (Summer):171–86.

Das Gupta, T. (1996): *Racism and Paid Work* (Toronto: Garamond Press).

Fry, M. (1983): *The Politics of Reality: Essays in Feminist Theory* (New York: The Crossing Press).

Ghosh, R. (1983): 'Sarees and the Maple Leaf: Indian Women in Canada', *in* G. Kurian and R.P Srivastava (eds), *Overseas Indians: A Study in Adaptation* (New Delhi: Vikas Publishing House).

Helweg, A. (1986): 'Indian Immigrant Professionals in Toronto, Canada: The Study of Social Network', *in* S. Chandrasekhar (ed.) *From India to Canada: A Brief History of Immigration: Problems of Discrimination, Admission and Assimilation* (LaJolla, California: A Population Review Book), pp. 67–79.

Helweg, A. (1979): *Sikhs in England* (New Delhi: Oxford University Press).

Hooks, B. (1984): *Feminist Theory: From Margin to Centre* (Boston: South End).

—— (1981): *Ain't I a Woman: Black Women and Feminism* (Boston: South End).

Kalra, S.S. (1980): *Daughters of Traditions: Adolescent Sikh Girls and their Accommodation to Life in British Society* (Birmingham, England: Diana Balbir Publications).

Kazi, H. (1986): 'The Beginning of a Debate Long Due: Some Observations on "Ethnocentric and Socialist Feminist Theory"'. *Feminist Review* 22 (Spring):87–91.

Kline, M. (1991): 'Women's Oppression and Racism: A Critique of the 'Feminist Standpoint', *in* Jess Vorst et al (eds), *Race, Class, Gender: Bonds and Barriers* (Toronto: Garamond Press and Society for Socialist Studies), pp. 39–63.

Kline, M. (1989): 'Race, Racism and Feminist Legal Theory', *Harvard Women's Law Journal* 12:115–50.

Kurian, G. and R.P. Srivastava (eds) (1983): *Overseas Indians: A Study in Adaptation* (New Delhi: Vikas Publishing House).

Kurian, G. and R. Ghosh (1983): 'Child-Rearing in Transition in Indian Immigrant Families in Canada', *in* G. Kurian and R.P. Srivastava (eds), *Overseas Indians: A Study in Adaptation* (New Delhi: Vikas Publishing House), pp. 128–38.

LaBrack, B. (1988): 'Evolution of Sikh Family Form and Values in Rural California: Continuity and Change 1904–1980', *Journal of Comparative Family Studies* 19 (Summer):287–309.

—— (1983): 'The Reconstruction of Sikh Society in Rural California', in G. Kurian and R.P. Srivastava (eds), *Overseas Indians: A Study in Adaptation* 215–240 (New Delhi: Vikas Publishing House).

LaBrack, B. and K. Leonard (1984): 'Conflict and Compatibility in Punjabi-Mexican Immigrant Families in Rural California, 1915–1965', *Journal of Marriage and Family* 46 (Aug.):527–37.

Lees, S. (1986): 'Sex, Race and Culture: Feminism and the Limits of Cultural Pluralism', *Feminist Review* 22 (Spring):92–102.

Li, P.S. (1983): The Chinese–Canadian Family', in P.S. Li and B.S. Bolaria (eds), *Racial Minorities in Multicultural Canada*, (Toronto: Garamond Press), pp. 86–96.

Mandell, N. (1995): *Feminist Issues: Race, Class and Sexuality* (Scarborough: Prentice Hall Canada).

Monture, P. (1993): 'I Know My Name: A First Nations Woman Speaks', in G. Finn (ed.), *Voices of Women, Voices of Feminism* (Halifax: Fernwood Publishing), pp. 328–40.

Monture, P. (1986): 'Ka-Nin-Geh-Heh-Gah-E-Sa-Nonh-Ya-gah', *Canadian Journal of Women and the Law* 2,1:159–71.

Mukherjee, A. (1993): *Sharing Our Experience* (Ottawa: Canadian Advisory Council on the Status of Women).

Muszynski, A. (2000): 'The Social Construction/Deconstruction of Sex, Gender, Race, and Class', in B.S. Bolaria (ed.), *Social Issues and Contradictions in Canadian Society* (3rd edn) (Toronto: Harcourt Brace Canada), pp. 95–131.

Naidoo, J. and J. Davis (1988): 'Canadian South Asian Women in Transition: A Dualistic View of Life', *Journal of Comparative Family Studies* 19 (Summer):311–27.

Ralston, H. (1996): *The Lived Experience of South Asian Immigrant Women in Atlantic Canada: The Interconnections of Race, Class and Gender* (Lewiston, N.Y.: The Edwin Mellen Press).

—— (1991): 'Race, Class, Gender, and Work Experience of South Asian Immigrant Women in Atlantic Canada', *Canadian Ethnic Studies* 23:129–39.

Ramazanoglu, C. (1986): 'Ethnocentrism and Socialist Feminist Theory: A Response to Barrett and McIntosh', *Feminist Review* 22 (Spring):83–6.

Ross, D.P. and P. Roberts (1999): *Income and Child Well-Being: A New Perspective on the Poverty Debate* (Ottawa: Canadian Council on Social Development).

Satzewich, V. (1998): 'Race, Racism and Racialization: Contested Concepts', in

V. Satzewich (ed.), *Racism and Social Inequality in Canada* (Toronto: Thompson Educational Publishing, Inc.), pp. 25–45.

Spelman, E.V. (1988): *Inessential Women: Problems of Exclusion in Feminist Thought* (Boston: Beacon Press).

—— (1982): 'Theories of Race and Gender: The Erasure of Black Women', *Quest: A Feminist Quarterly* 5,4:36–62.

StarPhoenix (1992): Visible Minority Population to Rise Three Million by 2001. (CP), 1 June.

Srinivas, K and S.K. Kaul (1987): *Indo-Canadians in Saskatchewan: The Early Settlers* (Regina: India Canada Association of Saskatchewan, Inc.).

Statistics Canada (1998): *Daily*, 12 May.

Thobani, S. (2001): 'Closing the Nation's Ranks: Racism, Sexism and the Abuse of Power in Canadian Immigration Policy', *in* S.C. Boyd, D.E. Chunn, and R. Menzies (eds), *[Ab]using Power: The Canadian Experience* (Halifax, N.S.: Feminist Publishing), pp. 49–64.

Thornhill, E. (1991): 'Focus on Black Women', *in* J. Vorst et al. (eds), *Race, Class, Gender: Bonds and Barriers* (Toronto: Garamond Press), pp. 27–38.

Vorst, J. et al. (eds) (1991): *Race, Class, Gender: Bonds and Barriers*. Toronto: Garamond Press.

The Sikhs
From India to Canada

❦

Introduction

The deracialization of immigration controls in the sixties and the influx of recent immigrants from Asia and Africa have had a profound impact on the composition of the Canadian population as well as the labour force characteristics. The increasing heterogeneity and presence of more diverse and visible groups have refocused debate on issues such as immigration policy, characteristics of immigrants, their settlement patterns and location within the Canadian mosaic, and patterns of social and economic inequalities linked to the racial and ethnic diversity of the Canadian population. The role of the state and state policies and programmes related to immigration controls and managing racial and ethnic diversity and inequalities form an integral part of this debate.

The Sikh immigrants and their Canadian born descendents are an important segment of the visible minority population in Canada. This sociological study and analysis of Sikh migrations and their location in the Canadian landscape are presented within broad political, economic, and social contexts. Their migration patterns are analysed within the broader context of international migrations, history of immigration policy, and the social and economic consequences for immigrants. Major sections of the book deal with procurement and use of immigrant labour, political economy of immigrant and migrant workers, racism, and the consequences of various policies for the formation of social institutions such as the family. The sections on Sikh religion and politics contextualizes the discussion on links between the Sikh community in Canada and their place of origin in Punjab. Historical analysis of immigration policies and controls help us to understand the contemporary situation of Sikhs and other visible minorities. Within a broad theoretical and contextual framework, the primary focus of this book remains on the historical and contemporary situation of Sikhs in Canada.

RELIGION, IDENTITY, AND POLITICS

Religious beliefs and practices form an integral part of the social structure, and religion continues to be an important part of people's personal lives, their ethical values, their social relationships, and political behaviour. Religion is an important source of community identity, internal solidarity, and cohesion. At the same time, religion is often the source of inter- and intra-group conflict and may form the basis of political divisions and struggles. Religion may often serve contradictory functions in the society; integrative and disintegrative; a conservative force that supports the status quo as well as an agent of social change.

Given the importance of religion and the current diversity of religious faiths in Canada, religious affiliation of a particular group and the knowledge of the beliefs, codes, and practices of that religion become crucial in understanding that community. This is particularly so in the case of the Sikhs, who have a distinct physical identity: the 5 Ks and the turban. Practice of their faith in accordance with religious teachings and strict adherence to the 5 Ks and turban may often come into conflict with the social practices, institutional requirements, and legal codes. For instance, initial strong opposition by some to the recruitment of Sikhs in the Royal Canadian Mounted Police (RCMP) was primarily based on the argument that Sikhs wearing turbans would violate the traditions of the RCMP and traditional codes regarding uniforms. Wearing a small sword by some students (ceremonial dagger) has often created tension in some schools. Sikhs have also sought exemption from bicycle safety helmet laws. They successfully lobbied in British Columbia for such an exemption in 1996, but in 2002 are faced with somewhat similar legislation in Alberta, which they vow to oppose. The Sikhs are asking for an across the country helmet exemption rather than recourse in individual jurisdictions.

Turbaned Sikhs now serve in the RCMP, school boards have made accommodations for practicing Sikh students, and Sikhs have gained exemption from helmet laws in some jurisdictions; all this has been made possible only through legal challenges and political lobbying. A knowledge of the Sikh faith and religious practices would perhaps help to create a better and wider understanding of these issues in the larger society and avoid future tensions and conflicts.

Thus, the section on Sikhs, Sikhism, and the Khalsa Panth is essential to understanding these issues and contradictions. The social context within which the Sikh religion emerged, the life, contributions, and teachings of the Gurus, religious codes and practices, also contribute to an understanding of the internal conflict within the community between the 'fundamentalists' and the 'moderates', and the links of these factions to the religious institution and place of religious authority in Punjab. The Sikh identity of self-sacrifice, bravado and valour are rooted in their historical experiences since the very foundation of the Sikh religion.

Social, economic, and political links of Sikhs in Canada to the 'old country' are not unique to this community, but are common to all immigrant communities to a degree. However, in the case of the Sikhs, these links have remained strong because of historical and contemporary immigration policy and practices. Even now about two thirds of the Sikhs are foreign-born, with their roots largely in Punjab. Religionization of politics intertwined with the politics of language, caste, class, regional, and communal loyalties continue to be important forces in people's lives. A full appreciation of the current situation in Punjab requires a historical–structural analysis of a number of forces and events both internal and external to the Sikh community. Our presentation covers the social, economic, political, and communal context of the historical and contemporary dimensions of the 'Punjab problem'. While the 'religious factor' has received most attention, the issues of the political economy and the development policies of the state have remained largely in the background. The communalization of politics, portrayal of regional issues as Sikh demands, and the sectarian and secessionist perception of the Punjab problem, helped to divert attention away from the underlying material conditions in the region. Political issues and agitations are rooted in economic development policy and its contradictions in Punjab, and embody broader economic forces of displacement, underemployment, unemployment, and increasing economic disparity.

Contending political interests played an important role in the social construction of the issues and problems. Polarization of politics between the 'moderates' and the 'extremists' in the Sikh community received encouragement even from the secular parties for electoral gains. External political interests and internal politics and contradictions among the Sikhs contributed to an increasing polarization of Punjab politics. The state, both at the provincial and central levels, also played an important role in shaping the political process and the construction of the Punjab problem and also the state's response and solution to the problems. Oppressive state policies were justified to root out 'extremists' and restore peace and order. While on the surface, the 'Punjab problem' appears to have been stabilized, the basic economic and social issues remain unresolved.

Our central point is that without a historical–structural analysis of the origin and development of the Sikh religion and religious codes and practices, one cannot fully understand the Sikh community in Canada, its internal contradictions and conflicts, and its relations with the larger community. While the communalization of issues remains a factor, the political economy of the province, economic development policies, and class disparities are fundamental to a full understanding of the Punjab problem. This type of analysis also contributes to a better understanding of religious, social, economic, and political links between the community in Canada and their primary place of origin in Punjab. Globalization of production and internationalization of labour and capital is likely to further extend these links.

MIGRATIONS AND LABOUR REPRODUCTION

A discussion of the salient aspects of theoretical and conceptual debates in migration studies and perspectives on racism and social inequality is essential to a full understanding of the migration patterns and their location in their places of destination. In the area of migration, theorizing, broadly speaking, falls into micro-level and macro-level perspectives. At its core, the focus of micro-level theorizing is on individualistic reasons or motivation for migration. The primary drive behind the migrants' decision is said to be self-interest and economic rationality to maximize their opportunities. The focus of macro-level theorizing, on the other hand, is on structural determinants in patterned migration movements determined by the dynamics of capitalist development and the interface between the needs of capital and the characteristics of labour. Capitalism as a world system is characterized by gross disparities and unequal accumulation of capital between the core and peripheral countries. Expansion of capitalist economies into the periphery produces disruptions and dislocations, which create conditions for further migrations. Similarly, in the study of racism and racial inequality, explanations range from individual racism with a focus on prejudicial attitudes and discriminatory actions of individuals, to institutional racism with a focus on institutional policies and practices that exclude racial minorities from equal participation and thus create differential opportunity structures. Studies of socio–economic status and mobility patterns of racial minorities are also guided by divergent perspectives. The assimilationist school sees social and economic inequality as a product of cultural value orientation and achievement motivation differences among various groups and their degree of assimilation into the 'mainstream' society. In their analysis of social inequality, structuralists focus on factors such as differential opportunity structures, labour market segmentation, and the persistence of race, class, and gender inequalities.

Our analysis in this book is informed by theoretical perspectives that see migrations as a product of global disparities and social inequality as a product of institutional racism and differential opportunity structures that create differential life chances for various social groups. Global disparities and internationalization of capital is accompanied by internationalization of labour. These developments have also enhanced capital's structural power over workers and have weakened labour in various countries and regions. In the context of the political economy of migrant labour, the circulation of workers across national boundaries helps to reduce labour costs and provide capital an increased access to labour resources and reservoirs. The state, by regulating the migratory flows and by controlling the legal–political status of migrants creates labour flexibility and judicial vulnerability of the workers, thus creating structural conditions for exploitation. Racialization of a segment of labour provides a pretext for extreme-exploitation of racial minority workers. The labour market allocation and labour market profiles of racial minority workers differ markedly from other workers, the former group more likely to be concentrated in the secondary labour market characterized by low-paying jobs, dangerous and unhealthy work environment, and seasonal work.

Sikh workers, and other workers from India, have been a racialized segment of the workforce in Canada. Racialized immigration controls have ranged from total exclusion to continuous journey stipulation and annual immigrant nationality quotas. In the case of immigrants from India, institutional racism has been most explicit in the racialized hierarchy of preferred immigrants, denial of legal–political rights, conjugal rights, and labour market inequalities. These measures created structural conditions for exploitation of the early immigrants at their workplace and social discrimination in their daily lives. Their material existence and everyday lived experience in Canada and its link to their colonial background formed an important dimension of the political consciousness of pioneer immigrants. While explicitly racist immigration controls and overt institutional racism are in the past, racial minorities continue to face socio–economic inequalities in Canada.

COLONIAL STATUS, RACISM, AND SIKH WORKERS

The urgent need for an alternate source of cheap, easily controlled, and exploitable workforce arose with the abolition of slavery. The Indian colony became the primary source of such labour. British colonial authorities developed wide-ranging policies for the supply, procurement, transfer, and use of Indian labour in various parts of the empire. While these policies varied somewhat depending upon the labour force requirements of specific economies, there were certain commonalities, including recruitment of single, male labour, denial of legal–political rights, social subordination, and racial labour policies. These policies were meant to create structural conditions for reproduction of a low-cost workforce.

The early Sikh workers in Canada were one of the most disadvantaged, racialized, and subordinated foreign-born workforce. The structural conditions and constraints under which they entered Canada made them the most vulnerable labour force. They were not allowed to bring their families and children with them and were denied legal–political rights. With limited alternative job opportunities, racial labour policies at their place of employment relegated them largely to low-paying and subordinated jobs in segregated work areas. The organization of the workforce and work along racial lines had various dimensions: racially segregated labour and living conditions; racial preference in employment and blocked alternative opportunities; differential wages and price of labour by race; racialized work and segregated work areas; racialized occupational and social hierarchy. They also faced racism and discrimination in their daily lives and had to endure and cope with discrimination in housing, restaurants, hotels, bars, and were denied many other services. Sikhs were also insulted and ridiculed for their appearance and mode of dress. Many of the discriminatory work and social experiences Sikhs shared with other Hindustanis. Their common shared experiences united them in their support for India's independence from colonial rule and aganist the racist immigration policy, racism, and racial discrimination.

In many respects Sikhs were a sub-proletarianized, marginalized and subordinated, workforce who were preferred as workers but considered as undesirable immigrants and permanent settlers.

POST-WAR CANADA: SOCIAL MOBILITY AND INEQUALITY

Post-war changes in immigration policy have had a profound impact on the sources of immigrants and their characteristics, and consequently the contemporary Canadian population is more heterogeneous and diverse. The recent arrivals are also better educated with professional qualifications and training than the early immigrants. They also tend to be better educated than their Canadian-born counterparts. While visible minority men and women have higher educational levels in comparison to other Canadians, they have differential labour market opportunities and employment earnings and incomes. Consequently the incidence of low income among visible minorities remains above the Canadian average. However, there is considerable inter- and intra-group variation among the visible minority groups.

The social and demographic characteristics of the Sikh community differ markedly from early immigrants from India. Their labour market opportunities and profile have also improved considerably in recent years. This is primarily due to the pre-immigration class and educational background of recent arrivals and the post-war changes in the occupational structure of Canada. The employment data indicate, however, that Sikhs and other Indo-Canadians still face inequality in the labour market and have low employment earnings and incomes. Notwithstanding higher educational attainment they are less likely to be in professional, managerial, and administrative jobs.

In the media the Sikh community is often 'problematized' and portrayed as undemocratic, conflict- and violence-ridden, a threat to the general public requiring inordinate use of public safety, law and order services. These portrayals have also contributed to the low social status (ranking) of Sikhs.

The visible success of a few Sikhs masks the economic and social inequality faced by many and glosses over the fact that a large number of Sikhs are far from being prosperous.

RACE, GENDER, AND FAMILY

The form and nature of the social institutions of racial minorities is often attributed to the cultural background, values, and practices of these communities. It is common to see family formation as a consequence of individual choice/preference and cultural patterns and practices. This orientation fails to consider the historical and structural forces that have had an important influence on family formation, family structure, and dynamics. Historically, the development of Sikh families was stifled because of racist and sexist immigration policies, recruitment of single male labour, denial of normal conjugal family life, and other restrictions and limitations placed upon their permanent settlement in Canada. The repeal of many of the statutory restrictions and changes in immigration policy saw the influx of better educated, professional–skilled workers, often from middle and upper-class urban backgrounds. Their family structure and family relations differ markedly from those Sikhs who arrived earlier and had relatively low educational levels, predominantly from a rural background and faced discriminatory state policies and a hostile social environment. Contemporary Sikh families show considerable diversity in family structure and dynamics, akin to that of families in the general population. There is considerable variation in cultural practices, gender relations, parent–child relations, and family attitudes toward courtship and marriage.

The incidence of low income among racial minority families remains above the Canadian average, which may limit the educational and other opportunities for their children and even their ability to successfully sponsor relatives to immigrate to Canada.

The economic well-being and internal dynamics of racial minority families are also linked to economic and social status of visible minority women. The socio–economic and labour market profiles of these women differ from those of their non-visible counterparts. In their analysis of gender inequality, most of the mainstream feminists assume a common experience of all women based on gender alone, separate from any other experiences. While gender affects social distribution of privileges it does not operate alone. Women of colour cannot overlook the simultaneity of experiences of racism, sexism, and class inequalities. The mainstream feminist discourse and theorizing largely based upon universalization of experiences of white women have failed to recognize and acknowledge the diversity and complexity of women's experiences. Race and racism continue to structure the experience of racial minority women in their daily lives and in the labour market. These experiences are, however, far from monolithic because of the diversity of origin and background, cultural practices, religion, educational level, and class status.

CONCLUSIONS

The sociological study and analysis of Sikh migrants and their descendants in Canada are presented within broad political, economic, and social contexts. It is only in this broader context that one can have a full understanding of the migrations and settlement patterns of Sikhs in Canada. Specific issues relating to them cannot be separated from the broader context of racial and social inequality in Canada and state policies to manage diversity which affects all racial minorities.

The sociological analysis in this book is informed by theoretical perspectives that see migrations as a product of global disparities and social inequality as a product of structural and institutional constraints and institutional racism that create differential opportunities for various groups. In short, race and colour matter in the life chances of individuals and groups, and are important bases of stratification in Canada. The structural forces also have a profound impact on the form and nature of social institutions of racial minorities.

We hope to have made contributions in a number of areas, these include our discussion and analysis of the social and economic history of early Sikh immigrants and their experiences in Canada. The structural conditions and constraints on their entry and labour market opportunities and the organization of the workforce and work on racial lines made them the most vulnerable and exploited segment of the labour force. Our presentation of the occupational and labour market data on post-war Sikh immigrants will also serve as a benchmark for subsequent studies of labour market profile of Sikhs. The crucial point to be recognized is that the immigrants enter a segmented and often segregated, racialized, and gendered labour market. The incorporation of immigrants by race and gender markers into the labour market determines their subsequent employment earnings and incomes.

There is no doubt that the labour market profile and opportunities for Sikhs have improved considerably in recent years. This is however primarily due to the pre-immigration class, educational, and occupational characteristics of recent arrivals and the post-war changes in occupational structure in

Canada. Yet the social (status) ranking of the Sikhs and other racial minorities remains low when compared with that of white ethnics. Canadians also continue to attribute negative personal and social qualities to racial minorities.

State policies on immigration and racial minorities also influence the characteristics of immigrants and the nature of social and economic inequality. Many social forces determine state policies, including the demographic imperatives and the labour requirements Canada will face in the future. The policies may also be influenced by the increasing presence of the visible minority population in Canada and their participation in the political process. Thus our discussion and analysis have much larger implications for Canadian society and public policy.

The overarching theme of this book is that the historical structural analysis is crucial for an understanding of the contemporary situation of Sikhs and other racial minorities. Our discussion and findings are more consistent with the view that structural barriers and constraints in the labour market and differential opportunity structures produce economic and social inequality rather than with individual and culturally based perspectives on inequality.